The NAUI Textbook

National Association of Underwater Instructors

Acknowledgments

Equipment:
Dacor, SCUBAPRO, Sherwood

Facilities and Support:
Ernie Polte, Fullerton College; Jack's Dive Shop; Sound Dive Center; Judi Jennett, Ocean Sports Hawaii; Susan Wells, Chapter Leader, Hawaii; Harry Ellis, Branch Manager, West Pacific Branch; Dirk Van Deusen, boat "Stella Maris," Hawaii

Photography:
Dennis Graver, plus file photos courtesy of Skin Diver Magazine and Sources' news contributors

Photographic Models:
Robyn Knowlton, Rhett Price, Tina Clothier, Jack Gillen

Illustrations:
Jim Mitchell, Derrick Story

Layout:
Lisa Ambrose

Word Processing:
Sally Bergquist

Content and Editing:
Jim Arkison
Jeff Bozanic
Nick Craig
Ronnie Damico
Roy Damron
Peter Davidson
Norris Eastman
Glen Egstrom, Ph.D.
Homer Fletcher
Don Freeman
Dennis Graver
Nancy Guarascio
Walt Hendrick, Sr.
Bill High
Bob Hoffman
Paul Heinmiller
Garry Howland
Marshall McNott
Lyn Nelson
Frank Nawrocki
Venda Schmid
Phil Sharkey
Lee Somers
Bob Widmann
Marcia Wieland
Bruce Zechman

Glossary:
Frank Wells

The NAUI Mission

To promote and encourage through purposeful activity the education and training of the general public in the safety and techniques of participating in underwater activities, and to educate people to preserve and protect the quality of the underwater environment.

Published in the United States of America by the National Association of Underwater Instructors (NAUI).

4650 Arrow Hwy., Suite F-1
Montclair, CA 91763

Eighth Edition
April, 1992

ISBN 0-916974-53-7

Table of Contents

SECTION 1

Introduction to Diving

Another World...   Have you ever wanted to be like an astronaut and walk on the moon? To experience the weightlessness and the thrill of being out of this world? To see things that few have ever seen? To explore the unknown, make exciting discoveries and be part of a great adventure? Many people fantasize about such things, but relatively few seem to be aware that such a world is readily available — a world with similar sensations waiting for the average person... It is the world beneath the waters.

Imagine being immersed in cool, clear, refreshing water. As you descend, the rays of sunlight dance and flicker as they are alternately focused and dispersed by the action of wavelets on the surface. They eventually diffuse to create intriguing lighting. As you descend slowly, it seems that you are suspended in space and that the entire bottom rises up to meet you. Details on a reef below become clearer as you approach. Clouds of colorful, timid fish come out of crevices and other places of hiding to investigate you and satisfy their curiosity. Exhaust bubbles instantly disperse the little creatures in unison. They disappear, only to reappear between breaths to complete their study of this strange newcomer to the reef.

The melodic sound of the bubbles from your exhalations rumbles pleasantly past your ears. You marvel at your ability to hang completely motionless in the water, totally weightless and suspended in space. A couple of easy thrusts of

There are similarities between visiting "inner space" and visiting outer space.

Scuba diving can be a wonderful experience.

your fins allow you to glide to a nearby crevice where movement was detected. Here you encounter a fascinating animal whose every movement holds your complete attention. Time passes so quickly that thoughts of a work-a-day world never even enter your mind. You can't believe you could ever be so relaxed wearing so much equipment while underwater, but now you marvel because you can barely feel the equipment. Scuba diving is not the strenuous activity you thought it would be.

You also never imagined the myriad of colors, textures, and life forms to be encountered. You thought the world under water was dark, cold, colorless, and dangerous. But now a smile comes to your face as you recall your initial unjustified apprehensions about diving. Your smile lines allow water to trickle into your mask, but a deft movement and a slight exhalation immediately clear the water. Before you know it, your buddy is showing his pressure gauge to you and signalling that it is time to ascend. Reluctantly, you acknowledge the signal and start the ascent. The bright light at the surface seems harsh at first, but the warmer surface water feels good. You would rather still be on the bottom though, exploring the remainder of the incredible reef. You can't wait to get back down, although you just left there seconds ago…

When you stop to think about it, scuba (Self-Contained Underwater Breathing Apparatus) diving in inner space is quite similar to being an astronaut in outer space. A life support system is needed, similar problems of weightlessness

and pressure differences require special skills, the environment is totally foreign, and there is so much waiting to be discovered and experienced. There is one great difference, however. Only a select few can become astronauts, but any healthy individual who is comfortable in the water can become a diver. You may never make it into outer space, but you can have all of the same thrills in inner space.

Training Just as an astronaut requires training before venturing forth, so does the new scuba diver. Actually, there are only a few things you need to learn in order to dive safely. You need to learn to handle the equipment properly, to prevent injury or discomfort from the effects of pressure, and to perform fundamental skills such as mask clearing, breathing patterns, and controlling buoyancy. These learning areas, coupled with an orientation to the local environment, will enable you to dive there.

NAUI COURSE RELATIONSHIPS
(Non-Leadership Programs)

Jr. = Denotes Junior Course available.
⓪ = Denotes number of open water dives required in course.
— — = Elective programs or optional progression paths.
——— = Primary progression path or core programs.

The NAUI Progression of Training

It all sounds rather simple, and it really is. The basics of diving are easily acquired, but there is more to diving than moving around underwater and looking at things. You will soon discover that diving is really a means to accomplish goals beneath the surface. You will want to explore mysterious wrecks, collect artifacts or shells, capture the interest and beauty on film, hunt for game, or pursue some other interest. Such specialized activities require specialty training, and NAUI — The National Association of Underwater Instructors, a pioneer organization in underwater education — offers such training. In fact, a progression of training, leading from the beginning levels of scuba all the way through expert diver ratings, is offered by NAUI Instructors. A program of continuing education is recommended to all who learn to dive. The more you learn, the greater your potential to have fun while diving.

NAUI Diving Courses Your first scuba experience might well be the ESE Program, which stands for Entry Scuba Experience. This introduction allows you to quickly experience what scuba diving is like. Not everyone begins with the ESE Program, but it can be a fun opportunity to try scuba before signing up for a full certification course.

The next step in the learning progression would be the Openwater I Diver course. This course covers all of the fundamentals of diving and qualifies those completing it to dive without professional supervision. As evidence of training and completion of required training, a certification card — commonly called a C-card — is awarded to those meeting the standards established by NAUI for a particular level of training. Your C-card will serve as your diving passport. It will allow you to buy or rent equipment, get air fills, go on diving charters, and participate in diving at resorts around the world.

You can be proud to bear a NAUI certification for diving. NAUI's requirements for certification are greater than those for other training organizations, and a NAUI C-card is widely recognized and respected because of this. Also, NAUI instructors are the finest educators in diving. You will enjoy the prestige that comes from being certified as a NAUI diver. Congratulations on your selection of NAUI to sanction your training!

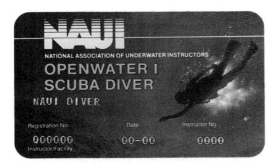

A NAUI Certification Card (C-Card)

Once you have acquired your Openwater I Diver certification, you will be aware of advanced skills needed to pursue many of the special interest areas of diving. Training in these additional skills, and added supervised diving experience, is the purpose of the NAUI Openwater II, Advanced Diver and specialty courses. You will want to complete one of these courses soon after obtaining your entry level certification.

This Book and Your Training   *The NAUI Textbook* is different than other diving texts. Most of the information is contained in seven chapters. Each chapter addresses a general topic area and is divided into seven parts. There are two reasons for arranging the information in this manner:

(1) It is intended that you will study only one or more parts of each chapter for each class, so a little about each topic will be learned for each area, rather than trying to learn everything at once about each topic area, and (2) your instructor has flexibility to organize the course and assign study material according to the training situation. The course can be structured to be completed in a few long sessions or in a series of shorter classes depending upon the needs and circumstances. Your instructor will tell you which parts of the chapters to study.

Your training will consist of three phases — academic, controlled environment, and open water. The academic phase is classroom instruction. The controlled environment phase is where the skills of diving are first introduced and are developed. This is usually done in a swimming pool, but it may be done in a calm, protected open water area. When you are proficient in the needed skills of diving in a controlled environment, you will have the opportunity to apply them in the third phase, open water.

After satisfactorily demonstrating your knowledge on a written exam and your skills in open water, you can be certified as a NAUI diver by your instructor. While that may seem a long way away, you will find the training so enjoyable that the day will arrive much sooner than you think.

The Entry Scuba Experience   Some of the information in this section is repeated in other chapters. Students enrolled in the Openwater I entry level course will not find it necessary to read or study all parts of the ESE section. ESE

Inter-relationships of classroom, pool, and open water training. Each effects the others.

A safe, enjoyable acquaintance with diving is the goal of the NAUI Entry Scuba Experience.

participants, however, will find all the information necessary to satisfactorily complete this introductory program without additional reading requirements.

This introductory scuba experience will be fun, exhilarating and will acquaint you with most of the skills and sensations of diving. Your ESE adventure will be instructed and guided by your NAUI instructor, a true professional who understands your feelings. The goal of the instruction is to make your initial underwater experience as safe and as enjoyable as possible.

The information in this section will prepare you for your first scuba session. The basic principles and skills presented are concise and easily understood. They serve two purposes: (1) They provide sufficient information to prepare you to make a supervised scuba dive. and (2) After becoming familiar with the knowledge and skills in this section and applying them in the water, you will have an excellent foundation for learning more detailed aspects of these subjects in a complete course leading to certification as a NAUI diver.

It's fun to study creatures underwater, but be sure to leave them there.

In the ESE program, you get to dive right away. You will be introduced to most of the basics of the ultimate aquatic activity. You will not learn enough to qualify to dive without professional supervision.

The First Concept: The natives are friendly. Who's afraid of the water? A few people are, but you shouldn't be. If you feel comfortable and

relaxed in a swimming pool, you should be able to have a great time scuba diving. The waters of our planet are filled with thousands of friendly, curious creatures. The opportunity to see, photograph, and play with these creatures is one of the things which makes diving so enjoyable. Still, a few people are a bit apprehensive at the thought of leaving our air-filled environment and venturing below the waves in order to visit these friendly underwater folk. If you are one of these

Fish feeding is fun!

people, here are a few facts which will help set your mind at ease.

First of all, you should be aware that when you go diving, you will be the most dangerous animal in the water. Really. If you are careless, you are far more likely to cause harm to the things which live underwater than they are to you. For example, it takes certain species of coral 20 years to grow a single inch. Break off a six inch piece of coral as a souvenir and you will have undone 120 years of growth. On the other hand, if you are careful and considerate of things underwater, they and you should get along just fine.

Next, know that the big ugly underwater things you see on TV and at the movies are generally found only there. Nearly anything you encounter diving will be much smaller than you are, and perfectly content to leave you alone. (Unless, of course, you want to lure them out with bread crumbs or other bait so they can pose for pictures. This is a lot of fun!).

The Second Concept: You can operate under pressure. You are under a lot of pressure while diving — water pressure, which is caused by the weight of the water above you. Consequently, the deeper you go, the more water you will be under, and the greater the pressure you will experience.

That's the bad news. The good news is that with a few minor adjustments, you will be relatively unaffected by this pressure.

Your body is comprised mostly of water and solids. These are unaffected by increases in pressure. Your body has several air-filled spaces in it, such as your lungs, sinuses, and middle ear spaces. When you scuba dive, your equipment automatically supplies you with air at a pressure equal to the surrounding water. All you have to do is breathe in and out, just as you normally do. Because air spaces in your body are constantly being filled with air at a pressure equal to the surrounding pressure, they, too, are unaffected by this increase in pressure.

It is important, however, that you do not dive if you have a cold, sinus congestion, or any other condition which would restrict the transfer of air from one body air space to another. It is also important that you work actively to equalize the pressure in the air spaces in your ears or "clear" them during descents.

By "clearing," we mean moving air from your lungs and throat to the tiny air space inside each ear. These middle ear air spaces are connected to the rest of your body's air spaces by small tubes which lead from the inside of your ears to the back of your throat. While these tubes are normally closed, they are not sealed. All you

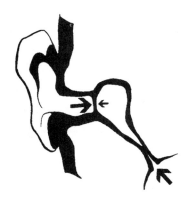

When "clearing" your ears during descent, you are actually moving air from your lungs into tiny air spaces inside your middle ear spaces.

have to do to "clear" your ears during descent is to get these small tubes to open so the higher pressure air from the rest of your system can travel through the tubes and into your middle ear spaces. This will keep the air pressure inside your middle ear spaces equal to the increasing water pressure outside.

How do you "clear?" It is fairly simple. You may be able to do it by simply yawning or swallowing, much like you do on an airplane. The easiest way for most people, however, is to block the nose by pinching it with your fingers (you can do this even when wearing a mask), blocking your mouthpiece with your tongue, and trying to exhale — firmly, but not forcefully. Since the air can't escape through either your nose or your mouth, it goes to the one remaining place it can — your middle ear air spaces.

The secret in ear clearing is not so much knowing how to clear as when to clear. A good rule to remember is "begin at the surface, then clear early and often." You only need to clear when descending, but you need to clear often — at least once every few feet of descent. An easy way to do this is to clear at the beginning of every exhalation. Your breathing pattern during descent should be, "Inhale, Clear, Exhale."

What if you have difficulty clearing? Well, if you are not troubled by a cold or congestion, the difficulty most likely stems from waiting too long before trying to clear. If you have difficulty clearing your ears, ascend a few feet and try again. The pressure will be less at a shallower depth, and clearing will be easier. If you can clear at the shallower depth, go ahead and continue your descent. Just remember to continue clearing every few feet. If you can't clear at the lesser depth, ascend a few more feet and try once more. Keep coming up a few feet at a time until you reach the point where your ears can clear, then continue your descent, continuing to clear your ears as you go.

The Third Concept: Breathing underwater is easy... and necessary. Your scuba equipment is designed to give you all the air you need underwater. All you have to do is breathe in and out — just as you do on the surface. This makes scuba diving just about the easiest of all water sports. It is important, though, that you do remember to breathe all the time when using scuba equipment. Here is why: The com-

Remember to breathe normally during ascent to allow expanding air in your lungs to escape.

Breathing underwater without a mask is a needed skill which can be quickly learned.

Look down to clear a mask which has a purge valve **Top Right**, or up to clear a mask which does not have a purge valve **Bottom Right**

pressed air you breathe under pressure contains molecules packed much more closely together than they are at the surface. For example, a lung full of air at a depth of 30 feet actually contains nearly twice as much air as a lung full of air at the surface. The increased pressure has merely compacted the air into the space.

As you ascend and the surrounding water pressure decreases, this air will want to expand. If you are breathing continuously, this expanding air will have no problem venting itself from your lungs. On the other hand, if you tried to hold your breath during this ascent, the expanding air would have no place to go. Eventually, it could cause a rupture in some of your lung tissues with very serious consequences.

Don't worry, though, for this "over-expansion injury" is very easy to avoid. All you have to do is something you have been doing all of your life — breathe. If you breathe in and out, you will vent any extra air and prevent any problems from occurring.

This whole explanation is expressed in the "most important rule of scuba diving" — When you are using scuba equipment underwater, *breathe naturally all the time. NEVER hold your breath when breathing compressed air.*

The Fourth Concept: Using mask and fins A mask is literally your window to the underwater world. With an air space in front of your eyes, you can see clearly, but if the space inside the mask fills with water, as it will occasionally,

everything appears blurred. To regain clear vision, simply restore air into the mask by exhaling into it through your nose. The air will rise to the top of the mask and displace the water out the bottom. The principle is very simple, but there are a couple of tricks to it. With the help of your instructor you will quickly learn to clear a mask of water.

You will need to be able to breathe in and out through your mouth from your scuba with your nose exposed to water. This requires a little concentration at first, but the skill can be mastered within minutes. Then you can take as much time as you need to clear a mask because there is no rush when you have air to breathe.

You may have a mask with a one-way valve at the nose. To clear this type of mask, simply make the valve the lowest point while sealing the mask against your face and exhaling into it. Masks without exhaust valves are cleared differently. The water needs to flow out over the skirt at the bottom, so, in addition to pressing the mask firmly against your face at the uppermost point to trap air, the mask needs to be tipped back while air is being added to it. This means simply that the head needs to be tilted back while exhaling. It is important to remember to start exhaling before tilting the head back. This keeps water from entering the nose and causing discomfort.

The last tip for mask clearing is to use a steady, moderate exhalation. Snorts of air are not as effective as a steady exhalation. You will find a mask can be cleared quite well by humming into it, and it doesn't make any difference which tune you select.

Remember these simple procedures, and with a little practice and some advice from your instructor, you will soon be able to clear your mask of water quickly and easily.

Swimmers use their arms for propulsion, but divers need to use their hands for other things. Fins are used because they make use of the large, strong muscles of the legs. The sooner you learn to stop swimming with your arms, the sooner you will develop the coordination of an experienced diver.

For optimum propulsion from fins, think of them as brooms attached to your feet and used to sweep the water away. To do this, extend the leg, point the toes somewhat, and use wide, slow strokes. This is exactly the way the fins should be kicked. You will discover that long, slow kicks work better than short, fast ones. If you will do this and keep your legs extended — not rigid, but with knees flexed — you will soon be looking just like an experienced diver as you move about under water.

The Fifth Concept: Controlling buoyancy. You can either float or sink or be neutral in water, which is one of your objectives in learning diving skills. Some of your equipment makes you float and some causes you to sink. Lead weights are used to offset buoyancy. The more buoyant you are, the more weights you will need. Your instructor will initially help you select the correct amount of weight. Later on, as you gain experience, you will learn to test and adjust weights independently. Buoyancy control is an important skill which requires practice to develop.

While descending, pressure compresses the material in protective suits and reduces their volume, so a reduction in buoyancy results. To compensate for this loss of buoyancy, divers wear buoyancy compensators (BCs), which restore buoyancy by means of air in an inflatable bladder. Most modern BCs are equipped with low pressure inflation devices so air from the scuba tank can be easily injected into the BC by simply depressing a button. During descent, a diver uses the low pressure inflator to add air to the BC to compensate for lost buoyancy and to remain neutrally buoyant — able to remain suspended at any depth. New divers sometimes overweight themselves and compensate with *over-inflated* BCs. This is a dangerous habit. (Learn to *properly* weight yourself at the surface without air in the BC.) Your instructor will assist you in selecting the minimum (optimum) amount of weight.

As we have already learned, *air in an air space expands during ascent* and this principle applies to the air inside a BC as well as to the air in body air spaces. The result of air expanding

Wide, slow kicks with legs extended and toes pointed— the keys to good use of fins.

A modern flotation system with a low pressure inflation device.

inside a BC is an increase in its volume and, therefore, an increase in buoyancy. Since you want to remain neutrally buoyant at all times underwater, it is necessary to release air from the BC during the ascent. This is easily accomplished by activating a dump valve or by opening the exhaust valve on the inflation/deflation hose. Since air rises in water, the air in a BC will always be at the highest point. It is necessary to make the dump valve or the exhaust valve also the highest point when venting air from the BC. In other words, with most BCs you need to be in an upright position to release air.

Being buoyant is desired at the surface, so the BC should be partially inflated there.

Remember these few points for controlling buoyancy: Vent the air from the BC in order to descend, add air as needed at depth to maintain neutral buoyancy, vent excess air during ascent to remain neutrally buoyant, and partially inflate the BC to achieve positive buoyancy whenever you are at the surface. These practices will become automatic with experience. In the beginning, your instructor will select your

weights and regulate the air in your BC to control your buoyancy.

The Sixth Concept: What if... New divers may have some apprehensions about the underwater world. This is natural because undersea environs are unknown to them and because Hollywood goes to great expense to depict some rather frightening events and creatures for those who trespass in Neptune's kingdom. The truth is, diving is very safe. The animals you encounter are seldom threatening. By following a few simple and logical rules, you can easily avoid problems under water.

Let's address a few of the concerns of new divers. They typically ask questions such as "what if... *I run out of air?*" First of all, you will have a gauge to monitor air pressure, just the same monitor the gas in your car, so you won't run out of air. Check the gauge from time to time and you will know when you are getting low. Your instructor will help you remember to do this. Secondly, your instructor and others diving with you will be equipped with an extra

If you leave alone those things with which you are unfamiliar, injury can be prevented.

regulator from which you can breathe if it should somehow be necessary.

I see a shark? This is highly unlikely. Most experienced divers have never seen a shark. And, in spite of the rarity of the occasion, the sighting of a shark is no cause for alarm. A diver who remains calm, moves slowly, and remains beneath the surface receives little attention from a passing shark.

There are a couple of rules to keep in mind with regard to potentially dangerous creatures. If you don't know what something is, don't touch it. Don't provoke animals. In short, *if you leave things alone, they will likely leave you alone.* Your instructor will point out things which are safe to touch and feel. This is part of the fun of diving.

My equipment fails? Modern diving equipment is rugged and reliable. The equipment is designed to be fail safe. For example, a regulator is more apt to free flow and deliver more air than is needed than it is to cut off the flow of air. Your instructor will help you inspect your equipment before you enter the water. If the gear is functioning properly when checked, you can be confident it will continue to work properly while you are diving.

You may have some small difficulty with an item of gear coming loose or needing an adjustment, but this certainly is no emergency. With air to breathe, there is no rush to correct the problem. Such nuisances can often be corrected more easily underwater than at the surface. Analyze the problem, determine how to correct it, and take your time in doing so. You can also bring the problem to the attention of your instructor, who will assist you. Your instructor will probably notice the problem before you and will point it out and help you correct it.

I get excited? Diving is unlike swimming, because divers exert as little energy as possible. The idea is to move slowly, take it easy, and feel comfortable. If this is not the case, and you feel apprehensive, you are probably working too hard and breathing too shallowly. To regain a relaxed feeling, all that is necessary is for you to reduce your activity level to a minimum, breathe deeply, and tell yourself to take it easy. Within a couple of minutes, you will feel better and can resume activity. This relaxation process is best implemented on the bottom. It is easier to relax there than at the surface.

Think of the adventure and fun of your first scuba experience.

Something goes wrong? You are going to do just fine, and you will not have any serious problems. How can we say this so confidently? Because millions of other divers have gone through a first scuba experience without problems. So will you. You will be diving with modern, reliable equipment in a controlled situation under the guidance of a professional. Think of the adventure and fun you will have, and of the good feeling you will have after your first scuba experience. That feeling is what motivates people to dive, and you are about to catch it, for it is highly contagious.

Time for Action   You should now be familiar with the key concepts required to use scuba. With some elaboration and demonstration by your NAUI Instructor, and some practice of a couple of the essential skills, you will soon be scuba diving in open water. Wonderful feelings of neutral buoyancy and breathing underwater will become part of the many exciting things you will want to tell your friends about. *Scuba diving is fun.* Enjoy your Entry Scuba Experience. And we will see you again for your Openwater I Diver training!

SECTION 2

1 *Equipment*

Diving is an equipment-intensive activity. When you first put on all of the equipment needed for open water diving, you may feel encumbered before you enter the water. Keep in mind that each item serves a purpose in the underwater environment and that the gear is designed to feel comfortable in water rather than on land. The sooner you get wet, the better it feels.

1.1. The Three Primary Items

The equipment needed for diving varies geographically, but you will always need a mask, a snorkel and fins.

Mask   To see clearly under water, an air space is required in front of the eyes. The mask fulfills this function. Masks are available in a large variety of types and styles. Numerous features are offered. As a minimum, the mask should be made of non-corrosive material, have a tempered glass lens (or lenses), an adjustable head band, and a means to block the nose (for ear clearing). This may be a pocket for the nose or finger wells on either side of the nose.

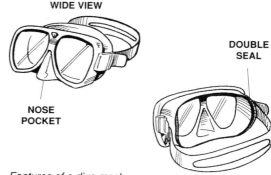

WIDE VIEW

DOUBLE SEAL

NOSE POCKET

Features of a dive mask.

Other features which may be desirable include:

1. A double seal for a snug but comfortable fit

2. Wide field of view for greater peripheral vision

3. A purge valve to clear water from the mask (not required, however)

4. Non-allergenic silicone material

5. Prescription lenses for visual correction (soft contact lenses may be worn with a standard mask)

The most important consideration of all in selecting a mask is the fit. To determine if a mask fits properly, place a mask without its strap very lightly against your face and inhale slightly through your nose. If the mask fits properly it will pull into place with the partial vacuum created and will remain there as long as the suction is applied. If you have to push the mask against your face to get it to sniff into place, the fit is not correct. A good approach to mask selection is to choose a number of masks with the features you want and test them all to see which one fits best.

New masks require some preparation for use. The strap needs to be adjusted so the fit is snug but not tight. There is also a thin film on the lens which must be removed in order to keep the lens

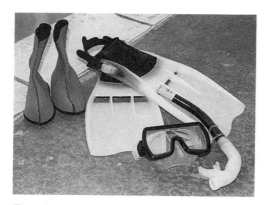

The primary items of snorkeling equipment.

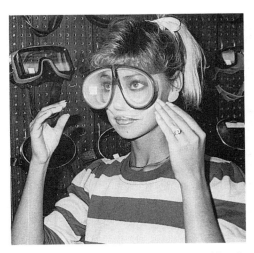

Testing mask fit — a most important consideration.

A snorkel allows you to float effortlessly at the surface.

free of condensation (which will obscure vision). The lens of a new mask should be scoured inside and out with toothpaste to remove this film. The toothpaste will not scratch the glass. Once the film has been removed, the lens can be kept free of condensation by coating it before diving with a commercial defog solution or with saliva.

Goggles are not an acceptable substitute for the mask. The nose must be included so air can be added to the air space to equalize pressure during descent. Don't try to economize when buying a mask—it is too important an item.

NOTE: Never wear ear plugs when diving.

Snorkel Have you ever noticed that you can lie on the surface of the water and float face down while completely motionless? If not, try it. Most people can float this way. The problem is that you cannot breathe without lifting the head, and that requires exertion. If you could float and breathe without exerting, wouldn't it be great? That's just what a snorkel allows you to do. Using a snorkel, you can rest or swim at the surface while watching the beauty beneath it without having to lift your head to breathe. This conserves energy and scuba air when at the surface.

There are several types of snorkels, including J-shaped ones, flexhose types and self-draining ones. Various available features include contour design, rotating mouthpiece for adjustment, and

special mouthpiece configurations. The two primary features to consider in the selection of a snorkel are comfort and breathing ease. The mouthpiece must be very comfortable in your mouth and should not twist when the barrel of the tube is placed over your left ear. Ease of breathing is determined by design. A good snorkel will have gentle curves, an inside diameter of about 3/4" (2 cm), and a length of not more than 12 to 14 inches (30-40 cm).

Fins and Boots Fins provide propulsion and stability in water and allow the hands to be freed for use. The strong muscles of the legs are employed; they handle the workload much better than the arm muscles.

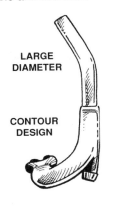

LARGE DIAMETER

CONTOUR DESIGN

SELF-DRAINING FEATURE

The desirable features of a snorkel.

Two basic types of fins are full-foot pocket fins and heel-strap fins. Full-foot pocket fins are typically used only in warm water areas or for snorkeling. Heel-strap fins are the most widely used. They are usually worn with neoprene boots. The boots provide protection and warmth and serve as shoes when walking about at a dive site.

When choosing fins, it is important to select ones with the right amount of stiffness and blade area. Large, stiff fins lead to fatigue and cramping while small, limber fins will not provide adequate propulsion. Your instructor will help you select the fin best suited for you and the area in which you'll be diving.

Fins are produced from various materials and with various designs and features. A snug, but not tight, comfortable fit (be sure to wear boots when trying on heel-strap fins) and the proper rigidity are the most important criteria. It is very helpful to try different fins in the water before purchasing them.

When selecting fins, try them on with boots. Look for a comfortable fit.

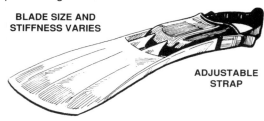

BLADE SIZE AND STIFFNESS VARIES

ADJUSTABLE STRAP

Full foot pocket-fins and heel-strap fins.

Maintenance   The maintenance of your primary items of equipment is similar to that for all dive gear — rinse the equipment in clear, fresh water after use; dry it thoroughly in the shade; and store it in a cool, dark place away from pollutants. The gear can be better pre-

served during prolonged storage if it is wrapped in plastic after it has dried completely.

Looking Back

You should now be able to answer the following questions regarding the three primary items of equipment.
1. The two most important criteria for the selection of mask, snorkel and fins are (select two: Type, style, fit, color, price, comfort, material, features).

A. _____

B. _____

2. A feature which is not required in a dive mask is (circle one: Non-corrosive materials, tempered glass lens, purge valve, nose blocking access).
3. List three factors which would reduce the ease of breathing with a snorkel.

A. _____

B. _____

C. _____

1.2   Scuba Equipment

Scuba equipment is the heart and soul of diving today. The main components are tank, tank valve, backpack and regulator. Let's examine each of these items as well as several types of back-up scuba equipment.

Tanks   Scuba tanks are a means of storing large quantities of air. This is done by compressing the air into a small, strong tank. The pressures involved are typically 3,000 psi (pounds per square inch) (210 atms/bars), and 2,250 psi (200 atms/bars). Different tank sizes and pressures result in different volumes of available air. Common tank volumes are 80 cu. ft., 71.2 cu. ft. and 50 cu. ft. (2600, 1,750 and 1,500 liters). Tanks are available in both single and double units. A single tank is quite adequate for recreational purposes. Tanks are produced from both steel and aluminum alloys. Both can corrode if water is admitted into them. The aluminum oxidizes and arrests corrosion while the steel rusts and accelerates corrosion. Aluminum tanks are slightly larger than steel tanks, are more easily damaged externally, and

require periodic servicing of the valve threads. All tanks require visual internal inspection by a trained inspector at least annually and a pressure test at a licensed facility every five years (annually or bi-annually in some countries). The pressure test is done hydrostatically, which means it is done with water.

Markings are placed on the shoulder of each tank to provide information concerning the cylinder. The illustrations below show the markings on a typical tank and indicate the meaning of each. The two with which you should be familiar are the service pressure and test date.

Proper care of your scuba tank includes rinsing it externally with fresh water after use, having it visually inspected annually (or more often under some conditions), and having it hydrostatically tested as required. You should also prevent moisture from entering the tank. If you always keep at least 100 psi of air in the tank (approximately 6.8 atms/bars) it is not likely that water will enter. Tanks should not be left standing upright when unattended. There is little danger if they fall over, but regulators and valves can be bent and toes can be smashed. So lay the tank down whenever you are not holding it. Also, be sure to block a tank securely when transporting it in a car so the tank won't roll around and damage itself or the car.

Left, Scuba tanks are available in various sizes in both aluminum and steel. *Right*, Typical markings on a scuba tank. In the first line, the four digit number (3000) is the working pressure of the tank. The markings on the right in the second line denote the months and year of manufacture.

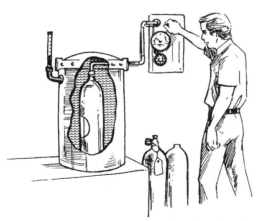

Hydrostatic (hydraulically in water) testing of scuba tanks is required every five years.

An internal inspection of your scuba tank is required annually. An inspection decal is affixed to the tank following inspection.

Tank valves: A K valve (left) and a J valve with the reserve lever (right).

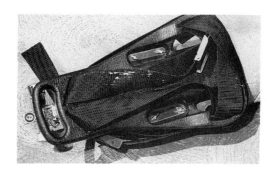

Backpacks for scuba tanks. Straps secured around a backpack to keep the straps and buckle from dragging.

Tank Valves Scuba valves are manual, high-pressure valves between the tank and regulator. They operate similar to a water faucet, allowing flow when turned counter-clockwise and shutting off flow when turned clockwise. Valves should never be forced by using tools for leverage, finger tight is adequate.

There are two types of scuba tank valves: J valves and K valves. A J valve has a reserve mechanism built in to retain a few hundred pounds (20 atms/bars) of air in the tank until released by turning a lever on the valve. The K valve is a simple on-off valve. Reserve valves are not totally reliable. They must be placed in the proper position (up) at the start of a dive and can be bumped and disabled during the dive. They also are more expensive to service than K valves. When used properly, they can be a good means to prevent a total depletion of air, but good divers prevent this by frequently monitoring remaining air with a submersible pressure gauge.

Every scuba valve is equipped with a pressure-relief disk. If a tank should be overfilled or if its pressure should increase greatly due to excessive heating of the cylinder, *e.g.,* from fire, the pressure-relief disk will rupture and release air, lowering the pressure. Pressure-relief disks should always be replaced by a professional dive store.

The tank valve should be serviced whenever your regulator is serviced, or whenever it fails to operate easily. Valves in aluminum tanks need to have their threads lubricated periodically (i.e., every 6 months) using a special lubricant. This should also be done at a professional dive store.

Backpacks A backpack is designed to hold the scuba tank securely and comfortably on your back. The pack may be a separate item of equipment or may be part of a BC jacket.

The pack should be comfortable and have an easily adjustable harness with quick-release buckles at the waist and on one shoulder. The band which secures the pack to the tank may be rigid or soft and flexible. The flexible bands should be easily adjustable and should lock onto the tank tightly to prevent the tank from slipping from the pack.

Backpacks should be rinsed after use and the straps should be secured around the pack so they do not drag and become frayed.

Regulators A scuba regulator is a mechanical device that delivers air at ambient (surrounding) pressure upon demand. As you descend and the water pressure increases, the regulator automatically compensates for the increased pressure. Modern regulators are rugged and reliable.

A regulator consists of a first stage which is attached to the tank (and represents one stage of pressure reduction) and a second stage (which has a mouthpiece and further reduces pressure to a breathable level). The two stages are connected by an intermediate pressure hose. Attached to the first stage of all regulators should be the mandatory submersible pressure gauge, which will be addressed later. Other handy attachments, such as the power inflator hose for the BC, may also be connected to the first stage. An optimum regulator setup is shown in the illustration.

Regulators are engineered in a variety of configurations and all fulfill the purpose for which they are designed. Some deliver air more easily than others. This should be the criteria used when determining which regulator to buy. All regulators will breathe easily at sea level, but some do not perform as well at depth. You will learn a lot about regulators from your instructor during your NAUI course. This will enable you to intelligently select the best regulator for you. Be sure to purchase a submersible pressure gauge along with the regulator.

Regulators have close tolerances, moving parts, and are subject to a harsh environment. While very dependable, they require preventive maintenance after every dive, and annual servicing by professionals who are factory trained and have proper tools, materials, equipment and parts for service. *You should make no attempt to disassemble, lubricate, or adjust a scuba regulator.* Have it serviced for any problems at a dive store. Delaying service on your regulator results in decreased performance and increased breathing effort; this can result in a feeling that you are not getting a sufficient amount of air. Such unpleasantness can be avoided by a thorough servicing once a year.

After each use, a regulator should be rinsed in clean water. Soaking is best, followed by rinsing. Water should be allowed to flow in and out of the holes in the first stage and into the mouthpiece and out of the exhaust on the second stage. Avoid strong water pressure, and *be careful not to depress the purge button on the second stage when water is present and the regulator is not attached to a tank.* With no air in the low pressure hose, depression of the purge allows water to flow through the second stage valve, up the hose and into the first stage, which must remain dry inside. There is a protective

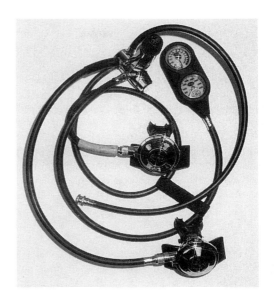

Above, *A modern scuba regulator with four hoses leading to a second stage, an extra second stage, a submersible pressure gauge, and a low pressure inflation device.*
Below, *When rinsing a regulator, use low pressure, avoid depressing the purge button, and be sure the protective cap is in place on the first stage.*

cap that seals the first stage input when it is not in use. This must always be replaced when the regulator is not in use, to prevent water from entering the first stage.

Avoid excessive force on the regulator hoses. They should not be coiled tightly for storage or pulled on when handling the scuba unit. Such actions break down fibers in the hoses and shorten their life.

In summary, select an easy breathing regulator and be sure it's equipped with a submersible pressure gauge. Care for it properly, have the recommended service performed each year, and the regulator will provide excellent service for years.

Contingency Scuba Divers should be able to avoid "out-of-air" situations the same as they avoid out-of-gas situations in their autos. For a variety of reasons, both situations can and do happen. Running out of air under water is certainly not desirable, but there are several options available to a diver for dealing with the circumstance. The preferred option is the use of contingency scuba equipment. Other options will be presented in other chapters.

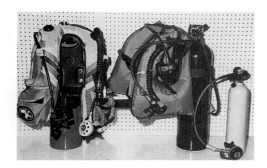

Above, *Different types of contingency scuba: An extra regulator second stage system (octopus) (left), a combination extra second stage and low pressure inflator (center), and a back up scuba unit (pony bottle) (right).*

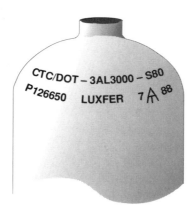

There are two basic types of back-up scuba: a separate scuba unit carried in addition to the primary unit, and an extra regulator second stage that allows two divers to breathe from one scuba unit. Redundant systems may be very small and compact, with built-in regulators, or may be a separate scuba tank with a standard regulator attached. Back-up scuba units are usually attached to the main unit.

Extra regulator second stages, which are called octopus regulators, are quite popular because they are relatively inexpensive (compared to another complete scuba unit), are easily installed, are lightweight and are easy to use. They lack the advantage of a separate air supply and a completely separate regulator. Octopus regulators serve well for most shallow-water situations where an air source is required by another diver.

The low-pressure hose on the octopus should be at least four inches (10 cm) longer than that of the primary regulator and should be secured in some manner so they do not dangle and drag. Your buddy should know where and how the regulator is secured. Back up scuba equipment should receive the same care and service as your regular scuba gear.

Looking Back

We have learned quite a bit about scuba equipment. Let's see if you can recall some of the key points.
1. In the adjacent illustration, circle the service pressure of the scuba tank and label it "A", then circle the hydrostatic testing information and label it "B". State when the next test is required.
2. Which three items of scuba equipment should be serviced each year?
3. Briefly describe the difference between a J valve and a K valve.

_____

_____

4. The recommended regulator configuration has four hoses coming from the first stage. List each hose and describe its use and value.
A. _____
B. _____
C. _____
D. _____

5. What is the most important criteria when selecting a regulator?

_____

6. What is it that should be avoided when rinsing a regulator after use?

_____

7. What are the two basic types of back up scuba units? _____

_____

A. Which one is most used?_____
B. Which is the best, but most expensive?

_____

1.3   Buoyancy Systems

Buoyancy control is one of the most important of all diving skills, so you will want to be very familiar with buoyancy control systems available.

There are three basic types of buoyancy compensators: The horse collar (which is worn around the neck), back flotation systems and buoyancy jackets. Let's address the advantages and disadvantages of each. Then we will look at some of the features of buoyancy systems and how to care for them.

Horse Collar   This device is similar to the old aircraft life vest, but is more refined. A horse collar BC can be used for both skin and scuba diving. Adjustment of the harness is critical to keep the BC from riding up when inflated. It must be donned and removed separately and

the diver must always remember to disconnect the low-pressure inflator hose when removing the scuba unit. Flotation, however, is not lost when the scuba is removed.

Back Flotation   These units are attached to the scuba tank so a separate flotation device is required if the diver wants to skin dive. Also, flotation is lost when the scuba unit is removed. Back flotation systems provide very good body positioning characteristics under water, leave the front of the diver uncluttered, and are popular for photography because of the neater frontal appearance. These systems are possibly more difficult to learn to handle; however, because the buoyancy in the rear tends to push you forward and into a face down position at the surface unless you lie on your back.

Buoyancy Jackets   Jackets tend to be the most popular system. As well as back flotation systems, they do not require the low pressure inflation hose to be disconnected when removing the scuba unit. Buoyancy jackets combine the benefits of both the horse collar and the back flotation system. They are comfortable to wear, provide very good body positioning underwater and give you a face up position at the surface, although some require use of the crotch strap to keep the unit from riding up when inflated.

Features   Buoyancy compensators are made of durable material and are designed for rugged use. They should be equipped with overpressure

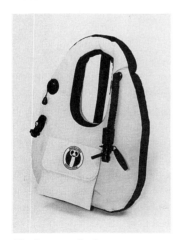

The horse collar buoyancy compensator.

The jacket-type buoyancy compensator.

A back flotation unit buoyancy compensator.

The most popular buoyancy system—the BC jacket.

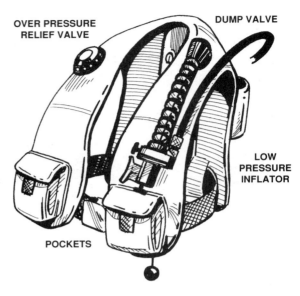

Features of a buoyancy compensator.

OVER PRESSURE RELIEF VALVE

DUMP VALVE

LOW PRESSURE INFLATOR

POCKETS

valves to prevent damage from excessive pressure. All BCs have an inflation/deflation hose which should be of at least 3/4 inch (2 cm) diameter and have an easy-to-work, comfortable mouthpiece. A dump valve mounted high on the unit (activated with a cord or cable from near the bottom of the BC) is easier to use when diving. Pockets are another useful feature.

One of the most important features is the low-pressure inflator which allows inflation to be achieved at the push of a button. Without this system, a diver is required to remove the regulator or snorkel, orally inflate the BC, re-insert and clear the mouthpiece, and repeat the process until sufficient buoyancy is obtained. It is much safer and convenient to have a low-pressure inflation system. At least one manu-facturer has combined a secondary regulator with the low-pressure inflation system for a BC. This has the advantage of eliminating one hose from the regulator and placing a secondary regulator in a position where it is convenient to use.

Carbon dioxide mechanisms are an optional item of some BCs and included on others. Their purpose is to provide flotation rapidly in the event of difficulty in the water. CO_2 detonators require regular maintenance in order to be dependable, and are a controversial item. You

Low pressure inflation system: Standard (top) and with integrated extra second stage (bottom).

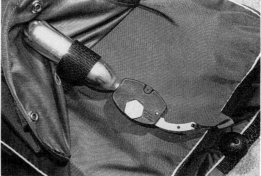

CO_2 mechanism for a BC. Normal position (left) and activated position (right).

should discuss the advantages and disadvantages of CO_2 mechanisms with your instructor and retailer to help you decide whether or not to include this feature on your BC.

Selection The best way to determine which BC is best for you is to obtain recommendations from your instructor, retailer, and other divers in the area, and then to try different types and models in the water. You want one which is comfortable, remains in position when 3/4 inflated, and which has controls that are easy to locate and operate. Be sure the BC you select includes a low-pressure inflation system.

Caring for your Buoyancy Compensator
Modern buoyancy systems are costly, but with proper care will provide long service. It is very important to rinse the unit both internally and externally after use. Salt water, dirty water or chlorinated water inside the BC will cause damage. Fill the unit with a couple of quarts of clean water through the oral inflator, slosh the water around inside, drain the water thoroughly, then fully inflate the unit to allow it to dry and to be sure it hasn't developed leaks.

If the BC has a CO_2 cartridge, it is necessary to remove and check the cartridge and clean and lubricate its threads each time the BC is used. Between dives, store the cartridge to protect it. This is important to insure reliability.

Looking Back

Let's review some of the important aspects of buoyancy systems.

1. Match the buoyancy system with the best description for each.

Horse Collar _____ a. Most popular system

Back Flotation _____ b. Provides good body positioning underwater

Buoyancy Jacket _____

c. Can be used for skin and scuba diving

2. Which of the following features is the most important one for consideration when selecting a BC?
a. Dump valve
b. CO_2 detonator
c. Low pressure inflator
d. Integrated back pack

3. Why do BCs need to be rinsed inside as well as outside?

1.4 Weighting Systems

To compensate for the buoyancy of your body, your protection suit, and other equipment, lead weights are used. As you will see, weights are available in many configurations. As you gain experience, you will be better able to determine which type is best for your needs. For now, let's just get acquainted with the systems and their features.

Weight Belts The most widely used system is the two inch (5 cm) wide nylon belt which holds various sizes of weights. The belt and 1-10 pound (.45-4.5 kg) weights are simple and easy to use. Once divers have determined the exact amount of weight needed for local diving, some prefer to use hip weights which balance well and keep the area beneath the tank clear. Belts that can be filled with lead shot are another option and offer the advantages of greater comfort and less danger of injury or damage occurring if dropped. Padded and covered weight belts are also available.

An additional feature a weight belt should have is a means to adjust its length. This is needed because different diving situations require different amounts of lead. As the weights are added and removed, the length of the belt changes. If changes in length can be made at the buckle end of the belt, excess lengths can and should be avoided on the free end when the belt is worn. A maximum excess of six inches (15 cm) is recommended. A popular feature of belts is some means to automatically take up the slack which is caused when a diver's circumference is reduced by the compression of the neoprene suit from water pressure. Belts which compensate for this change meet the need in several ways. This feature is desirable in areas where thick suits are required due to cold water temperatures.

The most important feature of a weight belt, however, is the quick-release buckle. Several types are available. The buckle should hold securely but release easily with a single motion from one hand. Find out the type of quick release preferred in your area.

Integrated Weight Systems To eliminate the belt and reduce the number of items needed to dive, weighting systems have been developed that are part of the scuba unit. This increases the weight of the unit and makes it difficult to handle out of the water, but the integrated units are preferred by some divers. It is important that these units have an easy, reliable means to release the weights included in them. Integrated systems without quick release options should be avoided. Periodic maintenance of the weights or lead shot and the release mechanism will probably be required to keep the weight release process functioning properly.

More information on weights, such as estimating the number of pounds of weight, preparing a belt for use and donning and handling techniques will be addressed in the Skills chapter.

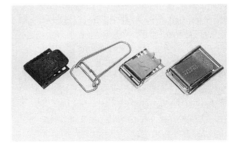

Above, Various types of weight belts for both regular weights and for lead shot.
Below, Lead weights are available in various shapes and sizes.

Above, Two types of compensating weight belts. *Below,* Various types of weight belt quick releases — The most important feature of the belt.

Looking Back

See if you can recall a few essential points regarding weighting systems.
1. What is the most important feature of a weight belt? _____
2. Describe the purpose of a compensating weight belt. _____

_____

3. Which type of weighting system requires maintenance. Why? _____

_____

1.5 Protective Clothing

Divers need protection against heat loss, cuts, scrapes, stings, and other injuries which are possible in the diving environment. We will examine various types and find out how to care for apparel worn for diving.

Wet suits Made of foam neoprene material in various thicknesses, ranging from 1/8 inch to 3/8 inch (3 mm to 9 mm), wet suits are the most widely used protective suits. They trap water inside which is quickly heated by the body. The insulation of the suit, which consists of tiny inert gas bubbles, prevents the heat contained within the suit from being lost. It should be apparent that a wet suit needs to fit snugly so the exchange of water inside will be minimal. The more cold water allowed into a suit, the sooner the diver will become chilled. It should also be obvious that the thicker the suit, the greater the insulation provided. What is not obvious is that the thicker the suit, the more weight required to overcome suit buoyancy, and the greater buoyancy loss as the suit is compressed by pressure.

"Shorty" suits are popular in warm water areas, while full suits are required for less temperate waters. For cold-water diving, wet suit divers opt for "Farmer John" suits to obtain an added layer of insulation over the trunk of the body.

Besides different colors and thicknesses, wet suit features include a nylon covering on one or both sides. "Nylon Two" suits endure better than those with nylon on the inside only, but sacrifice some elasticity. Zippers for the arms and legs are another option. In general, the warmer you

Today's wet suits are soft, comfortable, and attractive.

need to be, the fewer zippers the suit should have. Zippers make it easier, though, to don and remove the suit. You can also select from a list of other features offered by wet suit manufacturers. These include custom tailoring (recommended for greatest warmth), knee pads (also recommended), spine pad to reduce water flow down the back (a good idea, as well), pockets, knife sheaths, etc. Find out which features are preferred by local divers before ordering your suit. The type of suit worn by your instructor and its features will also serve as a good guide.

"Shorty" suits for warm water (left) and "Farmer John" suits for colder water (right).

Dry Suits For colder waters, dry suits are preferred. They are considerably more expensive than wet suits, but the increased comfort may be well worth it. There are at least three types currently available; foam neoprene suits, solid neoprene suits, and nylon shells.

Foam neoprene suits are one-piece suits that employ a waterproof zipper and seals at the extremities to exclude water. Insulation is provided by the suit itself. They are warmer than wet suits primarily because water is excluded from the suit and the diver is insulated by a layer of air as well as the insulation of the suit.

Dry suits are bulkier and require more weight than wet suits. They are more difficult to control underwater because they contain air. To reduce some of these problems, the solid neoprene suit was developed. It requires insulation to be worn under the suit. Because the thickness of the insulation worn can vary, the suit has versatility for diving in water of varying temperatures.

The third type of dry suit is the nylon shell. This is a loose-fitting type which allows a great deal of mobility and is very comfortable. Like the solid neoprene suit, the nylon shell requires special undergarments for effective insulation.

Because dry suits do not need to fit as closely as wet suits, the need for a custom-tailored fit is not as great. The cost will still be more than that of a wet suit due to the special water-tight zipper and other materials and labor needed to make the suit waterproof.

Because air must be added and vented from dry suits, they are equipped with the means to accomplish this. Low-pressure inflation valves are more desirable than oral inflators, so the well-equipped dry suit diver will have a hose from his regulator first stage leading to the suit inflator.

Special training is required for using dry suits. You will need to learn how to control them and to prevent and recover from runaway ascents (that can result from accidental loss of the weight belt and/or excessive air in the suits).

Dry suits have one great disadvantage. If the diver needs to urinate while using a wet suit it is easy to do so. But this isn't the case in a suit that's supposed to remain dry inside! On the other hand, a dry suit keeps you warmer so that the need to urinate shouldn't be as great or as frequent.

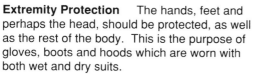

Above, A loose-fitting nylon shell dry suit (left) compared to a form-fitting typical wet suit (right).

Above Right, Protection for the extremities— hood, boots, and gloves. *Right*, Neoprene gloves (left) and mitts (right).

Extremity Protection   The hands, feet and perhaps the head, should be protected, as well as the rest of the body. This is the purpose of gloves, boots and hoods which are worn with both wet and dry suits.

Gloves of some type should always be worn while diving. Water softens the hands, so cuts and scrapes occur easily. Gloves are worn primarily to protect the hands from injury in warm water. Either gloves or neoprene mitts are worn in cold water to protect against heat loss as well as injuries. It is a good idea to learn to handle your equipment by wearing gloves during training so you will be better able to do so when you start diving on a regular basis.

Boots protect the feet from chafing by the fins, cushion them, provide protection against scrapes and cuts, prevent excessive heat loss, and serve as shoes on shore. These are all worthwhile reasons for divers to wear boots, even in tropical areas. Boots range from a simple neoprene sock to elaborate footwear with vulcanized, durable soles. Fit and comfort are,

once again, the most important considerations (along with the local requirements).

Half or more of the body's heat loss can take place from the head, so it is advisable to wear a hood when diving in temperate or cold water. These are standard hoods, cold water hoods — which have a large bib to provide greater insulation around the neck and shoulders — and dry suit hoods. The latter have special neck seals to mate against the neck seal of the dry suit itself. Some new divers dislike the feeling of a hood initially, but soon realize how much warmer they can be by wearing one.

Care and Maintenance   Protective clothing for diving requires the customary rinsing, should also be kept out of the sun as much as possible, and should be stored in a cool, dry place. Zippers require occasional lubrication with stick lubricant (available at dive stores). Small holes and tears can be easily repaired with suit cement, (also available from a dive store). You should prevent creasing foam neoprene items by avoiding folding them for prolonged periods. Creasing ruptures the insulating cells and reduces insulation along the crease. It is best to hang suits on special, wide suit hangers designed especially for the purpose. Hoods, boots, and gloves should receive the same care as the suits.

Top Left, Boots for diving. Molded sole (left) and hard sole boots (right).
Bottom Left, The tops of the boots should be worn under the wet suit pants. The pants are donned first, however.

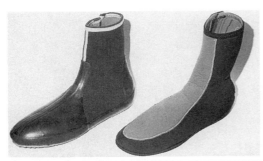

Looking Back

Can you answer these questions without referring back to the text? (It's okay if you need to look back.)

1. Protective clothing for diving is intended to protect against _____ and _____

2. Briefly describe why a dry suit keeps a diver warmer than a wet suit. _____
_____

3. What type of suit requires the greatest amount of weight? _____

4. To reduce heat loss in cold water, which of the following is of greatest value: gloves, boots or hood?

1.6 Diving Instruments

Just as an astronaut needs to rely upon instrumentation to know the time, location, and condition of a life support system, so a diver is dependent upon information provided by special instruments. You need to know where you are, where you are going, how deep you are, how long you can stay, and how much air remains in your tank. Let's look at the gauges available to provide this needed data.

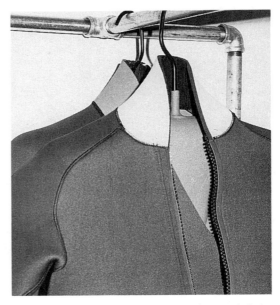

Store protective suits on wide hangers in a cool, dark place away from smog.

Submersible Pressure Gauge The Submersible Pressure Gauge (SPG) is an essential instrument for scuba diving. It monitors your air supply and is equivalent to the gas gauge in a car. You need to learn to interpret gauge readings and to refer to the gauge frequently while diving so you will be aware of a dwindling air supply and can avoid running out of air.

All SPGs perform the same function — they measure the pressure of the air in your tank. When the tank is filled, the working pressure is indicated on the gauge. When the tank is half full, the pressure will read only half as much, and so forth. By knowing the working pressure of the tank, you can determine the approximate amount of air in a tank by means of the gauge reading.

An SPG is a fairly sensitive instrument, so it should not be subjected to shocks or other abuse. Small leaks from the hose or connectors are no cause for alarm while diving, but the problem should be corrected at a dive store as soon as practical. A gauge with water inside requires servicing, and can become a hazard if repair is continually postponed.

Rinsing your SPG after use, avoiding harsh treatment, and having minor problems corrected promptly by a professional will result in many years of reliable service from your Submersible Pressure Gauge, which is a required item for all scuba dives.

Depth Gauges As you will soon learn, you are limited as to how deep you can dive and how long you can remain at a given depth, so a depth gauge is needed as a reference to help you avoid exceeding established limits.

There are two main types of gauges: capillary and Bourdon tube. The capillary gauge is a simple, inexpensive instrument that uses an air column in a piece of clear tubing. The air in the tube is compressed at depth, and the reading is indicated by the water/air interface inside the tube. The capillary gauge is very accurate for shallow depths up to about 40 feet (12 m) but is not recommended for use at greater depths.

Bourdon tube gauges use pressure to bend a curved metal tube. The straightening of the tube turns a needle on the dial through a linkage of levers and gears. An open Bourdon tube — seldom seen today — allows water inside the metal tube. A closed gauge has the tube filled with oil. The pressure is transmitted through a flexible part of the housing to the oil in the tube. Open Bourdon tube gauges require careful maintenance to keep the tube clear and open.

A Submersible Pressure Gauge (SPG) in use, plus a close-up of a typical gauge.

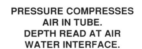

PRESSURE COMPRESSES AIR IN TUBE. DEPTH READ AT AIR WATER INTERFACE.

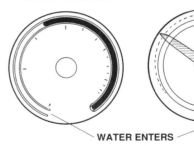

WATER ENTERS

PRESSURE TENDS TO STRAIGHTEN TUBE AND CAUSES NEEDLE TO MOVE.

A capillary depth gauge (left) compared to a Bourdon tube gauge (right).

Accuracy of these gauges is reasonable and fairly constant with depth, but initial and occasional accuracy checks are strongly recommended.

A desirable feature of a depth gauge is a means of memory for the deepest depth reached during a dive. The value of this will become apparent later. Some gauges have indicators which are pushed along by the needle on the dial.

Depth gauges need to be treated as the delicate instruments they are. They should be checked for accuracy when first obtained and at least annually thereafter. Reduced atmospheric pressure and high altitudes can be harmful to some gauges, so they should be transported in a pressure proof container when subjected to heights in excess of 1000 feet (300m).

Various types of depth gauges.

Timing Devices   Not only are you limited as to how deep you may safely dive, you are also restricted as to how long you can safely remain at a given depth. Dive watches or underwater timers are essential items.

Watches used for diving should be dive watches, not just waterproof ones. Divers need a way to measure elapsed time; this should be a feature of the watch. Analog watches accomplish this with a rotating bezel around the dial, while a stop watch mode is common for digital watches.

Underwater timers are designed to measure elapsed time, but have a valuable feature which may make them more desirable than a dive watch. A pressure-activated switch automatically starts and stops the time as you begin your descent and return to the surface, thereby automatically recording the elapsed time with no conscious thought required by a diver. When using a watch, you must remember to set the recording mechanism at the beginning of the dive and check it at the end. This action is sometimes overlooked.

Timing devices should be treated like the watches they are. They should be cleaned and lubricated as specified by the manufacturer. Wearing them in the shower or in a Jacuzzi is not advised.

An assortment of underwater watches and timing devices.

Compasses   When you are suspended in water and unable to see very far, a compass becomes an important reference instrument. Some divers use a compass on every dive, even in clear, tropical water. It can also be useful at the surface when fog suddenly appears.

The principle of a compass is simple. A magnetized, freely rotating needle, when not caused to deviate by local magnetic forces, aligns itself with the earth's magnetic field and points to magnetic north. This constant reference allows a diver to know position in relation to the north-seeking needle and to set and follow a course.

A compass used for diving should be a diving compass. This means it will be liquid filled, have a reference line called a "lubber line" and will have some means to specify a selected heading or direction. We will become more familiar with the compass and its use in the Skills chapter.

A compass should receive common sense care and should not be left in the sun for prolonged periods. The heat can cause the liquid inside to expand and leak.

Consoles   The various gauges sold for diving are available separately, but some divers prefer to combine them into an instrument console rather than wearing each gauge separately on the wrist. This makes it easier to suit up for a dive and keeps the arms clear. A console is formed around the submersible pressure gauge, so it can be heavy and should be supported in some way rather than allowed to hang free. The hose leading to the console should also have a hose protector added at the first stage end to prevent the weight of the console from damaging the hose. Hose protectors are a good idea for all hoses on a regulator.

Diving Compass

Diving compasses are available in a variety of sizes and types.

Dive Computers   Sophisticated computers to continuously monitor your time and depth are available to display information regarding how long you may remain at various depths. Information provided by other diving instruments, such as maximum depth, temperature – even tank pressure – may also be displayed. There are many dive computers currently available, and they offer a number of features. Selection is not an easy task, but your instructor and retailer can help you make a good choice when you become interested in a dive computer. These devices are extremely useful and desirable instruments, but they must be used properly. More information about dive computers and guidelines for their use is contained in Chapter Five of this text.

Looking Back

1. Which type of depth gauge is accurate only at shallow depths? _____

2. When should Bourdon tube depth gauges be checked for accuracy? _____

3. What is the main advantage of an underwater timer over a dive watch? _____

4. What four instruments are considered required equipment for diving?

A. _____   B. _____

C. _____   D. _____

1.7   Diving Accessories

With primary equipment, scuba equipment, protective clothing, buoyancy, weight systems, and instrumentation, you would think you'd be fully equipped for diving. You almost are, but not quite, Let's look at some major and minor accessories to the gear we've learned about thus far. Major accessories are actually required items, while minor accessories are merely nice to have.

Two Gauge Console

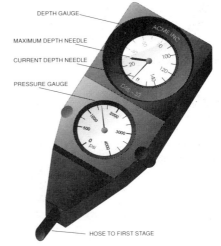

A typical instrument console.

Major Accessories   All divers should have a dive knife or a diver's tool with them while in the water. This item isn't for fighting off the denizens of the deep. It is a tool useful for cutting, prying, measuring and pounding. A sharp knife

A "Diver's Tool" (left) and different types of dive knives.

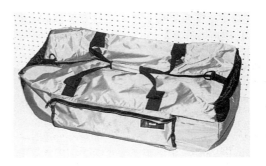

A gear bag is useful for transporting all of the equipment needed for diving.

The dive knife should be worn on the inside of the leg.

edge and a serrated part on a dive knife are needed to cut rope or line under water. This is probably the greatest need dive knives can meet, although they are designed to fulfill other functions as well. Dive knives and tools are available in many sizes and designs. A small one may serve very well, but the size and design best for you will depend on your locale and needs.

A sturdy sheath with straps is usually included with a dive knife. If worn on the leg, the knife should be strapped to the inside of the lower leg to avoid possible fouling.

Dive knives should be rinsed, dried and coated with a light film of oil to prevent corrosion. The edge should be kept sharp.

Another handy accessory is a gear bag. There are many styles and sizes from which to choose, but be sure to get one for transporting your gear.

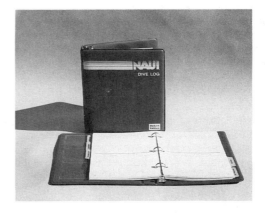

Your log book is a valuable record which should be maintained.

Dive flags are required in some areas. The flag warns boats of diving operations. Some states require that boaters remain at least 100 feet (30 m) clear of a dive flag. When using a flag, you have some obligations to fulfill. It should be displayed only when actually diving, and you should dive in its vicinity. Both the standard U. S. dive flag and the international "Alpha" flag are depicted. Your instructor will inform you of the local laws and practices.

A log book may not be an item of equipment, but it should be with you everywhere you go with your gear. It is a valuable record that is required by NAUI and should be maintained. In some areas, a record of logged dives is required as proof of recent diving experience. Also, as your diving career progresses, you may want to become involved in leadership positions. You'll need documentation of your diving experience. A well-kept log is the best means of documenting your underwater adventures.

It is always a good idea to have a first aid kit handy. By adding a few items to meet particular needs for diving, you can be prepared to quickly deal with minor injuries. The recommended contents are listed in the Appendix. For now, simply realize that having a compact first aid kit as part of your diving equipment is wise and recommended. And always carry your plastic NAUI Decompression Tables.

Minor Accessories   The following are some items which can be extremely useful:
Underwater slate - handy for recording data and communications.
Goodie bag - useful to hold game, specimens, artifacts and other "goodies."
Underwater light - obviously necessary for diving at night, but handy for daytime use as well to bring out vivid colors and to peer into holes and crevices.
Marker buoy - excellent for marking the location of items dropped or a specific area.
Spare parts - a kit of items which can save a dive. Includes such things as mask and fin straps, snorkel keepers, O-rings, etc.
Checklist - a great way to be sure you remember all the things you need for diving. Include personal articles as well as your dive gear. See sample in Appendix.

Dive Flags: The standard U.S. dive flag (left) and the International "Alpha" flag (right).

Looking Back

Can you recall these points regarding accessory equipment?
1. What is the most likely use for a dive knife under water? _____
2. What two responsibilities do you have when using the dive flag?
A. _____
B. _____
3. List two reasons why dives should be recorded in a log book.
A. _____
B. _____
4. List three minor accessory items that you feel will be useful.
A. _____
B. _____
C. _____

We said at the outset of the chapter that diving is an equipment-intensive activity. By now you should be a believer! Remember that all of this equipment helps you adapt to the underwater environment and to function there as safely and comfortably as possible. The more you work with the gear, the easier it becomes. Soon, using and handling equipment will be second nature, and you'll be able to devote much more of your attention to your surroundings and activities.

2 *Underwater Sciences*

2.1 *Water Compared to Air*

You are probably familiar with many of the differences in the properties of air and water. We need to examine them in greater detail because the better you understand these differences, the better you will be able to function within the underwater world and the safer you will be as a diver.

Composition You know that humans can't breathe water, and that no one has yet produced a practical artificial gill. We need to breathe oxygen in the form of a gas in order to live. Only about 20% of the air we breathe is oxygen. The remainder is primarily nitrogen, which is inert. But, as you will see, nitrogen does have some effects upon divers.

Compressibility Air can be easily compressed; but for all practical purposes, water is considered to be incompressible. The air surrounding the earth is compressed at the surface by the weight of the air above it, so the air at sea level is denser than it is high in the mountains. But, for all diving depths, water at depth can be considered equal in density to that at the surface. The effect of this is that a force applied to air will compress the air if it cannot escape, while a force applied to water which cannot escape is simply transmitted freely in all directions throughout the fluid. When you study pressure later in this chapter, you will see how this transmission of force can affect you as a diver. In another chapter, you will see how the decreasing density of air with altitude can also affect you.

Density We just mentioned that the density of air decreases with altitude. What is density? It is the quantity of something per unit of volume, such as pounds per cubic foot or kilograms per liter. If you pick up a bucket of air and a bucket of water, the water is much heavier than the air because the water is much denser than the air. A filled, standard scuba tank weighs over six pounds (2.7 kg) more than an empty tank of the same size. This is because the air weighs about .08 pounds per cubic foot (1.25 grams per liter). As you will see when you become familiar with the principles of buoyancy, this difference in weight will affect your diving.

The density or weight of fresh water is about 62.4 pounds per cubic foot (1.0 kg per liter); while sea water, containing dissolved salts, is slightly heavier, at 64 pounds per cubic foot (1.025 kg per liter). By comparing the densities

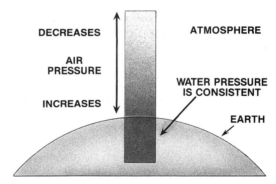

Varying air density with changing altitude compared to constant water density with changing depth.

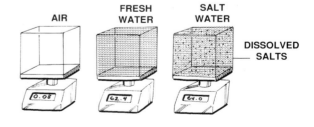

Densities (weight per unit volume) of air and water compared.

of air and water, you can see that water is 800 times more dense than air. Because of its higher density, water presents much greater resistance to movement through it than does air. The force of resistance to movement through a fluid is called "drag."

It is easy to see that drag must be greater in water than in air. In addition to the density of the fluid, drag is also affected by the frontal area of an object moving through it. The greater the frontal area exposed, the greater the drag. The effect upon you as a diver is that streamlining is important in water due to the great resistance to motion. A diver in a horizontal swimming position has much less resistance to forward progress than one in a semi-upright position, and the horizontal diver exerts much less energy for a given speed than does the upright diver.

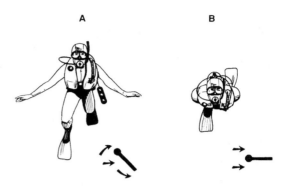

Streamlining reduces drag and the amount of exertion required. Diver A must exert more than Diver B.

Flow   You are probably familiar with the flow of water through a hose, but you also need to understand the flow of air as it relates to diving. The deeper you dive, the more resistance there is to the flow of air as you breathe. You have learned that air is compressible and is acted upon by the weight of the medium above it. Air becomes compressed and increases in density as depth in water increases. This produces increased breathing resistance and imposes limitations upon your exertion level as a recreational diver.

Heat Capacity and Transmission   When the air temperature is 80° F (27° C), you feel warm. When the water temperature is 80° F (27° C), it feels warm also, but you will become chilled enough to shiver in a relatively short time while relaxing in 80° F (27° C) water. You will probably be diving in water colder than this, so you need to understand how water can cause you to lose body heat rapidly. The first way occurs because water is much denser than air and can thus absorb a great deal of heat with only a small change in temperature. In fact, a given volume of water can absorb 3600 times as much heat as the same volume of air undergoing the same increase in temperature.

The second reason is also related to density. The molecules of water are closer together than those in air. Thus, heat can be conducted—transmitted by direct contact—at a rate approximately 20 times greater than it is conducted in air.

With the great heat capacity of water and its high rate of conductivity, it is easy to understand how you can lose large quantities of body heat and become chilled while diving. The effects of body heat loss and the prevention of it are addressed in another chapter.

Sound and Light Differences   Things look and sound differently underwater. Due to the density of water, sound travels through it rapidly. In fact, sound waves move so quickly through water that you are unable to determine their source.

While sound travels faster in water than in air — about four times faster — light travels slower. As light rays pass into the denser water, they are slowed and bending occurs. This bending, known as "refraction" causes visual differences which are presented in detail later in this chapter.

There is much more color in the underwater world than there appears to be. This is because daylight is composed of all of the colors of the spectrum and these colors are absorbed by water: first the warm reds and oranges, then the yellows and greens, until only blues and greys remain. The deeper you go in water, the less color you see, unless you provide an artificial light source at close range. When you do this, the undersea world comes alive with unbelievable colors.

Water will significantly affect your movement, warmth, senses and breathing. To become a diver you need to learn how to handle these

Due to the bending of light rays as the light passes from water into the air space of a mask, vision is affected. Objects appear larger and closer.

differences. This is what the equipment and skills of diving help you to do, so let's learn more about adapting to the underwater world by learning more about the physical effects on divers and the equipment and skills needed.

Looking Back

Test your retention and understanding with the following questions:

1. Air is about _____ % oxygen, and the balance consists primarily of _____

2. Air is more dense in the mountains than it is at sea level. True_____False _____

3. The density of water is much greater at 100 feet (30 m) than it is at 10 feet (3 m).
True _____ False _____

4. The difference in weight between a full and an empty 80 cubic foot (12 l) scuba tank is about _____ pounds (kg).

5. Briefly describe how a diver can reduce the effects of drag in the water.

_____

_____

6. In one sentence, describe why breathing resistance increases with depth.

_____

_____

7. List the two primary reasons for the high rate of loss of body heat in water.

A. _____

B. _____

2.2   Pressure

When you descend in water, the forces of the weight of the air and water above you will affect you. This force, measured in pounds per square inch or kilograms per square meter, is called pressure. In this part of this chapter, you will learn the rate of increase of pressure in water.

You already know that air has weight. The weight of the atmosphere surrounding the earth is approximately 14.7 pounds per square inch ($1.03 kg/cm^2$). This means that a one-inch square (one cm^2) column of air extending from the earth's surface to the outer edge of the atmosphere has a weight of about 14.7 pounds (1.03 kg). This constant force is referred to as one atmosphere of pressure. It acts upon us constantly, but we are adapted to it and scarcely notice any of the effects.

Remember that atmospheric pressure decreases with altitude. Later we will learn how decreasing atmospheric pressure by increasing altitude affects divers, but for now we will deal with atmospheric pressure as the pressure at sea level.

What we are concerned with in diving is the rate of change of pressure in water. To determine this rate of increase or decrease, you need to understand the amount of force resulting from the weight of water.

You know that salt water weighs 64 pounds per cubic foot (1.025 kg/l). If you were to take a one inch square (one cm^2) column of water and keep adding to it vertically, you would find that at a height of 33 feet (10 m) the one inch square (one cm^2) column of water is equal to atmospheric pressure. Thirty-three feet (10 m) of sea water is equivalent to one atmosphere of pressure. Because fresh water is less dense than salt water, one atmosphere of pressure in fresh water requires 34 feet (10.3 m) of water.

Since water is essentially incompressible and it transmits pressure freely, pressure in water increases at a constant rate and its effect is cumulative. Simply stated, if 33 feet (10 m) of water equals one atmosphere of pressure, 66 feet (20 m) equals two atmospheres of pressure, 99 feet (30 m) equals three atmospheres, and so on.

While diving, you are under the pressure of both the water and the atmosphere above it. Both pressures must be taken into consideration. At sea level, you are under one atmosphere of pressure. At a depth of 33 feet (10 m) in the ocean, or 34 feet (10.3 m) in fresh water, you are under two atmospheres of pressure — one from the air and one from the water. At 66 feet (20 m) in salt water you are under three

atmospheres of pressure. Since you are concerned with the rate of change of pressure, you must always take atmospheric pressure into consideration when working with changing pressures. This will become more evident in the next part of this chapter.

Since atmospheric pressure is nearly constant at sea level, most pressure gauges are adjusted so they read zero at sea level. When a depth gauge indicates 33 feet (10 m) it is saying that

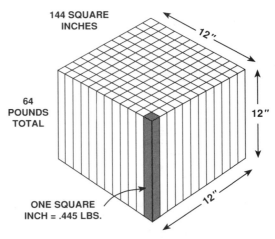

One cubic foot of salt water (64 pounds) exerts .445 pounds per square inch (64/144=.445). This pressure times 33 shows how 33 feet of salt water equals 1 atm of pressure (14.7 psi). One cubic meter (1,000 l) of salt water (1,025 kg) exerts 0.1025 kg per square centimeter. This pressure times 10 shows how 10 m of salt water equals one atm of pressure (1.03 kg/cm^2).

the pressure is one atmosphere greater than it was at the surface of the water. The pressure measured on a gauge is termed "gauge pressure," but it is not the total pressure present because it does not include atmospheric pressure. When atmospheric pressure is added to gauge pressure, the sum is termed "absolute pressure." This is the pressure to be used when determining the rate of increase or decrease of pressure for diving.

For example, if you descend from the surface to 33 feet (10 m), you are doubling the pressure, and if you ascend to the surface from 66 feet (20 m), you are reducing the pressure to one-third of what it was at 66 feet (20 m). Remember that

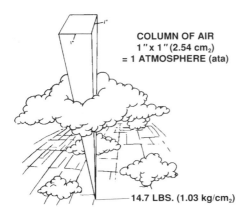

Atmospheric pressure is approximately 14.7 pounds per square inch (1.03 kg/cm$_2$) due to the weight of the air above the earth's surface.

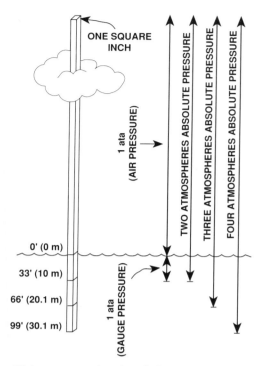

ONE SQUARE INCH

1 ata (AIR PRESSURE)

TWO ATMOSPHERES ABSOLUTE PRESSURE

THREE ATMOSPHERES ABSOLUTE PRESSURE

FOUR ATMOSPHERES ABSOLUTE PRESSURE

0' (0 m)

33' (10 m)

66' (20.1 m)

99' (30.1 m)

1 ata (GAUGE PRESSURE)

Water pressure alone is called "gauge pressure," but the weight of the atmosphere must also be considered. When combined, atmospheric and water pressure are called "absolute pressure."

absolute pressure is always one atmosphere more than the pressure of the water alone and that the atmosphere of air pressure must always be included.

You may be wondering how to determine the pressure at depths which are not equal to one atmosphere increments. Although you do not need to know this as a beginning diver, it may be of interest to note that pressure increases at a rate of .445 pounds per square inch (psi) per foot (0.125 kg per meter) of salt water and .432 psi per foot (0.1 kg per meter) of fresh water. By multiplying this constant by the depth in feet and adding 14.7 pounds (1.03 kg) (the average value for atmospheric pressure), you can determine the exact pressure at any depth in either fresh water or salt water.

For example, the pressure at a depth of 100 feet (30 m) in the ocean is 44.5 psi (3.09 kg) of gauge pressure plus 14.7 psi (1.03 kg) of atmospheric pressure, for an absolute pressure of 59.2 psi (4.12 kg). For your purposes, you

are more concerned with the rate of change of pressure than in the exact numbers. One hundred feet is only one foot greater than 99 feet (30 m) which is four atmospheres of pressure, so the increase or decrease of pressure compared to sea level is a factor of four. This is much more meaningful than the calculations in pounds per square inch or kg/cm^2 and is the approach we will use in the next part of this chapter involving pressure/volume relationships.

Looking Back

You have a good grasp of the concepts of atmospheric and water pressure if you can correctly answer the following questions:

1. One atmosphere of pressure is equaled by _____ feet (meters) of fresh water or by _____ feet (meters) of sea water.

2. The pressure is ____ times greater at a depth of 136 feet (40 m) in fresh water than it is at the surface.

3. What is the absolute pressure in atmospheres at a depth of 66 feet (20 m) in the ocean? _____

2.3 The Primary Effects of Pressure

With an understanding of the properties of water and some background on pressure, you will now be able to see how the effects of increasing water pressure directly affect you.

Let's start by illustrating some of the effects of increasing pressure with a simple "open system" — an inverted bucket filled with air and taken to depth in the ocean. As the bucket is forced below the surface, the pressure increases, causing the air inside the bucket to be compressed. The volume of air varies in proportion to the absolute pressure — as the pressure increases, the volume decreases proportionately. When the total pressure has doubled at a depth of 33 feet (10 m) the amount of air in the bucket will be one-half of its original volume. No air has been lost, it has only been compressed. When the bucket is taken to the surface, the air inside will expand to its original volume.

Let's compare a different situation, one where a constant volume of air is maintained in the

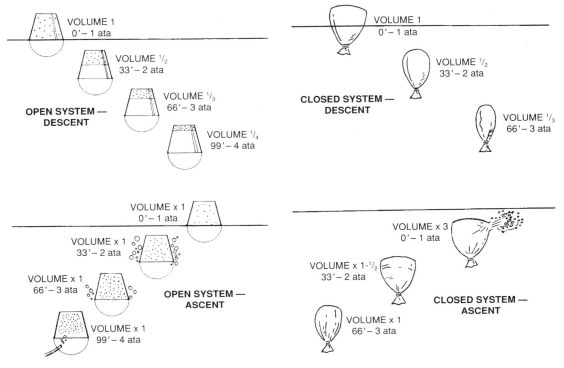

VOLUME 1
0' – 1 ata

VOLUME 1/2
33' – 2 ata

VOLUME 1/3
66' – 3 ata

**OPEN SYSTEM —
DESCENT**

VOLUME 1/4
99' – 4 ata

VOLUME 1
0' – 1 ata

VOLUME 1/2
33' – 2 ata

**CLOSED SYSTEM —
DESCENT**

VOLUME 1/3
66' – 3 ata

VOLUME x 1
0' – 1 ata

VOLUME x 1
33' – 2 ata

VOLUME x 1
66' – 3 ata

**OPEN SYSTEM —
ASCENT**

VOLUME x 1
99' – 4 ata

VOLUME x 3
0' – 1 ata

VOLUME x 1-1/2
33' – 2 ata

**CLOSED SYSTEM —
ASCENT**

VOLUME x 1
66' – 3 ata

Above, Effects of increasing pressure on an open system. Below, Compressed air expanding in an open system during ascent. Above right, Effects of decreasing pressure on a closed system during descent. Below, Compressed air in a closed system either expands its container or builds up pressure during ascents. For this reason, air in your lungs must be allowed to escape when you use scuba.

bucket during descent. This is done by adding air from an external air source to keep the bucket filled with air as the original quantity of air is compressed by pressure. As the bucket is taken deeper, more air is needed. Let's assume the bucket is taken to a depth of 33 feet (10 m) and filled with air, then raised to the surface. When the pressure is decreased from two atmospheres to one atmosphere, the volume of air in the bucket doubles. Since the bucket was filled with air at 33 feet (10 m), you should be able to visualize that one bucket of air will expand and escape from the container during the ascent to the surface. Can you also understand that three buckets of air will escape if the bucket is raised from a depth of 99 feet (30 m)?

The inverse relationship between pressure and volume is known as Boyles Law. Knowing the law is not as important as understanding the relationship between pressure and volume. If you like algebraic formulas, it may be helpful for you to see the relationship with the formula

$P1V1 = P2V2$, where P1 is the starting pressure, P2 is the new pressure, V1 is the starting volume and V2 is the new volume.

For example, if we substitute quantities for the bucket of air raised from 99 feet (30 m) (four atmospheres), we find that P1 = 4, V1 = 1, and P2 = 1. This means that 4 x 1 = 1 x V2. The answer is obviously four. Remember that absolute pressures must be used when making pressure/volume calculations.

Now let's examine the effects of pressure on a "closed system." Imagine a sealed plastic bag filled with air and pushed below the surface in the sea. During descent, the bag gets smaller as the air inside is compressed. When the bag is raised to the surface, the air inside expands and returns the bag to its original volume. If air can be injected into the bag at depth, a different situation will result during ascent than did with the bucket. If the bag is filled with air at depth and sealed and the bag is then raised toward the surface, the expanding air in the bag will be unable to escape. If the sealed bag was filled at a pressure of two atmospheres and brought to the surface, the pressure inside the bag would be twice the surrounding pressure, or the bag would burst. From a depth of three atmospheres (66 feet/20 m), the pressure differential would triple. To prevent the bag from rupturing, the excess air must be vented during ascent. In the next part of this chapter, you will see how this principle applies to your lungs when you breathe compressed air.

Increasing pressure also affects the density of air. In an open system, air is compressed as depth increases. The given amount of air occupies a smaller space as pressure increases. Thus, the density of the air is twice as great at two atmospheres, three times as great at three atmospheres, etc. If air is added to an air space to maintain the original volume, the air space will contain twice as much air at 33 feet (10 m) as the surface, three times as much air at 66 feet (20 m), etc. The overall effect is, the deeper you dive, the denser the air inside an air space. This explains why you use air faster when you dive deeper and why breathing resistance increases with depth. You are moving and consuming more molecules of air with each breath you take.

In Chapter 3 you will apply the primary effects of pressure to understand more clearly the basis for ear clearing, breathing habits and other aspects of the equalization of pressure. Since

we live on land without difficulty (while submerged in a sea of air and under the pressure of the atmosphere), we can also function well submerged beneath the pressure of water. We must do as we do on land, however — keep the pressure in the air spaces inside our bodies equal to the pressure outside. One of your most important goals is to learn to do this.

Looking Back

Complete the following charts for a given quantity of air in a balloon. An example is provided.

Pressure	Volume	Density
Doubles	Halves	Doubles
_____	One-third	_____
Halves	_____	_____
_____	_____	Quadruples

2.4 Buoyancy

Some things float, others sink and a few do neither. Let's find out why. Let's also find out how buoyancy can be controlled so you can float, sink or be neutrally buoyant at will.

The ancient scientist, Archimedes, discovered that an object immersed in water is buoyed up by a force equal to the weight of the water displaced by the object. If an object displaces an amount of water weighing more than itself, it floats. If the object weighs more than the amount of water displaced, it sinks. This actually relates to the density or specific gravity

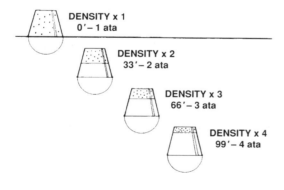

Above, Effect of pressure on the density of air.
Right, The average person can float motionless with the lungs filled with air. Exhaling reduces lung volume and displacement of water and results in a loss of buoyancy. Buoyancy control with lung volume is important for divers to understand.

of objects. Those denser than water sink, while those less dense than water float.

By examining actual diving situations, the principles of buoyancy will more easily be understood. The human body, with full lungs in the water, usually has a slight amount of positive buoyancy. This can vary significantly with changes in lung volume. Breathing out causes the chest to deflate, displaces less volume, and results in less buoyancy. When a wet suit — which is much less dense than water — is added, a person becomes more buoyant. To offset the buoyancy of the suit, lead weights — which are many times more dense than water — are worn. By selecting the correct amount of weight, buoyancy can be adjusted so a diver will neither float nor sink. This is termed neutral buoyancy, and is the recommended state of buoyancy under water.

Remember, buoyancy results from the displacement of water. This relates to the volume of an object or a diver as well as the weight. If the volume increases, more water is displaced and more buoyancy results. The opposite results if volume is decreased. If a cubic foot (liter) of salt water is displaced, the buoyant force will be 64 pounds per cubic foot (1.026 kg). That being the case, it is easy to see that if a half cubic foot (half liter) of water is displaced, only 32 pounds (0.51 kg) of buoyancy results.

With this in mind, let's follow a wet suited diver on a descent. The pressure increases and compresses the diver's suit, which now displaces less water, so buoyancy is lost. To compensate for this lost buoyancy, the diver adds air to the buoyancy compensator, thereby restoring the lost volume to regain lost buoyancy. You can see how the buoyancy compensator got its name.

It should be noted that during the ascent of a diver who added air to a BC at depth, the volume of both the wet suit and BC increase, thereby increasing buoyancy. This occurs because pressure is reduced. Air must be vented from the BC as the diver ascends in order to prevent an accelerated ascent.

Thus far we have identified two factors affecting buoyancy: the weight of an object and its volume. There is a third factor, which is the density of the fluid in which the object is immersed. Since salt water is denser than fresh water, more weight will be displaced by an

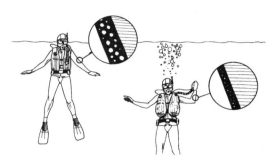

Pressure compresses a wet suit: Volume is reduced and buoyancy is lost. Adding air to a BC restores lost volume and buoyancy.

object in salt water than by the same object in fresh water. This simply means that there is greater buoyancy in salt water than in fresh water. A practical application of this is a diver who is weighted to be neutrally buoyant in salt water who wishes to dive in fresh water. This requires that the diver wear less weight in fresh water to be properly weighted. Conversely, fresh water divers need to wear extra weight when diving in the ocean.

As a diver, you will want to avoid negative buoyancy (sinking) most of the time. Neutral buoyancy is your constant goal beneath the surface. At the surface though, you will want to float so less exertion is required. Floating is termed positive buoyancy. Always re-check your buoyancy whenever you modify your equipment or change diving environments.

Looking Back

1. What are the three factors affecting buoyancy?

A. _____

B. _____

C. _____

2. List three ways in which a diver can change buoyancy.

A. _____

B. _____

C. _____

3. During descent a diver's buoyancy tends to

_____

4. (Circle one) An ocean diver needs to ADD/ REMOVE weight in order to be properly weighted for fresh water diving.

2.5   Thermal Effects

You already know that the heat capacity of water is over 3,000 times greater than air and that water conducts heat more than 20 times faster than air. We have also seen how a protective suit provides insulation to reduce the loss of body heat in the water and how pressure compresses closed cell suit material and re-duces the insulation it provides.

Body heat is also lost through respiration. Each breath taken is heated and the heat is lost with each exhalation. The amount of heat absorbed by the air we breathe depends upon the temperature and density of the gas. The deeper you dive, the denser the air being breathed and the greater the heat loss.

Besides heat loss in diving, you should be familiar with humidity and how it affects your regulator and mask, and about the effects of heat on a scuba tank.

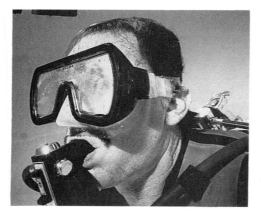

Condensation will fog a mask unless the mask has been treated with an anti-fog compound which causes the water to run off instead of beading on the glass.

Humidity   The amount of water vapor in the air is referred to as humidity. The higher the tem-perature of the air, the more water vapor it can hold. If air containing water vapor is cooled, the water vapor in the air condenses. As divers enter the water and descend, cooling occurs. This causes water vapor in the air to condense,which can fog your face plate or cause other problems. In extremely cold water, condensation can even cause scuba regulators to freeze and free flow, unless special precautions are taken.

When water condenses on the face plate of a mask, it tends to contract into beads unless the surface tension is reduced. Defogging solutions or saliva are used on masks to reduce the surface tension of water so it spreads out in a thin film instead of forming drops that can obscure vision.

You should be aware that the air in scuba tanks is very dry. Nearly all of the water has been removed from it following compression. This is necessary to keep moisture out of your scuba tank and prevent extensive corrosion.

Not only do you have to supply heat to each breath of air you take while scuba diving, you also have to humidify it. This can cause dehy-dration, so it's a good idea to drink plenty of fluids between dives and after diving. This helps replace the lost fluids.

Heat and Pressure   When a container filled with a gas is heated, the gas molecules inside the container become more active. One of two things will occur — the container will expand or the pressure inside will increase. In a rigid container, such as a scuba tank, the latter will occur. Scuba tanks should be cooled as they are filled, allowing more air to be stored in the cylinder at a given pressure than if the tank is hot. Once filled, if the tank is subjected to heating or cooling, the pressure in the tank can

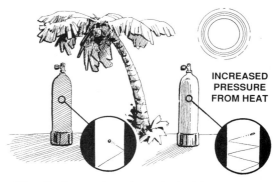

When the temperature of a scuba tank increases, the molecular activity inside increases, with a subsequent increase in the pressure.

vary by several hundred pounds. It will increase or decrease by approximately 5 psi for each degree change in Fahrenheit temperature (0.6 atm per degree Celsius). No air has been added or lost.

The phenomenon occurs simply because of the change in molecular activity caused by the change in temperature. Car trunks which can reach temperatures over 120° F (49 C) are not an especially good place to store air filled scuba tanks for prolonged periods. There is no danger from the pressure increase due to heat; but if a tank becomes hot enough, it will rupture the burst disk in the valve. Also, constant stressing of the tank metal may shorten the useful life of the cylinder. It is better to store tanks with a few hundred psi (15-20 atm) of air in them and to fill them just prior to use than just to store them filled to their service pressure.

Looking Back

1. The two primary ways in which divers lose heat underwater are _____ and _____

2. What causes water vapor in air to condense into a liquid? _____

_____

3. Briefly explain why a mask lens treated with saliva does not fog. _____

_____

4. Why should you drink lots of fluids when diving? _____

_____

5. Briefly explain the relationship between pressure and temperature for a rigid container of air. _____

_____

_____

2.6   *Other Effects of Water*

You are now familiar with some of the physical characteristics of water with regard to pressure, temperature and buoyancy. The main purpose of studying them is to learn how they affect you as a diver. In the next chapter, you will learn how your physiology is affected by the differences between the water and air environments. Right now, though, let's examine some of the effects of water on our senses.

Vision   You have already been told that light travels more slowly in water than in air and that light rays are bent or refracted when they pass through materials of different densities. But understanding the principles of physics is less important than knowing how your vision will be affected underwater. First, your eye is designed to focus light rays in air, so objects are blurry underwater unless an air space is before the eyes. Objects can be seen without a mask, but the objects are out of focus.

Next, refraction of light rays as they pass through water and then through your face plate causes magnification. Objects viewed underwater appear 25% larger and closer. Things are actually further away than they appear to be. They are also smaller than they appear to be. Remember this when you report the sighting of an animal or object. People tend to exaggerate anyway and, that trait, coupled with visual magnification underwater, results in some incredible stories.

Hearing   You can determine the source of sound on land by measuring the difference in time between sound reaching one ear and then the other. This is done subconsciously. While the interval is very short, you are able to distinguish it and can indicate the point or origin of a sound with your eyes closed, unless the sound is directly in front of you or directly behind you, in which case it reaches both ears at once.

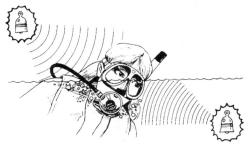

Because sound travels faster in water than in air, you can hear sounds well underwater, but the direction of the sound is difficult to determine when submerged.

Because water is dense it conducts sound very well. In fact, sound travels four times faster in water than in air. The effect of this is that you are unable to determine the direction of origin of the sound. There are many interesting things to be heard beneath the surface, but you just can't tell the direction from which they are coming.

Other Senses   Your senses of smell and taste are restricted underwater. Touch is an important sense in the underwater world: but cold numbs your sense of touch, so you may be able to feel things better by wearing bulky gloves that insulate. Remember also that cuts and scrapes acquired in water often go unnoticed until exposed to air after a dive. For these reasons gloves are important and should be worn.

Looking Back

See if your study of the effects of water was effective.

1. When looking at objects underwater, remember that they appear _____ and _____ than they really are.

2. If you were to signal a nearby diver underwater by tapping on your tank with your dive knife, what might you expect? _____
_____

3. List two reasons why your sense of touch is reduced underwater.

A. _____
B. _____

2.7   Air Consumption

The deeper you dive, the greater the surrounding pressure. The greater the pressure, the denser the air that you breathe, the denser the air, and the faster you empty your tank. The rate at which you consume the air in your tank is directly proportional to the depth of your dive. It should be easy to see that air will be consumed twice as fast at 33 feet (10 m) as at the surface, three times as fast at 66 feet (20 m), etc.

There are other factors affecting the rate at which your air is consumed. Next you will learn about these factors as well as how to simply and easily calculate and record your air consumption rate.

Air Consumption Factors   Besides depth, physical activity has the greatest effect on air

EACH BLOCK REPRESENTS AN EQUAL VOLUME OF AIR.

Air consumption is affected primarily by depth and activity.

usage. Exertion can use up to ten times more air than relaxation. A scuba diver should minimize exertion for several reasons: Conserving air is one of them. Beginning divers tend to be more active than is necessary, but learn to relax rather quickly. Air consumption rates usually decrease significantly during the first few dives after training because divers learn to relax and take it easy. The sooner you can do this, the more enjoyable diving will be.

Related to activity are the breathing rate and pattern. The more you exert, the deeper and more frequently you will breathe, and the more air you will use. It is possible, however, to waste a lot of air by poor breathing habits even when you are not exerting. You will learn more about breathing efficiency in the next chapter, but for now, be aware that shallow, rapid breathing (usually caused by unnecessary anxiety) wastes air and increases air consumption. By limiting exertion and feeling good about your dive you, will be able to maintain a slow, deep pattern of respiration, with long inhalations and exhalations. This is the best way to breathe underwater.

Another factor is physical size. Large people with larger lungs use more air than smaller people with smaller lungs. To compensate for these differences, smaller folks generally use smaller tanks.

Body temperature also affects respiration. The colder you are, the more you breathe. That's unfortunate because heat is also lost through respiration.

You can see how these factors or combinations of these factors can significantly affect your breathing rate under different conditions. Through experience you will learn to estimate the amount of air that you will use, based upon all of these factors.

Air Consumption   Calculation of air consumption is simple. Since the submersible pressure gauge measures the amount of pressure in your tank, and since pressure is directly related to volume, it is easy to measure consumption in pounds per square inch per minute (psi/minute or atmospheres per minute (atm/min). As an example, if you were using an 80 cubic foot (2,600 l) tank rated at and filled to 3,000 psi (210 atm), and your breathing rate was 50 psi (3.4 atm) per minute, the air in your tank could last about 60 minutes (3,000 divided by 50 equals 60) (210 divided by 3.4 equals 61) if used at the same rate and depth.

Measuring the rate of consumption is as easy as measuring the length of time it takes to use a given amount of air and dividing the air used by the time in minutes. For example, if you used 500 psi (34 atm) of air in 10 minutes, your breathing rate would be 500 (34) divided by 10 equals 50 psi (3.4 atm) per minute for that size tank. There is one remaining requirement. The rate must be converted to *surface consumption rate* in order to be applicable to a selected depth.

Your consumption rate can be determined with mathematical formulas or by using the NAUI Surface Air Consumption Rate (SAC-Rate) Calculator. You will first become familiar with the manual calculation procedure, then learn how to use the SAC-Rate Calculator.

If your breathing rate is 50 psi (3.4 atm) per minute at a depth of 33 feet (10 m), your surface consumption rate (SCR) will be only half as much, or 25 psi (1.7 atm) per minute. The SCR can be calculated for any depth by multiplying your air usage rate for the given depth times 33 (10 m) divided by depth plus 33 (10 m). This establishes the surface atmospheric equivalent pressure for the depth. To illustrate, if you use 75 psi (5.1 atm) per minute at a depth of 66 feet (20 m), your surface consumption rate is 75 times 33/66 plus 33 (5.1 times 10/20 plus 10 m). This equals 25 psi (1.7 atm) per minute (see example). It is also possible to rearrange the formula to calculate how long a given amount of air will last at a given depth.

American:

$$SCR = DCR \times \frac{33}{Depth + 33}$$

$$SCR = 75 \times 33/99 = 25 \text{ psi/min.}$$

Metric:

$$SCR = DCR \times \frac{10}{Depth + 10}$$

$$(5.1 \times 10/30 = 1.7 \text{ atm/min.})$$

Sample Problem: If you know your SCR to be 25 psi (1.7 atm) per minute for a given activity level using an 80 cubic foot (2,265 l), 3,000 psi (204 atm) cylinder, were diving at 95 feet (29 m) and noticed you had 1,000 psi (68 atm) of air remaining, how long would the remaining air last?

Solution: You use approximately four times as much air at 95 feet (29 m) as at the surface, or about 100 psi (6.8 atm) per minute. This means your air will only last about another ten minutes. Don't forget you are supposed to leave 300-500 psi (20-34 atm) of air in your tank, so the actual time available is more like five to seven minutes. If you can make this type of rough approximation, you have an adequate understanding of air consumption.

Determining your Surface Air Consumption Rate (SAC-Rate) is easy using the NAUI SAC-Rate Calculator. Mathematical formulas are tedious when compared to use of the NAUI calculator. Directions are included with the

The NAUI SAC-Rate Calculator simplifies the calculation of air consumption rates and is also useful for dive planning.

SAC-Rate calculator. Essentially, all you do is align the two outer discs for the amount of air used and the average depth, set the time during which the air was used on the inner disc, and view your surface consumption rate in psi per minute (metric version not yet available) in the window of the inner disc. For example, if you used 1,800 pounds of air in 30 minutes at an average depth of 50 feet, your SAC-Rate would be 24 psi per minute.

The SAC-Rate Calculator can also be used for dive planning when you know your typical air consumption rate. You align the two outer discs for the amount of available air and the planned average depth, set your air consumption rate in the window in the inner disc, and view the time that amount of air would last at that depth and consumption rate (next to "Set Time Here") on the inner disc. For example, with 2,500 psi of air available for a dive planned at 60 feet and a SAC-Rate of 24 psi per minute, the supply will last approximately 37 minutes.

It is important to note that your SAC-Rate as determined, using a tank of one size, may not be used for planning purposes if a tank of a different size is going to be used unless you recalculate the SAC-Rate for the new tank size or have an instructor assist you in converting your SAC-Rate to compensate for the change in cylinder size. It is easy to understand that a 50 cubic foot tank will not last as long as an 80 cubic foot tank, although both may be filled to 3,000 psi.

Your rate of consumption will change quite a bit during the first 10 to 20 dives you make. Until your rate stabilizes, you should figure your air usage rate for each dive and record it in your log book. This is a good practice to continue because you will learn how much your usual rate is affected by exertion, temperature and other factors, and you will be able to estimate the duration of your air supply, not only for a given depth, but will be able to adjust it for other factors as well.

That's all there is to it. If you have a good grasp of the factors affecting air consumption, how to calculate it and convert it to surface consumption rate and are able to approximate how long the supply will last at a given depth, based on a given rate, you know all you need to know for now.

Looking Back

1. List four factors affecting the rate at which air is consumed while diving.

A. _____

B. _____

C. _____

D. _____

2. If you use 1,300 psi (88.4 atm) of air during a 20-minute dive to 40 feet (12 m), your surface consumption rate is approximately _____ psi (atm) per minute.

3. List two reasons why you should calculate your own air consumption rate and record it in your log book.

A. _____

B. _____

③ *Your Body in Depth*

To skin or scuba dive safely, it is necessary that you understand how your body is affected by water and by changes in pressure. In this chapter you will learn many interesting things about anatomy and how specific parts of your body are affected as you descend and ascend underwater.

3.1 Air Spaces

The human body is comprised mostly of fluids and solids. There are air spaces such as lungs, sinuses, and the middle ear which must be considered when diving.

Lungs Your lungs are air sacs within the chest cavity. When you breathe in they expand, and when you exhale they deflate. They more closely resemble a sponge than they do a balloon. They are not large cavities, but are comprised of millions of tiny air sacs (called alveoli) in which air moves in and out to deliver oxygen to the body and to expel carbon dioxide.

As you know, the volume of air moved during breathing increases with activity. At rest, you normally exchange only a couple of pints of air with each breath. When exercising hard, you exchange as much air as possible during respiration to meet your body's increased demands for oxygen. Since you have a fixed amount of air when diving, you can see how exertion depletes your air supply much faster than relaxation.

Sinuses Sinuses are air cavities within the head that are lined with mucous membranes. There are four sets of sinuses. Each is connected by an air passage to the nasal airway. Normally, the air passages to the sinuses are open. Colds and other afflictions can clog the airways, isolate the sinuses, and prevent pressure equalization. Diving with a cold or with sinus congestion must be avoided.

Proper breathing habits are important.

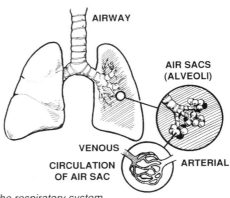

The respiratory system.

The sinuses are formed in bone, so are not compressible like your lungs. Pressure is transmitted to them through the solids and liquids of the body. If air pressure within the sinuses is not equal with the surrounding pressure, the effect pushes tissue into the sinus cavity where the pressure is less. As you might imagine, this can be painful. But it is easily avoided by making sure the sinuses are clear when diving.

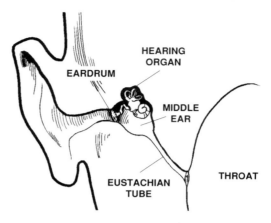

The middle ear air space is connected to the throat by a tube called the Eustachian Tube. Air passes through this tube to equalize pressure in the air spaces in the ear.

The head contains four sets of sinus cavities which need to be clear when diving.

Ears   The spaces inside the ears are of great concern to divers. The eardrum separates the outer ear from the middle ear, which is the air space of concern. The middle ear has an airway leading to it from the throat called the Eustachian Tube, which allows air to move from the throat to the middle ear. This is how equalization takes place in the ears. But equalizing is not automatic like it is in the sinuses. The Eustachian Tubes require a voluntary effort to open them and allow air to pass.

The eardrum transmits sound vibrations to the hearing organ of the inner ear by means of a series of small bones. The organ of balance is also contained within the inner ear. Sudden changes in pressure or temperature in one ear and not the other can cause dizziness to occur — especially when ascending — because of the different stimulus to the ears. By simply keeping the ears in equilibrium as far (as pressure and temperature are concerned), disorientation can be avoided.

Air space within the ears is formed by bone, so this space does not compress. The eardrum can be distended by pressure, but it will flex only

slightly before rupturing. When pressure in an ear is not equalized, discomfort is felt at once. *Such discomfort must be heeded and corrected in order to prevent damage to the ears. No discomfort or damage occurs when the air spaces in the ears are properly equalized.*

Mask   The mask creates an air space attached to your body. It is affected by pressure. During descent, ambient pressure increases on the mask and the diver's body. Since the mask is rather rigid, it will compress only slightly; a pressure imbalance will result. The effect of this low pressure within the mask can cause the mask to suck tightly against the face and for soft facial tissue to be "squeezed" into the mask causing tissue damage (barotrauma). There is no need for this to occur because the pressure inside the mask can be equalized easily (to equal the pressure on the outside of the mask) by exhaling through the nose into the mask as necessary while descending.

Looking Back

Ability to complete the following indicates good familiarization with the diver's air spaces:
1. Which body air spaces are affected by changes in pressure? _____

2. What problem might be expected if you were to attempt to dive with a cold? _____

_____

3. What action should you take if you felt a pulling sensation on your face and eyes while diving?_____

_____

3.2   Equalization of Pressure

You are already acquainted with the need to equalize pressure in air spaces, and even with some of the techniques. You will now become more familiarized with physiology and procedures of equalization.

Squeezes   During descent into water, the external pressure increases at a rate of nearly .5 psi per foot of depth (0.034 atm). If the pressure inside an airspace is not kept in balance with the outside pressure, the water pressure will squeeze the airspace and try to compress it. Whenever the pressure outside an airspace is greater than the internal pressure, the situation is called a "squeeze." Divers can experience ear squeeze, sinus squeeze, and mask squeeze, but can also avoid them with pressure equalization.

Squeezes on body airspaces can cause damage and should not be allowed to occur. The most common squeeze is in the middle ear. If not corrected, an ear squeeze can result in a ruptured eardrum, possible infection, and

perhaps even hearing loss. Additionally, if an eardrum ruptures (because a diver has carelessly ignored the pain which signals an ear squeeze), cold water entering the middle ear can shock the organ of balance and cause severe dizziness (vertigo). If this should happen, hold onto something securely or hug yourself and allow the water inside the ear to warm to body temperature. This doesn't take long. As soon as it is accomplished, your sense of orientation and balance will return. *Remember, though, this injury occurs only to the diver who disregards an ear squeeze.*

Sinus squeezes are also painful and can also be prevented. As long as the sinuses are clear, they will equalize pressure automatically. If the airways to them become swollen and congested, clearing the sinuses will become difficult or impossible. It is important to have healthy sinuses when diving.

The effect of a sinus squeeze — like ear squeeze — is to push tissue into the air space and reduce its volume. This pressure on the tissue ruptures small capillaries in the sinus membrane and effectively reduces volume by filling the cavity with blood. This is obviously undesirable and unnecessary.

You may think the solution to sinus congestion problems lies in medication. There are many sprays and tablets available to help relieve stuffiness. Some perform well. However, the effects of these drugs may be modified under pressure, and not much is known about potential problems. A drug which causes drowsiness on land may be dangerous underwater. For this reason, be sure to consult a diving physician

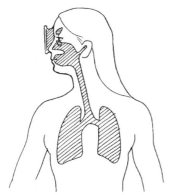

Body air spaces include lungs, sinuses, and ears. The mask is an attached air space which also requires pressure equalization.

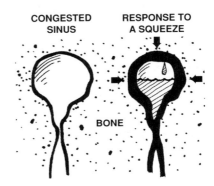

The effect of a squeeze in a congested sinus is the reduction of spation volume with associated tissue swelling and bleeding.

before using medication during diving. Be sure to avoid the influence of any medication that produces side effects.

Mask squeeze can rupture capillaries on the face and in the eyes and really ruin your appearance for a few days. It is a needless injury. Equalization of the mask is as simple as exhaling into it. The mask should never feel like it is pulling on your face.

While some squeezes are painful, they should not cause you undue concern. They can be prevented by pressure equalization or by responding to discomfort and reversing the pressure difference by ascending. Extreme consequences of squeezes on body air spaces have been presented only to familiarize you with the gravity of squeeze symptoms. With proper techniques, no pain or injury will occur from pressure increases during descent.

Equalization Techniques Understanding the anatomy related to pressure equalization in body air spaces will make it easier for you to equalize pressure on all air spaces during descent and to avoid squeezes.

The air space requiring the greatest attention is the middle ear. You have learned that the air in this space comes from your throat through a small tube. The opening to this tube is normally closed, but it can be opened by manipulating small muscles in your throat. If you listen closely, you can hear a slight crackling sound in your ears when you yawn, swallow, or jut your lower jar forward. This sound occurs because the tubes are opening. Obviously, any of the actions just described, such as swallowing, can be useful for equalizing pressures when diving.

Some people are very fortunate and can clear their ears by simply jutting the jaw forward and exhaling into the mask. Most divers, however, require more forceful measures to open the tubes and balance the pressure. *The most common method, known as the Valsalva maneuver, is attempted exhalation against closed nose and mouth.* This works well in most instances, especially when combined with jaw jutting. The key to successful ear clearing is to keep the difference in pressure between the water and the middle ear to a minimum. If the difference becomes too great (this requires only a few feet of water), pressure will hold the end of

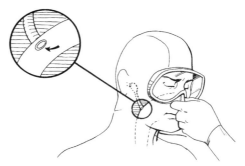

The Valsalva maneuver is the most commonly used technique for equalizing pressure in the ears.

the Eustachian Tubes closed and no action on your part will open them to allow equalization. If this occurs, your only recourse is to ascend a few feet and reduce the pressure difference until the tubes can be opened to allow equalization.

It is much better to clear the ears continually during descent and go down in an uninterrupted manner than it is to bounce up and down when clearing is done only occasionally. Your ears should be "pumped up" slightly before leaving the surface, then cleared every two feet (0.6 m) during descent. Descending feet first usually makes equalizing easier. Remember, equalize early and often.

Trying to equalize pressure in a squeezed ear by performing a very forceful Valsalva maneuver should not be done. Blowing hard against closed nose and mouth will not open the Eustachian Tube being held shut by pressure. It will actually seal the opening of the tube more tightly. Blowing hard increases the pressure on the inner ear and can damage it and your hearing. *For these reasons, you should perform a Valsalva maneuver firmly, but not with extreme force.*

Here are a few other techniques which may help for ear clearing: elevating the base of the tongue during Valsalva, swallowing while performing the Valsalva maneuver, wiggling the jaw back and forth during Valsalva, tilting the head to the side opposite an ear which won't clear while performing Valsalva, and descending feet first rather than head first. These methods should help keep your ears equalized while the other air spaces are cleared almost automatically. In the event of a cold, attempts to Valsalva and equalize middle ear pressure should be avoided. Mucous could be forced into the middle ear space and create problems.

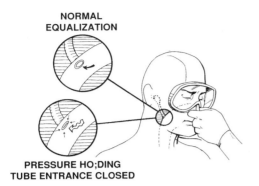

NORMAL
EQUALIZATION

PRESSURE HO;DING
TUBE ENTRANCE CLOSED

The "Trapdoor" effect caused by delaying ear clearing during descent. The pressure actually holds the ends of the Eustachian tube closed.

Looking Back

1. When the pressure outside an air space is greater than the pressure inside the air space, the situation is called a _____

2. List three possible consequences of failing to correct an ear squeeze.

A. _____

B. _____

C. _____

3. What is the most likely cause of a sinus squeeze?_____

4. Which type of squeeze is the easiest to prevent and is inexcusable?_____

5. In one sentence, describe the most commonly used ear clearing technique. _____

6. Describe two ways hearing injuries can be caused when diving.

A. _____

B. _____

3.3 Air Expansion Problems

In 3.2, you discovered the potential problems in air spaces during descent. During ascent, air in air spaces expands and must be vented to prevent damage or injury. You will now learn about air expansion problems of the ears, sinuses and lungs.

Reverse Blocks   A "reverse block" is the opposite of a squeeze and occurs when the pressure inside an air space is greater than the surrounding pressure. Blocks occur during ascent when the external pressure decreases. It is more difficult to get air into the body air spaces than it is for the air to get out, so blocks are much less common than squeezes. A reverse block in the ear can occur if the Eustachian Tubes become blocked. If the ear hurts and feels full during ascent, stop your upward progress, re-descend until the sensation is no longer present, jut your jaw forward, swallow, and re-ascend slowly. Repeat this as needed. If you must surface with the block, do so as slowly as possible. The block may release all at once. If this occurs, the sudden change in the middle ear pressure may cause dizziness, but this will pass quickly. Again, hold onto something, someone or yourself if vertigo is experienced.

Sinus blocks result from air trapped in a sinus cavity trying to expand during ascent. This can happen in two ways. A sinus that was unequalized during descent may have filled with body fluids. During ascent, the air in the sinus will try to expand to its original volume, but cannot due to the presence of the fluid. Thus, pressure differential increases and pain results. Another way in which a sinus block occurs is for a sinus which has been equalized during descent to close its airway. The most likely cause of this is when medication was used to open the airway initially. When the medication wears off, the sinus "rebounds" and closes the passageway even more than it was in the first place. This

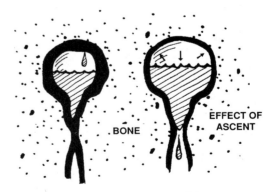

BONE

EFFECT OF
ASCENT

If sinus swelling closes a sinus while diving, pressure will develop inside the sinus during ascent. Avoid diving with a cold or with sinus problems.

rebound effect traps air in the sinuses and pressure increases in the cavity during ascent.

Prevention is the best means of avoiding a sinus block. Avoid diving with a cold or sinus congestion. Don't dive if you have to use medication to open your sinuses (unless directed to do so by a diving physician). If a sinus block does occur, a slow, gradual ascent is the best and only course of action.

Gas formed in the stomach and intestines while diving will also expand during ascent. This can cause discomfort, so gas-producing foods are not recommended in advance of diving activities. If problems are encountered during ascent, slow or stop your progress until the gas works its way out.

These difficulties with reverse blocks may arouse your concern, but they should not. They are uncommon and avoidable. By becoming familiar with them, you will be able to prevent them, recognize them, and handle them in the unlikely event one should ever affect you.

Lung Expansion Injuries   Air expanding in the lungs during ascent is easily vented by normal breathing. A serious problem exists, however, if you hold your breath and ascend. With your airway closed, air expanding in your lungs will cause them to rupture shortly after reaching their full volume. Unfortunately, there is no sensation of discomfort to alert you when this is about to occur. Since it is instinctive to hold your breath under water, you must program yourself to vent expanding air in your lungs during any ascent after breathing compressed air. (That is why training is absolutely necessary.)

A lung expansion injury can occur in as little as four feet of water, *so it is very important you understand the importance of not holding your breath during ascent.* If a lung rupture occurs, it is extremely serious and can be life threatening, so it must and can be avoided. As a result of lung rupture, a lung may collapse (pneumothorax), or the air from the lung may escape into the chest cavity (mediastinal emphysema) where continued expansion will cause further problems. Most serious of all, the air can escape into the blood stream. Air bubbles in the blood may migrate upwards to the head, block circulation to the brain, and cause unconsciousness and permanent damage. This blockage, known as an air embolism, is the most serious of diving injuries. As long as you keep breathing normally during ascent, there is no danger of this injury, but be aware of the consequences of breath holding. *Always keep breathing when using scuba equipment.*

Your reaction to this knowledge may be to want to keep your lung volume as low as possible during ascent by blowing out all the air you can, but this isn't good either. Small airways in the lungs collapse when lung volume is too low, and air trapped on the far side of the closure can expand and cause problems. It is best to maintain normal lung volume during ascent — not too full and not too empty. Normal breathing is the best and easiest action.

Looking Back

1. When the pressure inside a rigid airspace is greater than outside pressure, the condition is termed a _____

2. _____ is the best means of ensuring air does not become trapped in the sinuses.

3. Lung expansion injuries are caused by (three words) _____

4. Lung volume should be kept as _____ as possible during ascents when scuba diving.

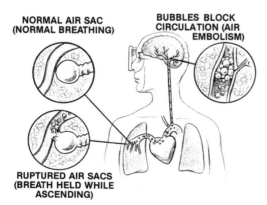

NORMAL AIR SAC
(NORMAL BREATHING)

BUBBLES BLOCK
CIRCULATION (AIR
EMBOLISM)

RUPTURED AIR SACS
(BREATH HELD WHILE
ASCENDING)

If the breath is held during ascent, a lung can rupture and introduce air into the bloodstream. The air bubbles can block circulation to the brain. The blockage is referred to as an air embolism.

3.4   Breathing and Circulation

Your body is a marvelous machine. It takes in oxygen, circulates it to your tissues, uses the oxygen to convert nutrients to energy, and exhausts spent nutrients and oxygen in the form of carbon dioxide. This is all done involuntarily by your circulatory and respiratory systems. It is even more amazing that you can assume voluntary control of your breathing. Let's examine these wonderful processes in greater detail. Knowledge in this area will help you understand the practical aspects of breathing underwater, and become a safer, more effective diver.

Basics   Muscles act on your diaphragm to change the volume of your chest and create pressure differentials that cause air to move in and out of your lungs. Oxygen in the air that is drawn into the lungs is absorbed into the blood through the thin membranes in millions of tiny air sacs. The oxygenated blood is pumped by the heart through arteries to body tissues where oxygen is used and converted to the waste product, carbon dioxide (CO_2). The carbon dioxide-laden blood returns to the heart through veins, and is then pumped back into the lungs where the CO_2 exits the blood into the lungs. The CO_2 is then exhaled, fresh air is drawn in, and the entire process is repeated.

Breathing Rate   Respiration is controlled by the amount of CO_2 in the blood stream. The respiratory center in the brain senses the CO_2 level in the blood stream and increases or decreases the muscular activity controlling breathing. The greater the amount of CO_2 present, the greater the breathing stimuli. Some people think breathing is controlled by oxygen levels, but the primary stimulus is CO_2.

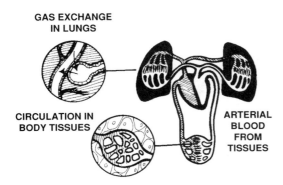

GAS EXCHANGE
IN LUNGS

CIRCULATION IN
BODY TISSUES

ARTERIAL
BLOOD
FROM
TISSUES

The circulatory system.

Breathing Patterns   Breathing takes care of itself on land, and it will do so underwater as well if modified slightly and kept within certain limits. The pressure and density of air ARE different underwater, so respiration needs to be changed somewhat to accommodate these differences. Generally, breathing needs to be deeper than normal when diving and kept at a slow pace by limiting exertion.

Shallow breathing exchanges little air in the lungs, so only a small amount of CO_2 is eliminated with each breath. The more CO_2 in the lungs, the less that can come out of the blood into the lungs. The more CO_2 there is in the blood, the greater the desire to breathe. This can become worse if the shallow breathing pattern continues. A high level of CO_2 in the blood stream stimulates a faster rate of breathing. But the increased rate fails to lower the CO_2 level because of the shallowness of breathing. The solution is deeper breathing. Unless you are aware of this situation, however, you may not recognize the symptoms of shallow breathing and might get caught up in the cycle of breathing faster and faster, yet feeling like you're not getting enough air.

The other extreme is breathing much deeper and more rapidly than is required. This overbreathing is called hyperventilation and has an effect on CO_2 opposite to that of shallow breathing. The CO_2 level in the lungs and blood is reduced, and can be lowered below normal levels if hyperventilation is extended. Since CO_2 is the stimulus to breathe, you feel less need to breathe following hyperventilation. This can either be useful or hazardous. If you have been breathing shallowly and feel some respiratory distress when it isn't justified, deep breathing will flush CO_2 from your system and increase your breathing comfort.

Controlled hyperventilation can be hazardous when followed by prolonged breath holding for skin diving. If the breath is held following excessive overbreathing, your body can utilize the available oxygen before the CO_2 level becomes great enough to stimulate breathing. Unconsciousness due to insufficient oxygen can therefore occur without warning. Controlled hyperventilation can safely extend breath-holding time if only a few deep breaths are taken. It is recommended that the number of breaths be limited to three or four.

A practice which is not recommended is attempting to increase the duration of the air supply by holding each breath for several sec-

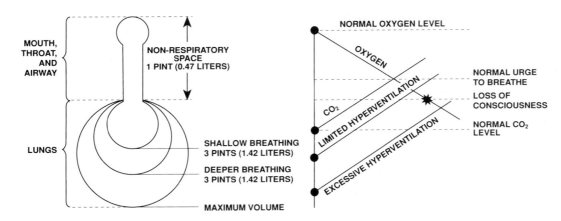

To use air efficiently, deeper breathing is required.

With limited hyperventilation, the stimulus to breathe occurs before unconsciousness, but with excessive hyperventilation, blackout can occur without warning.

onds. This is unwise because it results in a buildup of CO_2 in your system, can lead quickly to overexertion and develops unsafe breath holding habits. It is termed "skip breathing," is hazardous, and should not be practiced.

Another situation occurs when you exert yourself underwater and increase the demands on your heart and lungs. Both respiration and circulation are stepped up to meet the demands. More air must be moved at a faster rate to meet the body's need for oxygen. Due to the resistance to air flow at higher-than-normal pressures (and for other reasons as well), CO_2 can build up within your body even though you breathe hard. Finally, a point can be reached when you feel starved for air and you feel as if your regulator won't deliver enough air. Anxiety can set in unless you take prompt action to correct the problem. This involves stopping all activity, resting, and breathing deeply until (with emphasis on longer exhalations), you gradually recover from the effect. *The best course of action is prevention.* By taking it easy and learning the limits of exertion for various depths, overexertion can be avoided.

Now you can see why we said that breathing needs to be deeper than normal when diving and kept at a slow pace by limiting exertion. With experience, you will learn how to breathe properly underwater. By doing so, your breathing will become almost as automatic as it is above water. You can also see why your heart and lungs need to be healthy in order to dive.

Other Breathing Problems If it hasn't occurred to you yet, you will probably wonder what to do if you have to cough or sneeze underwater, or what to do if a drop of water causes choking. All of these problems can be handled with the regulator in place in the mouth. Just keep it in your mouth and cough or sneeze through it.

Choking can almost be eliminated as a problem if you always inhale cautiously when taking the first breath after clearing your regulator or snorkel of water. If you should happen to breathe in a little water and start coughing, do so through the regulator and speed recovery by swallowing repeatedly.

Breathing is a natural thing to do. It will soon feel natural underwater as well. Your familiarity with the process of respiration will help you avoid problems and allow you to safely enjoy the underwater world.

Looking Back

1. Breathing takes place because of a stimulus to the brain. This stimulus is the level of

_____ in the blood stream.

2. The recommended breathing pattern for diving is:

a. Rapid and shallow   c. Slow and deep

b. Rapid and deep   d. Slow and shallow

A key to enjoying diving is learning to relax and breathe properly.

3. If you feel starved for air while scuba diving, what actions should you take? _____

_____

4. What is the main concept to recall if you cough, sneeze, or choke while diving?_____

_____

3.5 Thermal Considerations

Your body must remain within a rather narrow temperature range in order to function properly. Your well being is jeopardized if you become too hot or too cold. Both situations are possible in diving. You need to know how thermal problems can occur, how to recognize them, what to do if they occur, and most importantly, how to prevent them from occurring.

Overheating   You tend to think of divers getting cold, so it is hard to imagine an over-heated one. This problem usually occurs on land, however, rather than in the water. When protective suits are worn to insulate against heat loss, they very effectively trap body heat when above the water. This can lead to overheating. Your body's first reaction is to perspire to lower

High heat loss areas of the body include the head and neck, torso, and abdomen. Less heat is lost through the arms and legs.

body temperature by evaporation. This is obviously ineffective when you are covered by a suit. If no action is taken to cool off, the next symptoms will be a pale, clammy appearance and a feeling of weakness, signifying heat exhaustion. You must take measures to lower body temperature at this point. Further increases will cause your heat-resisting responses to shut down. This can lead to a very dangerous condition known as heat stroke. Hot, dry, flushed skin is a symptom of heat stroke.

These problems need not occur. Their prevention requires only common sense. Avoid being in a protective suit for long periods of time before diving. Keep out of the sun. Get wet to cool off if there is a delay when preparing to dive. Remove insulation. Overheating is usually an avoidable problem.

Heat Loss Problems   You are aware that water absorbs much heat with little change in its own temperature and that it conducts heat very well. This means a warm body immersed in water will have heat drawn from it at a rapid rate. Remember, you heat the air you breathe: With each breath more heat is lost. This accounts for about 15-20% of your body's heat loss. This effect increases with depth as the density of the air increases. Finally, you know that insulation worn to protect against heat loss is compressed and reduced by pressure. This is unfortunate because the deeper the depth of the dive, the colder the water temperature. This is one good reason to limit recreational diving to relatively shallow depths. Diving is more fun when you are warm.

Light exercise can help a diver stay warm, but the activity must be controlled to prevent overexertion.

As your body loses heat, problems begin to develop. Muscles become cold and numb and lose their strength. The ability to think clearly and short-term memory are affected. If allowed to continue, heat loss can quickly create a serious medical emergency. Heart irregularities and unconsciousness can occur.

Fortunately, there are defenses against heat loss in water. Some of these are natural, and others require action on your part.

The body's defenses to cold include reducing circulation to the arms and legs. This conserves heat in the core of the body where the vital organs are located. You will shiver when your core temperature reaches a certain temperature. The purpose of shivering is to produce heat, but shivering in water cannot keep up with heat loss. Since shivering indicates chilling, and since it cannot generate enough heat in water to cause rewarming, prolonged shivering should be a signal to terminate diving activities.

Actions you can take to generate heat include eating well at least two hours before diving and exercising while diving. Heavy exertion must be avoided, however, for reasons already discussed.

Your best course of action is to insulate your body, particularly the high heat loss areas: Including your torso, groin, neck, and head. Many divers opt for an extra layer of insulation on the trunk of the body. A hood is especially important, because up to half of the body's heat loss in cold water can take place through the head. Your suit should fit well to prevent water exchange.

If you become cold while diving, re-warming is important afterwards. Get into warm, dry clothing as soon as possible. Warm drinks may help, but avoid alcohol because it contributes to heat loss. Depending on the circumstances, a warm or tepid bath may be advised. This is not recommended following deep dives, or if you are in the advanced stages of hypothermia. Your best course of action is to recognize heat loss as a potentially serious problem and either cease diving when cold or re-warm almost to the point of perspiring before resuming diving. If you insulate yourself properly, dive wisely, recognize the symptoms of heat loss, and respond properly , you will not have any serious problems. Learning to prevent problems is one of the main purposes of this course.

Looking Back

1. What are the two principal means by which body heat is lost in water? _____

_____

2. List at least three ways to conserve body heat in water:

A. _____

B. _____

C. _____

3. What body function is an indication that heat loss is approaching the critical stages? _____

_____

4. List one action that should be taken for rewarming after a dive and one which should be avoided: _____

3.6 *Secondary Effects of Pressure*

The primary effects of pressure are mechanical — the squeezing of air spaces and an increase in gas density. Increased pressure on the gas you breathe produces other more subtle effects which will now be presented by examining the gases: oxygen, carbon monoxide, and nitrogen. These subtle effects are referred to as secondary effects.

Oxygen Oxygen is needed to sustain life. Breathing a 100% concentration of it at depths of 25 feet (7.6 m) or more is dangerous. Under such conditions, it becomes toxic and is extremely hazardous. All you need to know is that scuba tanks should always be filled with compressed air, never with oxygen. The amount of oxygen in air isn't toxic at recommended diving limits, so no problems will occur as long as pure compressed air is used.

Carbon Monoxide Carbon monoxide is a "man-made" gas formed by incomplete combustion of fuels. It is found in the exhaust fumes of internal combustion engines. This gas is potentially dangerous even in small concentrations, especially when breathed at depth.

Divers can encounter problems with carbon monoxide if their air supply becomes contaminated when the pump intake of the compressor used to fill the tanks is too close to the exhaust of an engine. The engine exhaust gases will then be compressed along with the air. Faulty air compressors can also produce carbon monoxide. This produces a dangerous situation where carbon monoxide may seriously interfere with the ability of the blood to carry oxygen. Symptoms of carbon monoxide toxicity include headache, nausea, bright red lips and nail beds, and unconsciousness. Fresh air may be helpful, but pure oxygen and medical treatment are recommended.

Carbon monoxide toxicity can be avoided by always having tanks filled at a professional dive facility where the compressor is set up and

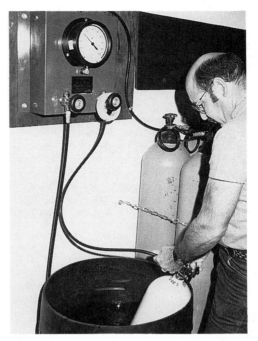

Tanks must be filled at a professional air station. NAUI PRO Facilities are a good source of pure compressed air.

maintained properly and where air quality is assured by periodic laboratory analysis of the air for purity.

Although carbon monoxide itself is colorless, odorless, and tasteless, contaminated air tends to taste and smell oily or foul. If the air from your tank seems suspect, it should not be used. The facility which filled the tank should be notified of the problem as soon as possible so they can investigate it.

Nitrogen Nitrogen is an inert gas that has no effect on you at normal pressures. As depth and pressure increase, however, nitrogen begins to affect your physiology.

At sea level, a certain amount of nitrogen is dissolved in the blood and tissues. As you breathe, some nitrogen molecules enter the blood stream and others leave it, at a one-to-one exchange rate: A state of equilibrium exists. This state becomes unbalanced when the pressure of the air you breathe increases. The deeper you dive, and the longer the duration of the dive, the more nitrogen is absorbed.

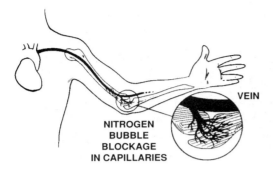

Excess nitrogen can form bubbles in the bloodstream which collect in the joints and cause an illness known as the "bends." This can be prevented with proper diving techniques.

A Recompression Chamber used for the treatment of decompression sickness.

Problems can occur if you absorb a great deal of nitrogen and then ascend too quickly. It took a while for the nitrogen to get into your system, and it takes time for it to get back out. If you ascend faster than the nitrogen can be eliminated through normal respiration, the excess nitrogen may form bubbles inside your body and produce an illness known as decompression sickness, or the "bends." If bubbles are present in your blood and tissues, they may impair circulation, distort the tissues, and produce varying symptoms (depending on the quantity and location of the bubbles). The symptoms range from skin rash, extreme fatigue, and painful joints to, in severe cases, paralysis and unconsciousness.

As with all problems encountered while diving, decompression sickness can and should be prevented. Tables of times and depths are available to provide time limits for various depths. Learning to dive is really a matter of learning to avoid potential problems imposed by the water environment. To avoid the bends you must learn about decompression tables and how to use them correctly.

Treatment of decompression sickness consists of recompressing a diver to a depth sufficient to cause the bubbles to return to solution and having him/her breathe high concentrations of oxygen. This must be done in a controlled environment with medical attention and cannot be carried out in the water. To accomplish the treatment, special hyperbaric chambers are available. A diver showing any signs or symp-

toms of bends should never be taken back underwater. Information on the location of recompression chambers for the treatment of diving accidents is included in another chapter.

Nitrogen under pressure can produce another effect. At depths approaching 80 feet (24 m), the gas may be intoxicating. The narcotic effect of nitrogen at greater depths will produce impaired thought and judgment and reduce physical ability. The danger exists that a diver could become unable to function well enough to ensure safety.

The prevention of this problem, which is called nitrogen narcosis or "rapture of the deep," is simple — avoid deep dives. Symptoms appear suddenly and increase in intensity with time. Recovery is as simple as ascending to reduce the pressure. The symptoms will leave as rapidly as they appeared. There are no after effects.

Looking Back

Problems caused by the secondary effects of pressure are avoidable. Do you know how to avoid them? How can:

1. Oxygen toxicity be prevented?
2. Carbon monoxide toxicity be prevented?
3. Decompression sickness be prevented?
4. Nitrogen narcosis be prevented?
5. What is the correct reaction to symptoms of narcosis?
6. List two reasons to avoid deep dives.

A. _____

B. _____

Narcosis can cause a diver to ignore depth limits and exercise poor judgment.

3.7 Health and Fitness Considerations

Health is the state of being sound in body and mind and is a prerequisite for diving. To enter the activity, you need to have a sound heart and lungs, clear ears and sinuses, and freedom from limiting disease or serious ailments.

You completed a NAUI Medical History Form at the beginning of this course. If you indicated any problems that might affect your ability to dive, you were asked to have a medical examination and medical approval prior to the commencement of training. Even if no problems were identified on your medical history form, a physical examination by a doctor who is familiar with diving is a good idea.

Women have special health considerations, due to menstruation and pregnancy. If a woman can engage in physical activities on land during menstruation, it is probably all right for her to dive. If cramps and other effects of menstruation are bothersome, a woman should refrain from diving when symptoms exist. With regard to pregnancy, not enough is known of the effects of pressure on an unborn child, so it is best to refrain from diving during pregnancy.

Fitness means the ability to meet the physical demands of a particular involvement. You need to be fit for diving. Initially, it means you need good aquatic ability, the ability to swim at least 220 yards (201 m) nonstop without aids. This demonstrates the aquatic fitness needed to learn the diving skills. Later you will need to develop fitness for using fins and performing other skills in the water. Fitness for swimming

More and more women are discovering diving.

may not necessarily mean fitness for diving, because different muscles are used in different ways. Playing ball does not necessarily keep you fit for diving. To get into shape for a particular activity requires a regular participation in that activity.

The best way to stay fit for diving is to dive regularly. An accepted alternative is to swim using mask, snorkel, and fins. One point to keep in mind is that your ability to dive safely is decreased by inactivity. Prior to resuming diving after a layoff of a month or more, fitness should be re-established by pool workouts prior to open water dives. Refresher courses offered by NAUI afford opportunities to polish skills, add new knowledge of the basics, and to help restore fitness and skill proficiency and are recommended.

Just as good health and fitness are important for diving safety, the use of drugs can lead to problems. Substances that alter your physiology or affect your ability to think clearly must be avoided. If you don't feel well, medication may mask the symptoms of your illness, but the illness still exists. If you don't feel well enough to dive without using a drug, you shouldn't be diving, even if you feel all right with medication. The effects of drugs can be changed by pressure. The best policy is to refrain from drug usage for at least 12 hours before diving.

Divers take pride in their health and fitness. If you are generally healthy at the outset of your scuba training, have good aquatic skills, dive or practice diving skills in the water frequently, and never dive under the influence of drugs, you will meet the health and fitness requirements for safe diving.

Looking Back

Now consider these questions on health and fitness.

1. Why is good health a prerequisite for diving?

2. When should a woman not dive?

3. True or False: Only people with medical history problems should have a physical examination for diving.

4. Complete this sentence: The best way to maintain fitness for diving is to _____

_____

5. If not feeling well but medication helps you to feel better, why shouldn't you dive?_____

_____

4 The Diving Environment

4.1 The Varying Environment

Underwater conditions vary significantly from one region to another. These differences influence the way divers dress for a dive and also what diving techniques they use. A quick review of the comparison chart below will show you how variable these conditions can be.

No matter where you go, you will discover special requirements pertaining to diving in that area. Before you enter the water you need to learn about the environmental characteristics which can affect your diving and how local divers deal with them.

In addition to the factors listed, there are other environmental and physical variations to be considered such as the season of the year, weather, dive site characteristics, and shore conditions. Let's examine more closely the last two parameters to better understand how diving techniques may change from place to place. Then we will learn more about variations in temperature, visibility, and aquatic life.

Dive Sites Divers will dive almost anywhere there is water, but generally they are attracted to interesting formations underwater. The formation may be man-made (such as an artificial reef, oil rig, breakwater or jetty) or natural (like submarine canyons and sheer drop-offs which are exhilarating to dive). Drift diving in a river can be exciting and fun. Diving inside and under things is popular with divers who enjoy penetrating wrecks and caves, exploring caverns, and diving beneath the ice in frozen lakes.

As you can see, there are many types of dive sites, each offering new and different experiences. While there are many fascinating places to explore underwater, many of them require special training beyond Openwater I. Any diving which does not allow direct vertical access to the surface is considered highly specialized and requires special equipment and training to be carried out safely.

Shore Conditions The easiest— and in some regions — the best diving is from a boat, but diving from shore is a popular alternative for thousands of sport divers. There are many things with which to contend when making a shore dive. Knowing what you may encounter can help in selecting or rejecting your next dive site.

	N.E.	M.A.	S.E.	Gulf	Tropics	Cen.	N.W.	M.P.	S.W.
Temp.	28-70°F −2-21°C	38-75°F 3-24°C	50-80°F 10-27°C	56-86°F 13-30°C	70-85°F 21-29°C	32-75°F 0-24°C	43-60°F 6-16°C	45-60°F 7-15°C	50-70°F 10-21°C
Visibility	1-80' .3-24m	0-60' 0-18m	3-30' .9-9m	0-100' 0-30m	40'+ 12+m	1-60' .3-18m	5-75' 1.5-23m	0-50' 0-15m	0-100' 0-30m
Currents	Moderate	Strong	Strong	Vary	Vary	Vary	Strong	Strong	Vary
Plants	Light	Light	None	None	None	Light	Moderate	Heavy	Heavy
Surf	Heavy	Heavy	Light	Varies	Light	Light	Varies	Heavy	Heavy
Hazardous Animals	Few	Few	Few	Some	Many	Few	Few	Some	Some

Typical environmental conditions. (See map on page 62.)

	North West
	Mid Pacific
	South West
	Central
	North East
	Mid Atlantic
	South East
	Gulf

Diving regions of the United States.

Diving takes place just about anywhere there is water. Underwater formations, whether natural or man-made, add interest to a dive.

The first difficulty may be simply getting to the water. Access can be difficult in areas with steep cliffs and rugged shores. You may have to walk or climb over rough terrain and cover considerable distances carrying your equipment. This can be exhausting and hazardous. You must plan ahead and know your capabilities and limitations.

When entering the water, other problems can be created by shoreline configurations. The shape of the shore may affect currents and wave action. The bottom may slope gradually, drop off suddenly, or have scattered holes and rocks. The composition of the bottom will affect the way you make your entry into the water. Wherever you go, you need an orientation to the dive site. This can best be done by diving new areas with a NAUI Instructor, Divemaster, or experienced divers from a local dive club. You need to know what to look for, what to look out for, and any diving techniques which may be unique to the area. The message is to always seek information about new dive sites from

experienced divers. Whenever possible, make your first dive with an instructor or divemaster who has local diving experience. As you gain diving experience and participate in advanced courses, you will be able to confidently explore new areas without supervision.

Looking Back

1. List from memory at least five environmental factors which affect diving.

A. _____

B. _____

C. _____

D. _____

E. _____

2. List at least four effects varying environment conditions can have on diving techniques:

A. _____

B. _____

C. _____

D. _____

Entry techniques vary with dive sites, so an orientation is required for each new location.

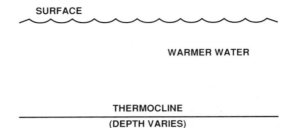

SURFACE

WARMER WATER

THERMOCLINE
(DEPTH VARIES)

COLD WATER

BOTTOM

The abrupt temperature transition of a thermocline.

3. List two actions you can take to minimize the problems you may encounter in the diving environment.

A. _____

B. _____

4.2 The Water

When you are immersed in water, you are subjected to heat loss. Your senses — especially your vision — are affected. Let's find out the extent of these effects and some guidelines for dealing with them.

Water temperatures can range from freezing to over 85°F. (29°C.). Diving in water colder than 65°F. (18°C.), however, requires special insulation. It is unlikely that you will ever dive in water warmer than 85°F. (29°C.). For the most part, diving takes place in fairly temperate water, yet you will chill rapidly without protection because of water's great capacity to absorb and conduct heat. The temperature of the water is a major factor to be considered when planning a dive. Water temperature usually lowers with depth. The deeper you go, the colder it becomes.

Frequently, particularly in fresh water, a phenomenon known as thermocline will appear.

This is a sudden change in temperature from warmer water to colder water. The two layers of water can vary in temperature as much as 20°F. (6.7°C.), are of different densities, and remain distinctly separated. If you are outfitted for the surface water temperature, you may find the drastic change in temperature at depth will force an early end to a dive. You need to have an idea of the water temperature at the depths at which you plan to dive. You need to select suitable protection for your warmth requirements.

Another major factor affecting dive operations is visibility, which can range from zero to more than 100 feet (30 m). Diving in water where visibility is severely restricted can be hazardous, and requires special training and equipment. If you can't see anything, you should postpone your dive until a day when visibility underwater is better. No-visibility diving is a necessary part of search and recovery training, but it is not fun when you are just learning to dive.

Underwater visibility is affected by the locality, season, weather, water movement, composition of the bottom, and other factors. In general, visibility is best during calm summer months and worst during winter rains and storms.

There are two primary problems related to visibility. The first is disorientation. With limited visibility, disorientation (and even dizziness) can result from a lack of visual reference while submerged. This can be avoided by refraining from diving in turbid water until you have been trained in the proper techniques. In extremely clear water, another phenomenon arises, that of estimating distance. As you have already learned, things appear to be just a few feet below you, and you can exceed your planned depth because the object turns out to be much deeper than it appeared. Frequent monitoring of your depth gauge is very important.

As you can see from the comparison chart at the beginning of this chapter, there are places where visibility exceeds 100 feet (20 m). The typical is from 5 (1.5 m) to 30 feet (10 m). With this in mind, you can see why divers need to remain close together underwater. You should start developing, from the very first time you get into the water, the habit of staying close — within touching distance of your diving partner.

Looking Back

1. Define a thermocline: _____

_____

2. List four factors affecting underwater visibility:

A. _____

B. _____

C. _____

D. _____

3. What is the primary hazard associated with zero visibility diving? _____

_____

4.3   Water Movement

Water is heavy. Reflect for a moment on the weight of a bucket of water and imagine the enormous potential energy contained in a large mass of moving water. It is useless to fight against such a force. You need to understand what sets water in motion, how the water moves, and how to function effectively in moving water.

Above, *Diving in low visibility can be interesting, but special training is needed.*
Below, *It is difficult to estimate distances and to maintain your planned depth when the water is very clear.*

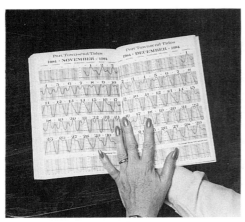

CURRENT
→

Above, Tide tables help a diver identify the times when currents will be at their minimum.
Right, Plan dives against currents. When diving from a boat, a safety line trailing the vessel is a good idea.

Tides   One cause of water movement in many areas is the tide, which is caused by the gravitational attraction between the earth and other heavenly bodies. The extent of tides ranges from negligible to a change in water level of over 40 feet (12 m). Typically, however, the difference between high tide and low tide is only a few feet (1 m) of water.

As a result of changes in water level, problems can arise. The entry and exit conditions change because of water level variations; ramps at docks and marinas become steeper as the tide recedes; and water must move in order to change levels. The movement of the water (tidal currents) is of great concern to a diver.

When tidal currents pass through restricted areas, they can be quite strong — strong enough to sweep you away no matter how hard you swim. In such areas, it is essential to consult tide and current tables, which are readily available, to help you plan dives for slack- water periods.

Water movement due to the tides can also affect underwater visibility. The best conditions are usually at high tide. There are exceptions, of course, and you will learn more about diving in currents from your instructor as part of your open water training.

Currents   Tides set masses of water in motion, but other influences can create currents as well, such as winds, gravity, and the earth's rotation. You must consider currents when planning a dive. Attempting to swim against a strong current can lead to exhaustion. You should usually begin dives against the current — no matter how slight it may be — so that it will assist you toward the exit point at the end of your dive if your entry and exit are to be the same. A buoyed safety line 100 feet (30 m) or more in length should trail behind an anchored boat. If you end a dive down current, you can grab the line and pull yourself to the boat. In advanced training, you can learn how to "drift dive," and use the current rather than fight against it.

Currents can be separated into three general categories: standing currents (the regular, steady type); tidal currents (which we have discussed); and transitory currents (which are rather unpredictable). An example of a transitory current is a rip current — a strong water movement which can pose problems for uninformed divers. A rip current occurs near shore and is formed when water is pushed up onto the shore by wave or wind action and then funneled back out through a narrow opening in a reef, sand bar, or other large formation which blocks the return flow of the water. The offshore current is narrow and can be quite strong.

If you find yourself being carried away from shore or unable to make progress toward shore, you may be in a rip current. You can escape the current by swimming parallel to the shore line until clear of the rip area, then you can turn toward shore and make progress. Rip currents can be identified with experience. If they occur in your area, your instructor will familiarize you with them and with the areas where they are likely to be present.

There are long shore currents, also, which run parallel to the coast line. It is important that you are aware of their direction and approximate speed when you plan your dive. A one-knot current means the water is moving at approximately 100 feet (30 m) per minute, which is about the same speed you can expect to comfortably swim underwater with scuba.

While these currents can carry you away from your point of entry, they can also transport you to a planned exit point and add to the fun and enjoyment of your dive. If you live near the ocean and participate in NAUI advanced training programs, you will learn how to use currents to make ocean diving easier and more exciting.

A classic rip current. You should learn to identify a rip and know how to escape one.

But, as a new diver, you will want to learn more about local currents and how to recognize them before you attempt to make unsupervised dives. The best way to accomplish this is by training with a NAUI Instructor who has plenty of personal diving experience in the local area.

Even with experience, advanced divers should inquire about local currents from local divers whenever they plan on diving a new ocean site. You just need to know the right

An understanding of the local current patterns is important before diving in a new area.

questions. After all, not everyone is trained in ocean diving. Your open water training may be confined to lake or quarry diving where tides and currents are non-existent.

Looking Back

1. List three causes of water movement:

A. _____

B. _____

C. _____

2. True or False: The best diving conditions usually occur at low tide. _____

3. True or False: Begin dives against the current. _____

4. Briefly describe how to escape a rip current.

_____

_____

4.4   The Bottom

The composition of the bottom affects your diving. You have already read about how it affects entry, exits, and visibility. You will now learn more about the various types of bottoms and various effects the differing compositions can have on diving.

As a rule of thumb, you can expect the underwater terrain at a dive site to be an extension of the shoreline. If the shore is rocky and rugged, similar conditions will usually be found beneath the surface. A wide, sandy beach indicates a vast expanse of sand offshore. There are exceptions, however, so while this general rule is often useful, it helps to check with others regarding a dive site whenever possible. Information on bottom conditions is also available on navigational charts.

Another general rule is that the more vertical relief there is to the bottom, and the more aquatic plants there are present, the greater the amount of life there will be in an area. Flat areas tend to be barren compared to kelp forests and coral reefs. Therefore, divers tend to seek sites which have abundant life and make for the most interesting diving.

The composition of the bottom ranges from mud and silt to clay, sand and pebbles, to rocks to coral. Mud and silt bottoms are stirred easily and can quickly reduce visibility to zero with suspended sediment. Sand bottoms are somewhat better, but tend to be underwater deserts. A rocky bottom provides a good base for aquatic plants and also provides many holes and crevices to serve as homes for aquatic animals. Aquatic plants do not grow well in tropical waters, but coral thrives there and makes for excellent diving. Coral, rocks, and other formations have sharp edges, so gloves are required to prevent cuts and scratches while diving.

Varying bottom composition requires varying procedures for diving. You will need to learn one entry technique for a sandy bottom, which provides good footing, and yet another for a muddy bottom, which can pose an entirely different set of problems. Once you have entered the water, you will find that very careful movement is required to keep from stirring up a silty or muddy bottom. You will do a lot of swimming over a sandy bottom, and you will move more slowly and see a great deal while exploring rock or coral reefs. The composition of the bottom affects your entire dive.

Plants and a rocky bottom make for interesting diving.

Looking Back

1. List three ways of knowing the composition of the bottom for a given location.

A. _____

B. _____

C. _____

These divers should be wearing gloves, especially when diving around sharp coral formations.

2. List four aspects of diving which can be affected by the composition of the bottom.

A. _____

B. _____

C. _____

D. _____

3. List four types of bottom composition and a problem which can result from each.

A. _____

B. _____

C. _____

D. _____

4.5 Diving with Potentially Dangerous Aquatic Life

Part of the fascination of the underwater world is the numerous forms of life found there. There are thousands of animals and plants to capture your interest and amaze you. There is beauty and color to be discovered underwater that surpasses anything you can imagine.

There are some hazardous creatures underwater, but if you watch out for them and leave them alone, injury can be avoided.

It is natural, however, to be concerned about animals and plants that could harm you; but, as you are about to learn, this is not an overriding concern for experienced divers. In fact, they sometimes look forward with excitement to the possibility of encountering these "critters" and organisms.

Yes, there are potentially dangerous animals and plants underwater, just as there are potentially dangerous creatures and plants on land. You have probably learned what to do to keep from attracting or agitating terrestrial life forms. By reading or through training and experience you have learned how to recognize and avoid those that can be harmful, so you can set out on a hike in the hills without undue apprehension.

Going beneath the surface of the water is similar to going up into the hills in that there are aquatic animals which can be just as harmful as dangerous terrestrial animals. But as you learn more about them, you will look forward without apprehension or fear of seeing many of them beneath the surface.

Aggressive behavior is rare underwater. Any injury you might receive from an aquatic animal would almost certainly stem from a defensive action on the part of the creature. You can cause an injury by inadvertently coming into contact with the animal or by agitating it. With this thought in mind, you can readily understand how to avoid potential problems. There are three rules to follow: (1) Learn to identify potentially hazardous life forms in the area where you will be diving, (2) Don't molest that which can hurt you, and look carefully while diving and (3) If you don't know what something is, don't touch it.

The diving environment varies, and so do the life forms within it. Each region has its own hazardous animals. There are creatures which can bite, some that can stick you, others that can sting, and a few that can even shock. Again, identification and avoidance are your keys to safety. How do you learn to recognize the dangerous animals in an area? Someone knowledgeable and experienced needs to show you. Not only do you need to know what an animal looks like, you need to know where you are most likely to come across it.

During this course, your instructor will teach you about the animals in the local area, but you will need to seek out similar information when visiting other regions. Aquatic life familiarization is one of the main reasons a formal orientation is recommended for dives in an unfamiliar region.

New divers frequently express concern about entanglement in large plants underwater. This may become a serious problem if you overreact when snagged and twist and fight to get free. The proper response is to stop, analyze the problem, and get assistance from your buddy to get clear or to slowly take steps to free yourself. You have air to breathe, so there is no urgency. With experience and confidence, you will find diving in dense growths of aquatic plants like kelp can be exciting and beautiful. You will consider snagging your equipment only a minor nuisance which can be dealt with quite easily.

The greatest predator you will encounter underwater will most probably be another diver. Your greatest enemy is panic. Train well, keep your dive equipment in good working condition, plan your dives, dive your plans, enter the sea as a friendly transient, and the underwater world will be kind to you.

Let's finish this section with a few words about conservation. Much of the life underwater can be taken as game or for souvenirs. If done in

A good rule for preventing injury: "If you don't know what something is, don't touch it."

Problems with marine plants are minimal when compared to their enhancement of diving.

excess or in violation of the fish and game laws, it affects the future. Remember that what you take has an impact on what will be available for others, as well as yourself, in the future. If all divers take all they can get from an area, the site will soon become barren. It can take years for an exploited area to recover, and some never do. You should take game or collect living things with conservation in mind. If you want to take something to remember a dive or to share the experience with others, the best thing to take is a photograph. It fulfills your purpose and doesn't deplete the environment. Underwater photography is one of the most popular of all diving activities, and you will be qualified to take a course in underwater photography when you become certified as an Openwater Diver.

Looking Back

1. Injuries from aquatic life usually stem from offensive behavior by an animal.

☐ True ☐ False

2. List three rules to follow to avoid injury from aquatic animals while diving.

A. _____

B. _____

C. _____

3. List two ways an orientation to a new diving area can help you avoid injuries from animals underwater.

A. _____

B. _____

4. What is the main reason for limiting what we take from the underwater world?_____

4.6 Boat Diving

Some of the best dive sites can only be reached by boat. You will want and need to learn the procedures for diving from boats — both commercial boats and smaller, private boats.

Be conservation minded. Take only photos and memories home with you.

A commercial dive boat.

Commercial charter boats depart at a set time, so plan to arrive at least 30 minutes prior to the departure time. Sign in when you board the boat and stow your equipment as directed by the crew. Tour the vessel for orientation and ask questions to familiarize yourself with the layout.

If you are prone to seasickness, suitable medication may be advised prior to departure; but make sure no side effects result from it. Adverse side effects, such as drowsiness or dizziness, can be dangerous when diving. Testing the medication in advance is a good idea. Non-prescription medicine is usually effective for most people; but if your doctor prescribes something, make sure he or she is aware that you will be diving while under the influence of the medication. If you feel the effects of motion sickness while the boat is underway, it is too late to take medication. It will help to get fresh air, watch the horizon, and stay near the center of the boat. Lying down with your eyes closed may bring relief also. Most people develop their sea legs fairly quickly.

It is important to get acquainted with the procedures for diving from a charter boat. Go with an experienced diver or group to learn the correct techniques. You need to know how to enter, exit, get your tank filled, keep your gear together, etc.

Diving from a small boat requires you to learn yet another set of procedures. You will probably have to dive even more compactly than when aboard a charter boat due to space limitations. For example, you might don your wet or dry suit on shore and then take the boat to the dive site.

The procedures for entering and exiting the water vary, depending on the size and configuration of the vessel. Care may be required to keep the boat balanced as you enter or exit. It is often helpful to don and remove your scuba equipment in the water rather than aboard a small boat. Some means to get back aboard the boat must be available.

Safety procedures are necessary for small boat diving. A written plan of your destination and expected time of return should be left with someone so help can be summoned if you do not return within a reasonable period of time. Good seamanship is important, and more than one person aboard the boat should be trained to operate it competently. The deployed anchor should be checked at the beginning of the dive to make sure it is secure and at the end of the dive to ensure it is clear for lifting. Someone who can operate the boat should remain aboard during dives.

For both large and small boats, you should dive in the vicinity of the vessel and remain up current from it during your dive. A trail line with a float behind the boat is always a good idea when currents are present.

As you can see, there is much to learn through practice in order to dive properly from boats. As with every new aspect of diving,

The techniques and procedures for diving from a private boat are different than those for diving from a large, commercial boat.

Boat diving is fun diving!

You will need to learn the proper procedures for diving from a charter boat.

training is recommended, followed by initial participation with an experienced diver — especially for specialized boat diving activities such as drift diving. Having someone point out what to do and what not to do helps greatly to prevent embarrassment, frustration, and unpleasant incidents. You should get all the training you can for your diving so you can get all the diving you can from your training.

Looking Back

1. To dive safely from a boat, what are the first two actions you should take?

A. _____

B. _____

2. List three steps you can take to help prevent seasickness.

A. _____

B. _____

C. _____

3. What training is recommended for diving from small boats that is not required for charter boat diving? _____

4.7   Other Considerations

With regard to the environment, the main idea is to know what to expect, to be prepared, to know what to do to have fun safely, and to exercise good judgment based on your knowledge and experience. Some divers take chances in unfavorable environmental conditions because they travel a long way to reach a particular location. It is always a good idea to have a contingency plan.

In addition to the topics presented, there are other environmental considerations with which you should become familiar. Sunlight is one example. It varies in intensity on different parts of the earth. The sun's rays are more intense in tropical areas than in temperate ones. Sunburn is preventable, and can ruin a diving vacation if precautions are not taken. Note that you can become sunburned while diving. Keeping in the shade as much as possible, covering up with light clothing, and the use of sun screen are all wise precautions.

You should find out if there are any obstructions or hazards you might encounter at a diving location. Examples include fishing line, hooks, and nets, rubble and debris, (such as wire and cable), trees, or brush. Just knowing such

Have an alternate site selected in case conditions are bad at your intended location.

Don't let sunburn ruin your dive trip. You need protection, even when in the water.

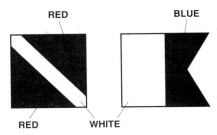

Dive flags: U. S. flag (left) and international alpha flag (right).

activity. As you explore new dive sites, you will want to explore others. Every place is different. Diving activities, as well as physical environments, vary from region to region and from site to site. Learning more about the special qualities of the diving environment amplifies your diving enjoyment and your safety underwater. One of NAUI's specialty courses is Underwater Environment. Ask your NAUI Instructor about it.

Looking Back

1. List three ways to avoid sunburn during a tropical diving vacation.

A. _____

B. _____

C. _____

When you display a dive flag, you have a responsiblity to dive nearby (within 100 feet).

things are present and being on the lookout for them can aid greatly in preventing difficulties. You can also plan in advance how to cope with a possible nuisance.

Boat traffic is a consideration deserving special attention. To caution boaters and to let them know of diving activities, special flags, which are known to most boaters, are flown. The standard U. S. dive flag and the international dive flag are illustrated. They signal boaters to remain at least 100 feet (30 m) clear of an area and should be flown only when divers are actually in the water. To be afforded protection by the flag, you must surface close to it. Not all boaters know or respect a dive flag, so be prepared for those who trespass into the area supposedly protected. It is always a good idea to pause before surfacing and listen for the sound of approaching vessels. A power boat poses a serious threat to divers in the water, so exercise caution.

An infinite variety of underwater environments makes scuba diving a lifelong recreational

2. List three precautions to be taken to avoid entanglement in underwater obstructions.

A. _____

B. _____

C. _____

3. List three practices divers use to avoid being struck by a boat while in the water.

A. _____

B. _____

C. _____

　　We hope you have gained one overall impression from this section on the environment. The fundamental and underlying concept is that you must be trained and oriented for each new set of conditions and every new activity.

5 Dive Time Planning

5.1 Nitrogen Absorption and Elimination

We have mentioned several times the limitations of time and depth on diving. In this chapter, you will learn the basis for these limitations, become familiar with dive computers, and learn how to use both the NAUI Dive Tables and the NAUI Dive Time Calculator to plan dives with correct time and depth limits.

The various gases comprising the air you breathe dissolve into your body according to the concentration of each gas in the air. Air is essentially nitrogen and oxygen and oxygen is consumed by the body. Thus the gas with which we are primarily concerned is nitrogen. We have a certain amount of nitrogen dissolved in our blood and tissues at all times. When we breathe at sea level, nitrogen molecules are exchanged for nitrogen previously dissolved in the body. The exchange rate between new and old nitrogen is constant; the amount of nitrogen in solution remains constant.

Ingassing of Nitrogen When you are subjected to changing pressures under water, the balance of nitrogen absorption and elimination is upset. Under increased pressure, the air you breathe is denser, which means the concentration of nitrogen is increased. There is more nitrogen in the air you breathe than there is within your body. The result is an "ingassing" of nitrogen into the body until a state of equilibrium is reached between the amount of nitrogen being breathed and that dissolved into the sytem. The ingassing occurs rapidly at first, then proceeds more and more slowly until equilibrium results many hours later, assuming the pressure remains constant. There are no negative effects experienced while the ingassing of nitrogen occurs at moderate depths.

The different tissues of your body — fat, muscle, bone, etc. — absorb gas at differing rates. Nitrogen is absorbed quickly by muscle tissue, but very slowly by bone tissue. There

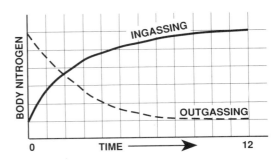

Above, Ingassing and outgassing (accumulation and elimination) of nitrogen in the body depicted graphically.
Below, The bubbles form because of the sudden drop in pressure.

are different ingassing rates for each kind of tissue. The cumulative effect of these various rates involves complicated mathematics; fortunately the rates are all taken into consideration in dive computers, tables, and calculators, so you need not concern yourself with varying absorption rates.

Outgassing of Nitrogen After spending time under pressure, you absorb a quantity of nitrogen greater than that found in your body at sea level. When you ascend and reduce the pressure, the balance between the nitrogen in your system and the amount being breathed is mis-matched again. There is a greater concentration of nitrogen in your blood and tissues than there is in the air you are breathing. The result is an "outgassing" of nitrogen from your body until a state of equilibrium is reached. The excess nitrogen passes from the body tissues to the blood, from the blood into the lungs, and is then expired. This process occurs rapidly during the first few minutes, but takes many hours to complete.

As long as the reduction of pressure is not too rapid for the amount of nitrogen present, the outgassing of nitrogen can occur without physiological problems. If the change in pressure is sudden, however, the nitrogen may come out of solution in your system so rapidly that bubbles form in your body. These bubbles can damage tissues and cause a painful condition known as "decompression sickness", "DCS" or the "bends".

A can of soda can be used to illustrate the principle of decompression sickness. Carbon dioxide is dissolved in the soda under pressure and remains in solution until the pressure is dropped suddenly by opening the sealed container. The rapid drop in pressure causes the carbon dioxide to form bubbles within the liquid and produce effervesence within the drink. If the pressure in the container was relieved very slowly, no bubbling would occur, and the soda would eventually be devoid of effervesence. To lessen the chance of bubbling within your body, *it is important to control both the amount of nitrogen absorbed while diving and the rate at which it is eliminated from the body.* This is the purpose of the information provided by dive time planners, which include dive computers, dive tables, and dive calculators.

Be aware that several factors can cause decompression sickness which would normally not occur. These factors include old age, obesity, fatigue, injuries, and the effects of drugs or alcohol. Be fit for diving, and dive conservatively.

A specific pressure reduction is required for bubble formation to occur. If you dive deeper than approximately 20 feet (6 m) and then ascend, the pressure change may be sufficient for bubble formation to take place if the amount of nitrogen absorbed is sufficently high. If you dive to depths of 20 feet (6 m) or less, decompression sickness is not likely to occur unless you reduce the pressure below that at sea level by going to altitude and thus further increasing "outgassing".

For depths of 21 feet (6.4 m) or greater, time limits called "dive time limits" have been established. The length of time spent at a given depth is not to exceed these limits or decompression sickness — a very serious condition — could be experienced during or after the ascent from the dive.

Time limits for various depths were established decades ago by the U.S. Navy based on field testing of military personnel. While the 1958 Navy time limits have been the standard of the diving community for many years and are still being used by many experienced divers today, physiological research and accident analysis of decompression have resulted in the recommendation by many highly qualified experts that lesser time limits than the U.S. Navy tables be used for recreational diving. Reduced time limits have been incorporated into the NAUI Dive Tables and Dive Time Calculator to reduce the risk of decompression sickness for recreational diving activities. Divers who choose to use time limits in excess of those currently recommended recognize and accept the increased risk associated with longer dive times.

Depth	NAUI Limit	U.S.N. Limit
0-20' (0-6 m)	No limit	No Limit
21-40' (6.4 - 12 m)	130 mins.	200 mins.
41-50' (12.5 - 15 m)	80 mins.	100 mins.
51-60' (15.5 - 18 m)	55 mins.	60 mins.
61-70' (18.6 - 21 m)	45 mins.	50 mins.
71-80' (21.6 - 24 m)	35 mins.	40 mins.
81-90' (24.6 - 27 m)	25 mins.	30 mins.
91-100' (27.6 - 30 m)	22 mins.	25 mins.

Note: Diving to depths in excess of 60 feet (18 m) is discouraged for entry level (NAUI Openwater I) divers. Intermediate (NAUI Openwater II) divers are qualified to dive to a maximum depth of 80 feet (24 m); NAUI Advanced Scuba Divers are qualified to dive to a maximum depth of 100 feet (30 m); and NAUI Deep Diving Specialty divers are qualified to dive to 130 feet (39 m), which is the maximum depth limit for recreational diving.

You do not need to memorize the dive time limits. Most of them are included on your NAUI Dive Tables and on the NAUI Dive Time Calculator. The times are presented here merely to acquaint you with typical time limits for diving. Note, however, that the length of allowable time decreases as the depth increases.

The outgassing of nitrogen occurs at different rates for various body tissues, so the outgassing of different tissues becomes the controlling factor for the time limits of various depths. It helps to be familiar with the concept, which forms the basis for dive computers, tables and calculators, but a thorough understanding of the principle is not necessary at this point in your diving education. You will learn much more about ingassing and outgassing theory in your NAUI Advanced Scuba Diver course.

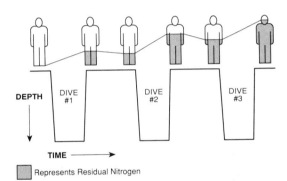

■ Represents Residual Nitrogen

Residual nitrogen is the nitrogen remaining in the body from dives made within the past 24 hours. It accumulates from dive to dive.

Residual Nitrogen   To understand the use of dive computers, tables and calculators, you do need to become familiar with the concept of "residual nitrogen". You already know that many hours are required to either fully absorb or to fully eliminate nitrogen into or from your system. Based on this concept, if you absorb some nitrogen at depth, ascend to the surface, and then descend again within 24 hours of your first descent, there will still be nitrogen remaining in your body from your first dive. Nitrogen from the second dive will be added to that remaining from the first dive. The net result after the second dive is that you will have more nitrogen in your system than you would if you had not made a

prior dive. You must always take into account any nitrogen remaining in your system from dives made within the past 24 hours. This "Residual Nitrogen" reduces your allowable dive time for any given depth.

Looking Back

1. Briefly describe "ingassing" as related to diving. _____

2. What causes bubble formation during "outgassing"?   _____

3. What is the deepest depth to which you can dive with no dive time limit? _____

4. According to the table presented, what is the no decompression limit for a dive to 52 feet? ___

5. Define in one sentence the term "residual nitrogen". _____

Determining Time Limits   There are three ways in which you can determine how long you may dive and then ascend within the dive time limits. You may use information displayed by a dive computer or may plan your dive time using either the NAUI Dive Tables or the NAUI Dive Time Calculator. Each offers certain advantages and has certain limitations. You should become familiar with each method so you will be able to minimize the risk of decompression sickness by the proper use of any of your options.

As previously mentioned, different body tissues absorb and release nitrogen at different rates. Mathematical models have been developed to estimate ingassing and outgassing for various tissues, and dive computers with mathematical programs can continuously calculate the amount of nitrogen in several "compartments" (a component of the mathematical model used for the calculator) for any given depth. This information is used to determine time/depth limits which are displayed for the diver.

Dive tables are also based on mathematical models. The time limits provided by tables are in increments of ten feet (3 m) of depth and are based on the assumption that the entire time of the dive is spent at the deepest depth. This is one disadvantage of the use of the tables as compared to a dive computer. A dive computer calculates ingassing and outgassing in one foot (0.3 m) increments and only for the depth to which you are diving, even as that depth varies during your dive. With a computer you are not penalized by being required to count all of your dive time at the deepest depth. You absorb less nitrogen at shallower depths, so when you spend part of your dive in water shallower than the maximum depth of a dive, a dive computer takes this into consideration and computes only the amount of nitrogen a mathematical model predicts is absorbed or eliminated. The results of a dive with progressively shallower depths (called a multiple-level or "multi-level" dive) using a dive computer are longer dive time limits and less residual nitrogen penalty than when the fixed-calculation dive tables are used. Dive computers are expensive, however, compared to dive tables.

There are dive tables available which can compute multi-level dives. The manual planning and execution of multi-level dives are complex and are not recommended for recreational diving. If you wish to receive credit for reduced nitrogen absorption during multi-level dives, obtain and use a dive computer, but only after becoming proficient in dive table usage.

The following overview of dive tables will prepare you to learn to use the NAUI Dive Tables and Dive Time Calculator. A "letter group" designation is used in the tables as a simple means of expressing the amount of residual nitrogen within your body. The letters range in sequence from "A" to "L". A very small amount of nitrogen is represented by Group A, and the amount increases as the letter groups progress toward "L". You are designated with a group letter following a dive, and are assigned to lower groups as you outgas nitrogen while at the surface between dives. When you dive again to a given depth, your group letter at that time is used to determine an amount of time that would represent the residual nitrogen in your system. This time is then subtracted from the normal dive time limits, which results in a reduced time limit for your repetitive dive. The residual nitrogen time is also added to the amount of time you actually spend diving, and that total time is then used to determine a new letter group.

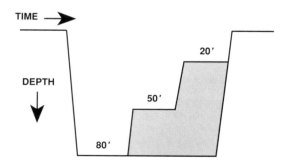

Multiple level dives involve diving at progressively shallower depths during a dive. The nitrogen absorption depicted by the shaded area is counted when dive tables are used, but not when a dive computer is employed.

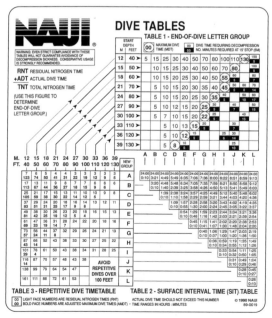

The NAUI Dive Tables

Manual dive calculators are based upon the dive tables, but eliminate the calculations tables required in order to determine letter group designations when more than one dive is made. A dive calculator also reduces errors often made in reading dive tables. It is easy to learn to use a dive calculator, but this should be done only after you become familiar with the procedures for planning dive time limits with the dive tables. A dive calculator may not always be available, but dive tables are usually readily available at dive sites.

It is important to know and understand that there are a variety of dive tables and computers and that these vary in the information they provide. Some are more conservative than others. Always use the type of table, calculator or computer with which you are familiar. If your dive buddy is using a different type, you should agree to abide by the most conservative dive planning information.

5.2 Dive Table Terms and Rules

To use the NAUI Dive Tables and Dive Time Calculator properly, you must become familiar with certain terms as well as rules which must be followed.

Dive Table Terms

1. *Dive Schedule:* The schedule of a dive is an abbreviated statement of the depth and duration of a dive and is expressed as depth/time, *e.g.,* 70 feet (21 m)/40 = 70 feet (21 m) for 40 minutes.

2. *Maximum Dive Time (MDT):* The length of time that may be spent at a given depth without being required to stop during ascent to prevent the likelihood of decompression sickness.

3. *Decompression Stop:* The time a diver stops and waits at a specified depth during ascent to allow nitrogen elimination before surfacing.

4. *Precautionary Decompression Stop:* Three minutes spent at a depth of 15 feet (5 m) as a safety precaution even though the Maximum Dive Time has not been exceeded. This procedure is recommended at the end of every dive.

Time spent decompressing is considered "neutral" time and is not part of Dive Time.

5. *Required Decompression Stop:* An amount of time specified by dive tables, a calculator or a computer to be spent at a specified depth (15' (5m) for NAUI Tables and Calculator) whenever the Dive Time Limits are exceeded.

6. *Actual Dive Time (ADT):* The time from the moment you begin your descent until the time you return to the surface. (Time spent doing precautionary decompression may be excluded.)

7. *Letter Group Designation:* A letter symbol used to designate the amount of excess nitrogen in your system. The nearer the beginning of the alphabet, the less the amount of residual nitrogen in your system.

8. *Surface Interval Time (SIT):* Time spent on the surface between dives. During this time, excess nitrogen is eliminated from your body and your letter group designation changes, moving closer to the beginning of the alphabet.

9. *Residual Nitrogen:* The nitrogen remaining in your system from a dive or dives made within the past 24 hours.

10. *Repetitive Dive:* Any dive made within 24 hours of a previous dive.

11. *Residual Nitrogen Time (RNT):* On repetitive dives, the amount of time you must consider you have already spent at a given depth for a planned dive. This time is based on the amount of residual nitrogen remaining in your system from a previous dive. Residual Nitrogen Time is obtained from a table and is based on your letter group designation following your Surface Interval Time (SIT).

12. *Adjusted Maximum Dive Time (AMDT):* For repetitive dives, AMDT is the Maximum Dive Time for the depth of the dive minus the Residual Nitrogen Time (RNT) for the dive.

13. *Total Nitrogen Time (TNT):* This is the sum of your Residual Nitrogen Time (RNT) and your Actual Dive Time (ADT) following a repetitive dive. This total is used to obtain a new letter group designation after the repetitive dive. TNT is expressed as RNT + ADT = TNT.

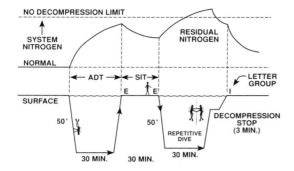

NO DECOMPRESSION LIMIT

SYSTEM NITROGEN

RESIDUAL NITROGEN

NORMAL

ADT — SIT

LETTER GROUP

SURFACE

50'   50'

REPETITIVE DIVE

DECOMPRESSION STOP (3 MIN.)

30 MIN.   30 MIN.   30 MIN.

Dive table terms.

Looking Back

1. What is the Dive Schedule for a dive to 60 feet (18 m) for 30 minutes?_____

2. Identify the Surface Interval Times in the following series of dives: 50' (15 m)/35, 1:25, 40' (12 m)/35, 2:20, 30'(9 m)/40. _____

_____

3. If your Residual Nitrogen Time is 36 minutes and your Actual Dive Time is 19 minutes, your Total Nitrogen Time for the dive is _____ minutes.

4. How is the amount of nitrogen remaining in your system after a dive expressed in the dive tables?_____

_____

5. You should decompress at a depth of _____ feet (meters) for _____ minutes following dives in which the Maximum Dive Times are reached.

Dive Table Rules

1. On any dive, ascend no faster than 60 feet (18 m) per minute. This is only one foot (0.3 m) per second, and this slow pace is the *maximum* rate of ascent. The use of a timing device and depth gauge (or a dive computer) is required to measure your rate of ascent.

2. Use the exact or next greater number when referring to the dive tables. If a number in a table is exceeded, use the next greater number. For example, for depths from 40 to 130 feet (12-39 m), the dive tables increase in ten foot increments, so a dive to 41 feet (12.3 m) is considered

a 50 foot (15 m) dive and a dive to 61 feet (18.3 m) is counted as a 70 foot (21 m) dive.

3. When determining the dive schedule for a dive, use the deepest depth attained during the dive. If part of the dive was spent at 60 feet (18 m) while the majority of it was spent at 40 feet (12 m), the dive must still be considered as if the entire time were spent at 60 feet (18 m).

4. When making a series of dives, plan repetitive dives to the same or shallower depth as the previous dive. This allows you to outgas nitrogen on progressively shallower dives instead of carrying a large amount of residual nitrogen on deeper repetitive dives.

5. Consider all dives made shallower than 40 feet (12 m) as 40 foot (12 m) dives when planning repetitive dives.

6. A Surface Interval Time (SIT) of at least ten minutes is required before entering the Surface Interval Timetable. NAUI recommends a minimum of one hour between dives, however.

7. If a dive is particularly cold or strenuous, use the next greater bottom time. An example of this is included later in this section.

The general rules for using the dive tables include use of the deepest depth reached during a dive.

Looking Back

1. Ascend from all dives at a maximum rate of _____ feet (meters) per minute and allow a minimum of _____ minutes between dives.

2. Arrange the following dives into the preferred sequence: 30' (9 m)/40, 60'(18 m)/30, 50'(15 m)/20. _____

_____

3. A dive to 25 feet (7.6 m) for 40 minutes should be considered as a dive schedule of _____ when planning a repetitive dive.

5.3 Finding Time Limits

Now that you know the concepts behind the tables, the terms used for them and the rules for their use, you are ready to learn how to refer to the NAUI Dive Tables. In this section, you will learn the general organization of the tables and how to use them to determine Dive Time Limits for both single and repetitive dives.

General Organization The NAUI Dive Tables are based upon the U.S. Navy Decompression Tables and have been specially designed by

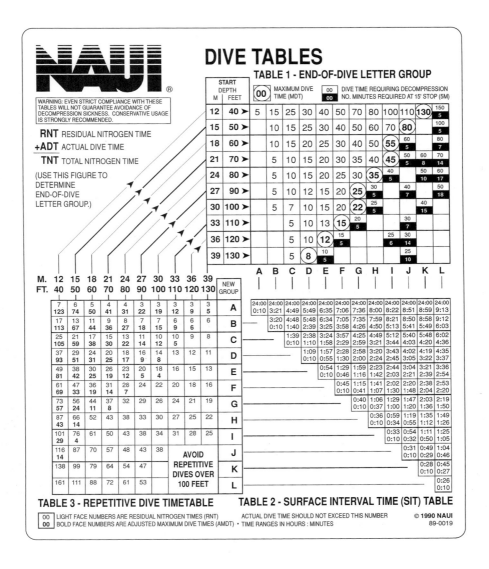

NAUI for recreational diving. The NAUI tables are configured so that each of three tables flows into the next. You begin with Table 1, which is called the "End-of-Dive Letter Group" table. Not only does it give you a letter group designation at the end of a dive, it also contains the Maximum Dive Time information for depths from 40 to 130 feet (12 to 39 m). Look at Table 1 and note that Maximum Times are circled for each depth.

Table 1 is entered horizontally from the left. The numbers on the table represent bottom time in minutes. Find the row for the appropriate depth and move to the right along the line until you find a bottom time that meets or exceeds your dive time. Now follow that column downward, exit the table, and find the letter group designation that indicates the amount of nitrogen remaining in your system following a dive. For example, a person who dives to 50 feet (15 m) for 30 minutes would have an "E" letter group designation.

letter group. The times are expressed as hours and minutes (Hours:Minutes).

The SIT table is entered vertically coming down the column from Table 1 and followed downward until you find a range of times into which the length of your surface interval falls. Then follow that row horizontally to the left, exit the table, and receive a new letter group designation. For example, if you enter the table with an "E" letter group and have a surface interval of three hours, you will exit the table on the third horizontal line and end up with a new letter group of "C". Note that the maximum time in the table is 24 hours. All excess nitrogen is considered to be eliminated after 24 hours, so a dive after that amount of time is not a repetitive dive.

TABLE 1 - END-OF-DIVE LETTER GROUP

START DEPTH M	FEET	00 = MAXIMUM DIVE TIME (MDT)									00 / 00 = DIVE TIME REQUIRING DECOMPRESSION / NO. MINUTES REQUIRED AT 15' STOP (5M)		
12	40	5	15	25	30	40	50	70	80	100	110	(130)	150/5
15	50		10	15	25	30	40	50	60	70	(80)	100/5	
18	60		10	15	20	25	30	40	50	(55)	60/5	80/7	
21	70	5	10	15	20	30	35	40	(45)	50/5	60/8	70/14	
24	80	5	10	15	20	25	30	(35)	40/5	50/10	60/17		
27	90	5	10	12	15	20	(25)	30/5	40/7	50/18			
30	100	5	7	10	15	20	(22)	25/5	40/15				
33	110		5	10	13	(15)	20/5	30/7					
36	120		5	10	(12)	15/5	25/6	30/14					
39	130		5	(8)	10/5	25/10							
		A	B	C	D	E	F	G	H	I	J	K	L

Table 1 - "End-of-Dive Letter Group" table.

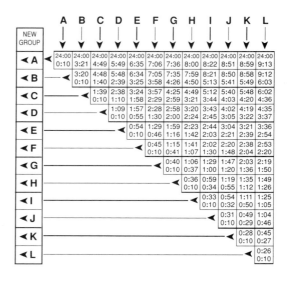

Table 2 - "Surface Interval Time (SIT)" table.

The longer you remain out of the water, the more excess nitrogen you eliminate. Crediting you with the loss of the nitrogen is the purpose of Table 2, the "Surface Interval Time (SIT) Table". It consists of blocks containing two numbers which represent the minimum and maximum times for assignment to a particular

Table 3 is the "Repetitive Dive Timetable". It tells your Residual Nitrogen Time (RNT) based on your current letter group and your planned depth and provides Maximum Dive Times that are reduced by the amount of your RNT. Your Actual Dive Time (ADT) must not exceed the Adjusted Maximum Dive Time (AMDT). Your Residual Nitrogen Time (RNT) must be added to your ADT to obtain your Total Nitrogen Time (TNT). This formula is illustrated in the upper left corner of your NAUI Dive Tables.

To use Table 3, enter it horizontally from the right on the row representing your letter group designation after your SIT and move to the left until you intersect the column corresponding to the depth of your planned repetitive dive. Depths are listed across the top of the table. At the coordinates of the depth and the letter group you will find two numbers. The top number represents RNT for that depth; the bottom number represents the Adjusted Maximum Dive Time (AMDT) for the depth. If you compare the totals of the AMDT and the Residual Nitrogen Times for any depth, you will find they all total the Maximum Dive Time Limit for that depth in Table 1. The AMDT is found by simply subtracting RNT from Maximum Dive Time for a given depth. Table 3 has already done the work for you. Your Actual Dive Time must not exceed your AMDT during a repetitive dive.

An example of the use of Table 3 is a "C" letter group diver planning a dive to 50 feet (15 m). At the coordinates "C" and 50 feet (15 m), you find the number 21 over the number 59. This means the diver has 21 minutes of RNT and the duration of the ADT must not exceed 59 minutes. The diver proceeds with the dive, keeping the ADT within the 59 minute Adjusted Maximum Dive Time, then adds the ADT to the 21 minutes of RNT and uses the dive schedule of 50 feet (15 m)/TNT to re-enter Table 1 and obtain an End-of-Dive letter group. Note how the cycle has been completed with the three tables.

Exercises Use the NAUI Dive Tables to find the Dive Time Limits for both single and repetitive dives.

1. What is the Maximum Dive Time for a dive to 60 feet (18 m) for your first dive of the day?

Answer: Because you have no residual nitrogen, you are allowed the Maximum Dive Time for the depth: 55 minutes.

2. What is your letter group designation following a dive to 55 feet (16.7 m) for 39 minutes?

Answer: Remember, when you exceed numbers in the tables, you use the next greater number. There is no 55 foot (16.7 m) depth in Table 1, so you use the 60 foot (18 m) schedule. The first time not exceeding 39 minutes in the 60 foot (18 m) row on Table 1 is 40. Thus the dive schedule for a 55 feet (16.7 m)/39 dive is actually 60 feet (16.7 m)/40 in the tables. Following the 40 minute column to the bottom of the table, you find that your letter group designation is "G" following this dive.

M.	12	15	18	21	24	27	30	33	36	39	NEW
FT.	40	50	60	70	80	90	100	110	120	130	GROUP
	7 / 123	6 / 74	5 / 50	4 / 41	4 / 31	3 / 22	3 / 19	3 / 12	3 / 9	3 / 5	◄ A
	17 / 113	13 / 67	11 / 44	9 / 36	8 / 27	7 / 18	7 / 15	6 / 9	6 / 6	6	◄ B
	25 / 105	21 / 59	17 / 38	15 / 30	13 / 22	11 / 14	10 / 12	10 / 5	9	8	◄ C
	37 / 93	29 / 51	24 / 31	20 / 25	18 / 17	16 / 9	14 / 8	13	12	11	◄ D
	49 / 81	38 / 42	30 / 25	26 / 19	23 / 12	20 / 5	18 / 4	16	15	13	◄ E
	61 / 69	47 / 33	36 / 19	31 / 14	28 / 7	24	22	20	18	16	◄ F
	73 / 57	56 / 24	44 / 11	37 / 8	32	29	26	24	21	19	◄ G
	87 / 43	66 / 14	52	43	38	33	30	27	25	22	◄ H
	101 / 29	76 / 4	61	50	43	38	34	31	28	25	◄ I
	116 / 14	87	70	57	48	43	38	AVOID REPETITIVE DIVES OVER 100 FEET			◄ J
	138	99	79	64	54	47					◄ K
	161	111	88	72	61	53					◄ L

Table 3 - "Repetitive Dive Timetable"

It is very important to keep track of your time and depth on all dives.

3. If your initial letter group is "G", what is your new letter group after a surface interval of one hour?

Answer: The correct answer is "F". To obtain it, enter Table 2 vertically at the Group G column and follow it down until you find the time range (0:41-1:15) corresponding to your surface interval. At that point on the table, follow the row to the left and obtain your new letter group.

4. With an "F" letter group, what is the Adjusted Maximum Dive Time for a dive to 50 feet (15 m)?

Answer: Table 3 is the Repetitive Dive Timetable providing the Adjusted Maximum Dive Time (AMDT) information. As an "F" diver going to 50 feet (15 m), the AMDT is 33 minutes. This is found as the lower number at the coordinates of F and 50 feet (15 m) in Table 3. Your Actual Dive Time must not exceed this number.

5. What is the Residual Nitrogen Time of a diver making the 50 foot (15 m) dive with an "F" letter group designation?

Answer: Table 3 also provides RNT times. At the 50 foot (15 m) and F coordinates, the top number (47) is the RNT.

6. With an ADT of 32 minutes on a dive to 50 feet (15 m) with a letter group of "F", what is the Total Nitrogen Time (TNT) of the dive?

Answer: TNT is the sum of ADT and the RNT, so TNT in this instance is the 32 minutes of ADT, plus 47 minutes of residual time, for a TNT of 79 minutes.

7. What is the End-of-Dive letter group for the dive in question six?

Answer: The dive schedule is 50 feet (15 m)/79. This information is taken to Table One to obtain an End-of-Dive letter group. For a depth of 50 feet (15 m), you find that the first time not exceeded by your TNT is 80 minutes. The letter group for a total time of 80 minutes is "J".

Looking Back

You have just used the NAUI Dive Tables to become acquainted with their arrangement. You should now be able to determine the Maximum Dive Time for single and repetitive dives and should also be able to determine your correct letter group designation following a dive. You will next learn how to use the tables so your combined dive plans do not exceed the Dive Time Limits.

Dive Table Planning When making repetitive dives, you will find that at times you are unable to dive to the depth you would like, for the duration you would like, due to the Adjusted Maximum Dive Times imposed upon you by residual nitrogen. In this part of Chapter 5, you will learn three ways to plan dives within the Dive Time Limits.

Limiting Your Actual Dive Time The first means of keeping within the Maximum Dive Times is easy — limit your ADT. Your first dive of the day should not exceed the Maximum Dive Time for the depth of the dive, and your repetitive dives should not exceed the Adjusted Maximum Dive Time for your planned depth. As you are about to see, this can be rather restrictive.

Suppose you wish to make three 25 minute dives to a depth of 60 feet (18 m). Assume a surface interval time of one hour between dives and an ADT of 25 minutes for the first dive. Following the first dive your letter group designation is "E". After a surface interval of one hour, your letter group changes to "D". According to Table 3, your AMDT for the second dive is 31 minutes. If you repeat the Actual Dive Time of your first dive (25 minutes) your TNT for the second dive is your ADT (25 minutes) plus your RNT of 24 minutes for a total of 49 minutes. Your End-of-Dive letter group following the second dive is "H". An hour after surfacing from the second dive, your letter group is "G", and a "G" diver planning a dive to 60 feet (18 m) is limited—according to Table Three—to a maximum ADT of 11 minutes. Now let's use this three-dive example to find other ways to allow us to safely spend more time underwater.

Planning your Surface Intervals A good way to control your residual nitrogen, and your Adjusted Maximum Dive Time for a repetitive dive, is with the surface interval. The longer you remain at the surface between dives, the less nitrogen remains in your system and the longer you can safely stay beneath the surface on your next dive. What you want to be able to do is to determine exactly how long a surface interval is required in order to safely carry out a planned dive.

Let's use the third dive from our initial series of three dives as an example. After the second

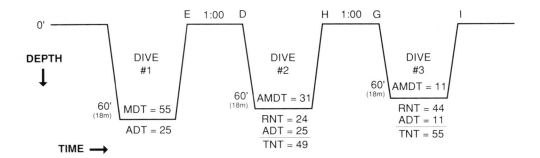

DEPTH
↓

E 1:00 D   H 1:00 G   I

0' ─────┐   ┌──────┐   ┌──────┐   ┌──────
        │   DIVE   │   │   DIVE   │   │   DIVE   │
        │   #1   │   │   #2   │   │   #3   │
        │   │   │   │ 60' │ AMDT = 11   │
   60' │ MDT = 55   │ 60' │ AMDT = 31   │(18m) │   │
  (18m) │   │(18m) │   │   │ RNT = 44   │
        │ ADT = 25   │   │ RNT = 24   │   │ ADT = 11   │
        │   │   │ ADT = 25   │   │ TNT = 55   │
                                │ TNT = 49   │

TIME ──▶

The dive time on the third dive is very limited due to residual nitrogen from the previous dives.

dive, the letter group designation was "H". To plan the dive, start with Table 3 and the bottom time you want for the planned depth and work backwards. Here is how it is done: For a desired ADT of 25 minutes at 60 feet (18 m), find the first group in the 60 foot (18 m) column that has an AMDT equal to or greater than 25 minutes. The group that does this is "E", which has an AMDT of 25 minutes. You now have half of the problem solved. All that remains is to determine how long it will take you to change from letter group "H" to letter group "E", and Table 2 quickly provides that information. Just look at the coordinates of letter group "E" horizontally (the ending group) and "H" vertically (the starting group) and find the minimum time required (1:42). By waiting just 42 minutes longer between your second and third dives, you can safely make that third dive for 25 minutes. Planning your surface interval is the second way to plan your dives.

Limiting Your Depth   Your third option is to increase your bottom time by limiting your depth. If you were not able to extend your surface interval between the second and third dives in our example series, and did not want to make a dive of a very short duration, you could dive to a shallower depth and safely spend more time diving. Let's see how that works and how you would plan the dive.

Again, assuming a letter group designation of "G" following a one hour surface interval after

| M. | 12 | 15 | 18 | 21 | 24 | 27 | 30 | 33 | 36 | 39 | NEW |
FT.	40	50	60	70	80	90	100	110	120	130	GROUP
7 123	6 74	5 50	4 41	4 31	3 22	3 19	3 12	3 9	3 5	◄ A
17 113	13 67	11 44	9 36	8 27	7 18	7 15	6 9	6 6	6	◄ B
25 105	21 59	17 38	15 30	13 22	11 14	10 12	10 5	9	8	◄ C
37 93	29 51	24 31	20 25	18 17	16 9	14 8	13	12	11	◄ D
49 81	38 42	30 25	26 19	23 12	20 5	18 4	16	15	13	◄ E
61 69	47 33	36 19	31 14	28 7	24	22	20	18	16	◄ F
73 57	56 24	44 11	37 8	32	29	26	24	21	19	◄ G
87 43	66 14	52	43	38	33	30	27	25	22	◄ H
101 29	76 4	61	50	43	38	34	31	28	25	◄ I
116 14	87	70	57	48	43	38				◄ J
138	99	79	64	54	47		AVOID REPETITIVE DIVES OVER 100 FEET			◄ K
161	111	88	72	61	53					◄ L

You will learn how to work the tables in reverse for planning safe repetitive dives.

your second 25 minute dive to 60 feet (18 m), refer to Table 3 and look for the maximum depth which will permit you to make a 25 minute dive with a letter group of "G". Enter Table 3 on the "G" line and follow it to the left until you find an AMDT equal to or greater than 25 minutes. In this instance, the time is 57 minutes and the depth is 40 feet (12 m). You can see that by

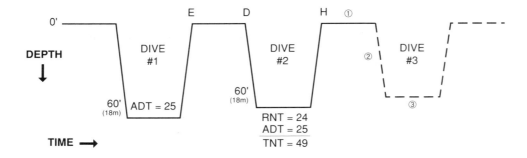

To avoid required decompression for the third dive, you can extend the Surface Interval Time ①, limit the depth ②, or limit Actual Dive Time ③.

diving 20 feet (6 m) shallower on your third dive you can make your 25 minute dive. This is making good use of the dive tables.

Looking Back

You have just learned three ways to use the dive tables to plan your dives within the Dive Time limits. Now see if you can solve the following problems. Your instructor will provide more information on planning procedures.

1. After a dive to 65 feet (19.8 m) for 28 minutes and a surface interval of two hours, what is the maximum time you can dive on a second dive to a depth of 60 feet (18 m)?

2. After a dive to 70 feet (21 m) for 30 minutes, what is the minimum surface interval that will allow you to repeat the dive without exceeding the Adjusted Maximum Dive Time?

3. With a letter group designation of "E" following a series of dives, what is the maximum depth to which you can dive for at least 20 minutes?

5.4   Using the NAUI Dive Time Calculator

The NAUI Dive Tables are the basis for the calculator, which eliminates the calculations required with the tables. When you are familiar with the NAUI Dive Tables, it is very easy to learn to use the NAUI Dive Time Calculator.

General Organization   Tables 1 and 3 of the NAUI Dive Tables are combined on the base plate. Letter group designations appear around the circumference, and Actual Dive Times in minutes appear in the window. End-of-Dive letter group designations appear to the right of the ADT numbers in the disc window. Table 2 —the Surface Interval Timetable—is printed on the disc and is identical to Table 2 on the NAUI Dive Tables.

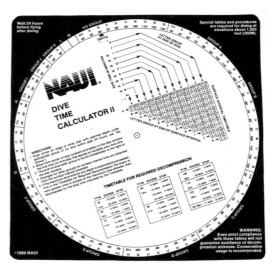

The NAUI Dive Time Calculator is easier to use than dive tables.

Dive Planning Using the Calculator For your first dive of the day, find the "No Group" section on the base plate and align the depth arrow on the edge of the disc with the planned depth of your dive. The Maximum Dive Time for the dive appears as the largest number in the window. As an example, a "No Group" diver planning a dive to 60 feet (18 m) would have a Maximum Dive Time of 55 minutes.

Assuming you made your first dive of the day to 60 feet (18 m) and that your ADT for the dive was 23 minutes, your next step would be to determine your letter group designation following the dive. This is done by aligning the disc as described in the previous paragraph, reading bottom times from the center of the disc outward, and finding the first time you do not exceed. For our schedule of 60 feet (18 m)/23 minutes, the first time not exceeded is 25 minutes. Our End-of-Dive letter group appears to the right of the window next to 25: letter group "E".

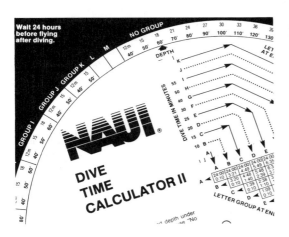

Use "No Group" portion of the calculator for the first dive.

Letter group changes with surface intervals are determined the same as with the NAUI Dive Tables. An "E" diver after a surface interval of one hour would have a letter group designation of "D".

For planning of repetitive dives, find your new letter group on the circumference of the base plate and align the depth arrow on the disc with the planned depth of the repetitive dive. If, as a

Group "D" diver, you wish to return to 60 feet (18 m), you will find in the window that your ADT is not to exceed 31 minutes. If you made a second dive of 23 minutes as a "D" diver, your End-of-Dive letter group (found adjacent to the first ADT number not exceeded in the window) would be 26 and your End-of-Dive group would be "H". Note that the design of the calculator eliminates Adjusted Maximum Dive Time and the need to add Residual Nitrogen Time to Actual Dive Time to obtain Total Nitrogen Time for the determination of your End-of-Dive letter group. All of this is rendered unnecessary by the design of the calculator, but the answers you obtain with the calculator are exactly the same as if you calculated the dive schedules using the NAUI Dive Tables.

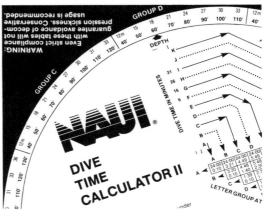

It is simple to find repetitive dive time limits using the NAUI Dive Time Calculator.

Dive Planning with the Calculator The same three methods of dive planning used with the dive tables can be used with the Dive Time Calculator. You may limit your bottom time to the maximum number indicated for a given depth and group, extend your surface interval to obtain a lesser group letter, or dive to a shallower depth. As an example of dive planning using the calculator, assume you are a Group "F" diver and wish to dive for at least 25 minutes. Looking in the window below Group "F" on the calculator, you find, by moving the window back and forth, you may dive up to 19 minutes at 60 feet (18 m) and up to 33 minutes at 50 feet (15 m). Thus, you would have to dive no deeper than 50 feet (15 m) in order to remain 25 minutes and not exceed the Maximum Dive Time.

If you wanted to dive to 60 feet (18 m) for 25 minutes, but could not because you were a group "F" diver, you would need to determine the group letter designation that would allow you to make the dive and the minimum surface interval required to achieve that letter group. To determine the group that will allow a 60 feet (18 m)/25 dive schedule, simply align the depth arrow with 60 feet (18 m) in Group "F" and then work back one group at a time, realigning the depth arrow with 60' (18 m) for each group, until you find a MDT that equals or exceeds 25 minutes. In this instance, the first group allowing a Maximum Dive Time of 25 minutes is Group "E".

In some instances, the words "DO NOT DIVE" appear in the window of the calculator. This means you have too much residual nitrogen to permit a dive to the depth selected for a particular letter group. You will need to extend your surface interval to dive to the depth or select a shallower depth that indicates you may dive.

You can see already that using the Dive Time Calculator is easier than using the Dive Tables.

Exercises   Use the NAUI Dive Time Calculator to find the Dive Time Limits for both single and repetitive dives and for the planning of repetitive dives.

1. What is the Maximum Dive Time for a dive to 60 feet (18 m) for your first dive of the day?

Answer: You have no letter group designation for your first dive, so you align the depth arrow of the disc with 60' (18 m) under the "No Group" section of the base plate. Find that the Maximum Dive Time is 55 minutes.

2. What is your letter group designation following a first dive to 55 feet (16.7 m) for 39 minutes?

Answer: Just as with the dive tables, whenever a number is exceeded, you use the next larger number. There are no 55 foot (16.7 m) depths on the Calculator, so you must use the 60 foot (18 m) schedule. The first number under 60 feet (18 m) greater than 39 in the "No Group" section is 40 minutes. The dive schedule becomes 60 feet (18 m)/40 and the letter group is found to the right of the window beside 40—letter group "G".

3. An hour after your first dive, your letter group is "F". With this new group designation, what is

the Maximum Dive Time for a dive to 50 feet (15 m)?

Answer: Align the depth arrow on the disc with 50' (15 m) in the Group "F" section of the base plate and read the Maximum Dive Time of 33 minutes in the window.

4. If a Group "F" diver makes a 32 minute dive to a depth of 50 feet (15 m), what is the End-of-Dive letter group designation?

Answer: Align the depth arrow on the disc with 50' (15 m) in the Group "F" section of the base plate and find the first time not exceeded by a 32 minute dive. In this case, that number is 33 minutes. Find the End-of-Dive group letter, which is "J", on the disc next to 33 in the window.

5. As a Group "H" diver, what is the minimum surface interval required to allow you to dive to a depth of 60 feet (18 m) for 25 minutes without exceeding the Dive Time Limits?

Answer: A Group "H" diver may not dive to 60 feet (18 m), as is stated in the window of the calculator. This is because a diver with this letter group designation has a large amount of residual nitrogen. Moving the depth arrow of the disc to 60 feet (18 m) to lower letter groups on the base plate shows that the time limits for Groups G, F and E are 11 minutes, 19 minutes, and 25 minutes, respectively. This means that you will need to attain letter group "E" before you can dive for at least 25 minutes without exceeding the Maximum Dive Time. Since you are in Group "H" and know you need to attain group "E", determining the surface interval is now merely a matter of referring to the Surface Interval Timetable and seeing how long it takes to move from group "H" to Group "E". At the coordinates "H" and "E" on the Surface Interval Timetable, we find the minimum time to be 1:42.

If you will check back to the dive table exercises you did previously, you will find you have just solved the same problems with the Dive Time Calculator you did using the Dive Tables and that the solutions are identical!

5.5   The Worksheet

A means to systematically keep track of depth, bottom time, surface intervals, letter group designations and other information is needed when working with the dive tables or the dive calculator. On the back of your NAUI Dive Tables is a Dive Planning and Recording Worksheet. This part of Chapter Five explains how to use the Worksheet, which is recommended for the prevention of errors.

The NAUI Worksheet on your dive tables can be written on with a standard pencil and erased or scoured clean without damaging the tables. It is intended for use, so take a pencil when you go diving and write dive information directly onto your NAUI Tables Worksheet. Your NAUI Dive Tables are also waterproof, so you can record information on them in the water or refer to planning information previously entered.

The concept of the worksheet is quite simple. Time is plotted horizontally to the right, and depth vertically downward.

The concept of the worksheet is simple.

Four simple rules make the worksheet easy to use.

1. Enter the appropriate time (T) on each top corner of each dive profile. Include the appropriate letter group (LG) designation in the blanks above the times.

2. Enter the maximum planned depth (PD) for each dive profile (left side) prior to a dive and the actual depth (AD) after the dive (right side of the profile).

3. Enter either the Maximum Dive Time (MDT) or Adjusted Maximum Dive Time (AMDT) for each dive profile. The reason for MDT and AMDT being listed twice at the bottom of each profile is that the time limit for both the intended maximum depth plus the next greater depth should be included for contingency planning.

4. Enter the formula for Total Nitrogen Time (RNT + ADT = TNT) beneath each repetitive dive profile.

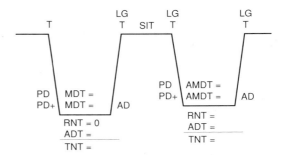

The basic rules for use of the worksheet. T = Time, PD = Planned Depth, AD = Actual Depth, LG = Letter Group, SIT = Surface Interval Time. The remaining terms have been previously defined.

Step one is to plan your first dive by entering the planned depth and MDT on the first dive profile. Enter the Maximum Dive Times (MDT) for the dive along the bottom line of the profile as shown in the example. Then record the time at the beginning of your descent on the upper left corner of the profile. When you return to the surface, the elapsed time is recorded in the upper right corner along with your end-of-dive letter group. The deepest depth of the dive should be recorded on the right side of the dive profile.

When a repetitive dive is planned, the procedure is nearly the same except that you now use the Adjusted Maximum Dive Times at the bottom of the repetitive profile and, (unless using the Dive Calculator) add your RNT to your ADT at the bottom of the profile to obtain Total Nitrogen Time (TNT).

When precautionary decompression is carried out, the time spent decompressing is shown next to a short horizontal line drawn through the ascent side of the dive profile. This appears as the number "3" in the following illustration.

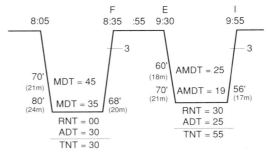

Example of a completed dive worksheet.

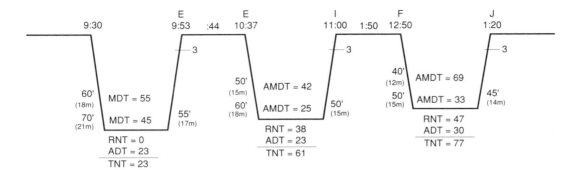

Now let's record a series of dives on a worksheet as an example. You will then be given another series of dives to record for practice.

Sample Worksheet Problem   The first dive of the day is planned to a depth of 60 feet (18 m), begins at 9:30 a.m., and lasts for 23 minutes. The actual depth of the dive is 55 feet (16.8 m). You surface at 9:53 and remain out of the water until 10:37. Your next dive is to a depth of 50 feet (15 m) for a duration of 23 minutes. You surface at 11:00 and have a surface interval of 1:50. At 12:50 p.m. you begin your third dive to a planned depth of 40 feet (12 m), but you end up reaching a depth of 45 feet (13.7 m) with an ADT of 30 minutes. You surface from the third dive at 1:20 p.m.

Note: When the Worksheet is used in conjunction with the calculator, "RNT + ADT" for a sum of "TNT" is disregarded. Only the Depth and the ADT are required to determine the "End-of-Dive" letter group when using the Dive Time Calculator.

Exercise Problem   Record the following dives on the worksheet and take them to class for review with your instructor. Work the exercise once using the NAUI Dive Tables and once using the NAUI Dive Time Calculator. Compare your results, should be the same.

Your first dive of the day begins at 8:00 a.m. and is to 60 feet (18 m) for 31 minutes. Time up is 8:31 and the surface interval time is 1:31. The second dive begins at 10:02 to a depth of 55 feet (16.8 m) and lasts for 24 minutes. Time of surfacing from the second dive is 10:26 and you remain out of the water for two hours. The third

dive, started at 12:26, is to a depth of 50 feet (15 m) for 31 minutes. What are the time of surfacing and the End-of-Dive letter group?

Do not rely on your memory to keep track of dive times, maximum depths, or surface intervals. This information must be recorded. The NAUI Worksheet provides an easy and convenient way to accomplish this. Get into the habit of recording your dives on the Worksheet, and it will become easy to keep track of your diving. This also makes it easier to complete your log book at the end of the day.

5.6   Special Rules and Sample Problems

To be prepared to handle situations related to the dive tables, there are a few special rules and procedures you need to learn. How long do you decompress if the Maximum Dive Time is exceeded? What is the procedure for decompression? How can you keep from getting decompression sickness if you are to fly after diving? What if you want to go diving at some altitude above sea level or fly in a plane after diving? How do you handle a cold or strenuous dive? The answers to these questions follow.

Decompression   Intentionally exceeding the Maximum Dive Time is unwise, unsafe, and discouraged. As you will learn in your Advanced or Specialty training for deep diving, there are many requirements that must be met to carry out decompression dives properly. Even if these requirements are met, dives requiring decompression are still discouraged. The long term

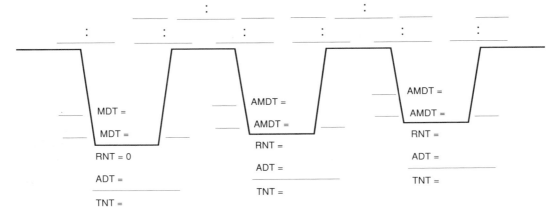

Worksheet for exercise problem on previous page. (Precautionary decompression time is not to be included as part of Actual Dive Time.)

If decompression is required, maintain the stop depth at chest level and limit activity to light exercise.

effects of decompression diving are still not clearly understood, so this type of diving is deemed inappropriate for recreational purposes.

If you accidently exceed a Maximum Dive Time, you will need to decompress. This involves stopping at a depth of approximately 15 feet (5 m) during your ascent and remaining there for a specified number of minutes to allow excess nitrogen to be expelled. During a decompression stop, your activity should be kept to a minimum. You should have some means of support to help you maintain a constant depth during decompression stops. An ascent line, a

decompression "bar" suspended from a boat, or the contour of the bottom in shallow water are examples of support. It is difficult to remain at one depth in shallow water without something to grasp. Swimming and hovering decompression are possible, but not easy. If you think you may need to decompress, have a means available to help you remain at a depth of approximately 15 feet (5 m).

Refer to Table 1 of the NAUI Dive Tables. You are already familiar with the Maximum Dive Time for each depth. To the right of the MDT are split squares containing two sets of numbers. The top number represents dive time, and the lower number represents the amount of decompression time required for that dive time. This decompression information tells you how long to remain at a depth of approximately 15 feet (5 m) to avoid decompression sickness if you should mistakenly exceed the Maximum Dive Times. For example, if your Total Nitrogen Time on an 80 foot (24 m) dive was 45 minutes, a ten minute decompression stop would be required.

Refer to your NAUI Dive Time Calculator. Required decompression information is handled differently on the calculator than it is on the dive tables. A separate Decompression Timetable is provided. To use the table, simply find in the first column the depth of your dive, find in the second column the first time that equals or exceeds your dive time in excess of the Dive Time limit for the depth, then decompress at 15 feet (5 m) for the time indicated in column three.

In addition to required decompression stops, you will want to stop at 15 feet (5 m) for three minutes as a safety precaution at the end of every dive. These "Precautionary Stops", while not required, are a good idea. Taking this action is recommended both to prevent decompression sickness and to maintain control of ascents near the surface. You may wonder how to document the time spent decompressing. Time spent doing decompression is simply "neutral" time. As an example, if you had an elapsed dive time of 45 minutes on a dive to 70 feet (21 m), you should stop at 15 feet (5 m) for three minutes. Determine your End-of-Dive letter group by

TABLE 1 - END-OF-DIVE LETTER GROUP

(00) = MAXIMUM DIVE TIME (MDT)   00/00 = DIVE TIME REQUIRING DECOMPRESSION / NO. MINUTES REQUIRED AT 15' STOP (5M)

M	FEET	A	B	C	D	E	F	G	H	I	J	K	L
12	40 ➤	5	15	25	30	40	50	70	80	100	110	(130)	150/5
15	50 ➤		10	15	25	30	40	50	60	70	(80)	100/5	
18	60 ➤		10	15	20	25	30	40	50	(55)	60/5	80/7	
21	70 ➤	5	10	15	20	30	35	40	(45)	50/5	60/8	70/14	
24	80 ➤	5	10	15	20	25	30	(35)	40/5		50/10	70/17	
27	90 ➤	5	10	12	15	20	(25)	30/5		40/7		50/18	
30	100 ➤	5	7	10	15	20	(22)	25/5			40/15		
33	110 ➤		5	10	13	(15)	20/5		30/7				
36	120 ➤		5	10	(12)	15/5		25/6	30/14				
39	130 ➤		5	(8)	10/5			25/10					

Above, When TNT exceeds the no-decompression limit, decompression time is noted in Table 1.
Below, Wait 24 hours before flying after you have been diving.

using the schedule 70 feet (21 m)/45. Including stop time as part of your Actual Dive Time may also be done as an added precaution.

To document your decompression stops — either precautionary or required — enter the decompression time on your worksheet next to a short horizontal line drawn through the ascent line of the dive profile, as shown on page 91.

If decompression is required, refrain from further diving activities, or flying after diving for at least 24 hours.

Omitted Decompression   If you surface from a dive and discover required decompression was omitted, discontinue diving, rest, breathe oxygen if it is available, drink plenty of fluids, and watch for symptoms of decompression sickness. If you suspect you may have symptoms of the bends, proceed to the nearest recompression facility. No matter how well you feel, refrain from diving for at least 24 hours. Do not re-enter the water in an attempt to make up for the omitted decompression.

Cold/Strenuous Dives   If you become cold during a dive or work hard, use the next greater time for your dive schedule. For instance, a first dive to 60 feet (18 m) for 40 minutes would be considered a 50 minute dive. If you become cold **and** work more than usual, use both the next greater time and depth.

Flying After Diving   You are aware that decreasing the pressure below that at sea level following diving can lead to decompression sickness. What you need to know is how long to delay flying after diving to avoid problems related to decompression. Here are guidelines for going to altitudes of up to 8,000 feet (2,438 m) after diving. (Note: Commercial airliners pressurize the cabins of the craft to maintain an altitude equivalent to 8,000 feet (2,438 m) or less. For recreational diving, NAUI recommends you wait at least 24 hours before flying. If you make dives requiring decompression (which you are advised not to do) or if required decompression is omitted, wait more than 24 hours before flying.

Diving at Altitude   Atmospheric pressure decreases with altitude. This means the rate of change of pressure is greater when descending into water at altitude than it is at sea level. To take this difference into account, special altitude dive tables are used and special procedures must be followed. The maximum rate of ascent changes with altitude, as do the decompression stop depths. Before diving at altitudes above 1,000 feet (300 m), you need to be trained in the use of the special tables and procedures. If altitude diving is common in your area, your instructor may provide additional information as part of your training, or recommend that you participate in a high altitude specialty training program subsequent to your being certified as an Openwater I or II Diver. High altitude training is beyond the scope or purpose of this textbook. For now, what you need to know is: Do not attempt high altitude diving without first completing a high altitude training program.

Looking Back

1. When is it appropriate to make a precautionary decompression stop? _____

2. How much decompression is required for a Total Dive Time of 50 minutes spent at a depth of 80 feet (24 m)? _____

3. The dive schedule for a first dive of the day to 80 feet for 21 minutes is _____ if you become chilled during the dive.

4. As a rule of thumb, how long should you wait before flying following some conservative diving? _____

5. Special diving procedures are in order above what altitude? _____

Sample Problems

You have learned a great deal about the NAUI Dive Tables and the NAUI Dive Calculator and their uses. Now it is time to pull together all you know and apply it to typical diving situations. The following problems contain all of the aspects

of dive table and dive calculator usage you will need to know for recreational diving. Explanations are included. When you understand how to work problems such as these correctly, you will be able to plan your dives to avoid decompression sickness.

First Problem   Use the worksheet provided. Include a three minute precautionary stop at 15 feet (3 m) for all dives. Do not include the decompression time as part of dive time.

The first dive is to 60 feet (18 m) for 30 minutes and is followed by a 30 minute surface interval. The second dive is to 50 feet (15 m) for 30 minutes. Question: What is the End-of-Dive letter group after the second dive?

Answer: 60 feet (18 m)/30 results in Group "F". After a 30 minute SIT, the letter group remains "F". An "F" diver using the dive tables and going to 50 feet (15 m) has an RNT of 47 minutes which is added to the ADT of 30 minutes for a Total Nitrogen Time of 77 minutes. A schedule of 50 feet (15 m)/77 minutes results in an End-of-Dive letter group of "J". Note: The addition of the RNT to the ADT is not required when using the NAUI Dive Time Calculator. Simply look up the ADT of 30 minutes under 50 feet (15 m) in the Group "F" section and note that the End-of-Dive letter group is "J".

Second Problem   The first dive is to 55 feet (16.8 m) for 31 minutes followed by a SIT of an hour. The second dive is to 51 feet (15.3 m). What is the Maximum Dive Time for the second dive, and what is the End-of-Dive letter group if the Adjusted Maximum Dive Time is reached?

Answer: 55 feet (16.8 m) for 31 minutes is actually a 60 feet (18 m)/40 schedule resulting in a letter Group "G" designation. A one hour SIT leads to Group "F", and an "F" diver going to 51 feet (15.3 m) [60 feet (18 m) on the tables] has an RNT of 36 minutes. The Adjusted Maximum Dive Time (AMDT) for an "F" diver at 60 feet (18 m) is 19 minutes. Remember that your Adjusted Maximum Dive Time must include your ascent time (approximately one minute for this

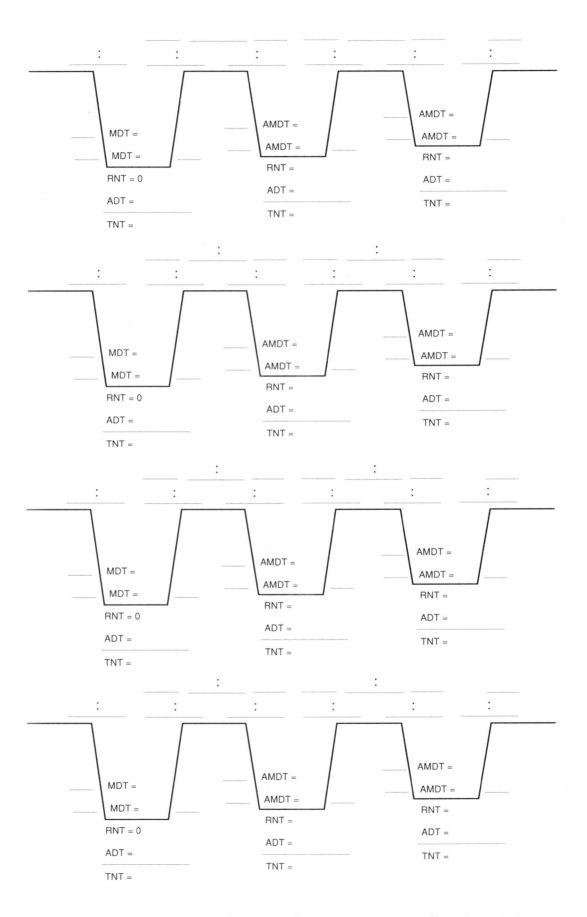

Panel 1 (top):

:   :   :   :   :   :

MDT =
MDT =
RNT = 0
ADT =
TNT =

AMDT =
AMDT =
RNT =
ADT =
TNT =

AMDT =
AMDT =
RNT =
ADT =
TNT =

Panel 2:

:   :   :   :   :

MDT =
MDT =
RNT = 0
ADT =
TNT =

AMDT =
AMDT =
RNT =
ADT =
TNT =

AMDT =
AMDT =
RNT =
ADT =
TNT =

Panel 3:

:   :   :   :   :

MDT =
MDT =
RNT = 0
ADT =
TNT =

AMDT =
AMDT =
RNT =
ADT =
TNT =

AMDT =
AMDT =
RNT =
ADT =
TNT =

Panel 4 (bottom):

:   :   :   :   :

MDT =
MDT =
RNT = 0
ADT =
TNT =

AMDT =
AMDT =
RNT =
ADT =
TNT =

AMDT =
AMDT =
RNT =
ADT =
TNT =

dive) so you will need to begin your ascent at or before 18 minutes of bottom time. Your TNT, if your ADT is 19 minutes, is 36 RNT plus 19 ADT for a total of 55 minutes. The dive of 51 feet (16.8 m)/55 is a 60 feet (18 m)/55 schedule producing an End-of-Dive letter group of "I".

Third Problem   After the second dive in the previous problem, a SIT of how long is required in order to make a 25 minute dive to 50 feet (15 m) without exceeding the Adjusted Maximum Dive Time? Also, what is your End-of-Dive letter group following the third dive if your ADT is 25 minutes? (Use the worksheet from the previous problem.)

Answer: To plan the minimum SIT with the dive tables, refer to Table 3 and determine the letter group required to allow the dive to be made. In this instance, to make a 25 minute dive to 50 feet (15 m), you need to achieve a Group "F" designation, which has an AMDT of 33 minutes. When you know the letter group required to make the dive, you go to the Surface Interval Timetable and work it in reverse to determine the minimum time needed to achieve the necessary letter group. Since you want the new group to be "F" and since your starting group is "I", the minimum time required is one hour and 30 minutes. Now let's determine the End-of-Dive letter group. Your ADT (including ascent time) is 25 minutes and your RNT for an "F" diver to 50 feet (15 m) is 47 minutes, producing a TNT of 72 minutes for a schedule of 50 feet (15 m)/80 and a letter group of "J". Note that when planning dives, you may at times need to use the tables in reverse order.

To solve this problem using the Dive Time Calculator, start at the Group "I" section on the base plate and move the depth arrow from one 50 feet (15 m) depth to the same depth for the next lesser letter group until the desired time of 25 minutes is permitted. In this instance, the first group allowing a 25 minute dive to 50 feet is "F". The Surface Interval Timetable on the calculator is used exactly the same way as that described for use of the table with the NAUI Dive Tables. A dive schedule of 50 feet (15 m)/25 minutes as a "F" diver produces an End-of-Dive letter group of "J".

Fourth Problem   Complete the Worksheet for three dives to 52 feet (15.8 m) for 25 minutes each with a SIT of one hour between dives.

Answer: This problem is tricky because it is not asking you to plan the dive to avoid required decompression and because decompression is required. It illustrates what can happen if you do not document your dive schedules and do not use the tables to plan your dives. Your first dive places you in letter group "E". A one hour SIT leads to Group "D". A "D" diver returning to 52 feet (15.8 m) has an RNT of 24 minutes. The TNT for the second dive is 49 minutes, so the dive schedule is 60 feet (18 m)/50 and results in an End-of-Dive letter Group "H". An hour later, the new group designation is "G", and a "G" diver going to 52 feet (15.8 m) has a Adjusted Maximum Dive Time of 11 minutes (which is exceeded) and an RNT of 44 minutes. Although you should not exceed the AMDT, it is exceeded during this dive of 25 minutes. The TNT is 44 RNT plus 25 ADT for a total of 69 minutes. So you are required to decompress for seven minutes, as indicated by the tables, when the TNT is greater than 60 minutes and equal to or less than 80 minutes.

To use the Dive Time Calculator to determine the decompression requirement, find in the timetable at the bottom of the disc the exact or next greater time in excess of the time limit for the dive, then determine the decompression schedule. For this example, the ADT was exceeded by 14 minutes. Seven minutes of decompression is indicated for dive times at 60 feet (18 m) which exceed the limits by more than five minutes and up to 25 minutes.

By working with the tables and the calculator, you will soon feel very comfortable with their use. Your instructor will be glad to help you with any difficulties you have. Remember the importance of recording and planning your dives to prevent decompression sickness.

5.7   Using Dive Computers

When you are able to afford a dive computer, you will find this instrument allows you more dive time due to its capability to continuously calculate multi-level dives, only charging you for the nitrogen actually absorbed. You will also find dive planning is easier because you do not have to make calculations. You must not become totally dependent on a computer, however, because electro-mechanical devices are subject to failure.

Dive computers differ greatly. Different computers offer various features, and different mathematical models are used by different manufacturers. This results in dive schedules ranging from the conservatism of the NAUI Dive Tables to more liberal profiles. Since dive computer designs and features are subject to change, NAUI does not recommend particular types. We suggest you discuss the types and features of various computers with your instructor and your retailer and choose a model they recommend.

Computer Terms   There is some additional terminology with which you will need to be familiar in order to use a dive computer. These terms include:

1. *Ceiling:* Most dive computers do not use the standard depths for decompression stops, but instead calculate the shallowest depth to which you may ascend without risk of forming bubbles in your system. This minimum depth is called your "ceiling" and must not be passed. Whenever a computer displays a ceiling, you have entered a decompression situation, so you should dive with a computer in such a way as to prevent a ceiling from being established.

2. *Scrolling:* Before a dive, a computer will continuously flash the Maximum Dive Times for various depths in sequence. This feature is an aid for dive planning and is called "scrolling".

Computer Usage   A dive computer has the potential to become the "ultimate instrument" for diving activities. Some computers combine information that would usually require several instruments and present the information on a single digital display. A computer may be able to display several or all of the following items of information:

1. Current depth
2. Maximum depth attained
3. Elapsed bottom time
4. Surface interval time

Typical decompression computers and the NAUI Dive Tables.

5. Temperature
6. Minutes remaining within Dive Time Limits
7. Minutes remaining based on air supply and consumption
8. End-of-Dive letter group designation
9. Rate of ascent
10. Dive number
11. Profile of the dive
12. When flying is safe
13. Scrolling of Dive Time Limits
14. Ceiling

The following rules are to be followed when using a dive computer:

1. Each diver relying on a dive computer must have a separate unit. One computer may not be shared by a buddy team. A dive computer used by one diver may not be used by another diver for a subsequent dive until the time period required for complete outgassing has been completed.

2. The dive computer instruction manual should

be studied carefully and the computer used in accordance with the manufacturer's instructions. Completion of a dive computer specialty course is highly recommended.

3. If a dive computer fails at any time while diving, the dive must be terminated and appropriate surfacing procedures (precautionary decompression) should be initiated immediately.

4. You should not dive for 24 hours before using a dive computer.

5. Once a dive computer is in use, it must not be switched off until it indicates complete outgassing has occurred, or 24 hours have elapsed, whichever comes first.

6. When using a computer, non-emergency ascents are to be at the rate specified for the make and model of the dive computer being used. Several computers specify ascent rates that are slower than the rate used for the dive tables.

7. A five minute decompression stop is recommended for all dive computer repetitive dives to 60 feet (18 m) or greater even if the computer does not indicate a ceiling.

8. Repetitive and multi-level divers should start the dive or the series of dives at the maximum planned depth, followed by subsequent dives or depths of shallower exposure.

9. Repetitive dives in excess of 100 feet (30 m) should not be made.

Some people suggest planning dives with the dive tables or a dive calculator as a contingency plan for computer diving. Due to the multi-level calculating capability of the computer, this practice is not usually feasible, although it is possible with some computers. You usually cannot revert to the dive tables in the event of a computer failure or the accidental switching off of your computer. Your only options in this event are to discontinue diving for 24 hours or to limit any subsequent dives during the day to depths of 20 feet (6 m) or less.

Computer diving is easier than diving with manual calculations, but you should always be able to use the dive table and dive calculator calculations in the event a computer is not available for use.

Take your NAUI Tables whenever you go diving.

Looking Back

1. A "ceiling" display on a dive computer indicates the _____ to which you may _____

2. If a computer is shut off or fails between dives, the maximum recommended depth for any repetitive dive is _____

3. The maximum recommended depth for a repetitive dive when using a dive computer is

_____

4. True or False: Planned dives using a dive computer should be calculated in advance with dive tables. _____

You are now familiar with dive time planning and should be capable of solving repetitive dives using either the NAUI Dive Tables or the NAUI Dive Time Calculator to avoid required decompression. It is important to note that decompression sickness cannot be entirely prevented, no matter what device you use to plan dives, due to individual factors and susceptibility. For this reason, conservative usage of all diving planning devices is strongly recommended.

Risk-reducing Recommendations

Some experts recommend the following practices, which you may wish to consider:

1. Limit diving to three dives per day.

2. Avoid multiple-day, multiple depth dives.

After three days of repetitive diving, wait 24 hours before diving again.

3. Avoid multiple complete ascents (surfacing) during dives. Also avoid repetitive dives of short duration — called "yo-yo" dives — following a surface interval of less than one hour. The minimum time between dives specified by the dive tables is ten minutes, but a minimum surface interval of one hour between dives is recommended.

4. No dive tables, dive calculators, or dive computers will absolutely ensure against decompression sickness. They merely provide time limits based on statistical conclusions, so you must use them properly, conservatively, and with common sense to prevent injury.

6 Diving Skills

In the introduction, you were told of three things you must learn in order to dive safely: handling equipment properly, preventing injury or discomfort from the effects of pressure and the environment, and performing fundamental skills. This chapter is an orientation to gear handling and diving skills. The application of this information plus the guidance of your NAUI Instructor will have you looking and performing like a seasoned diver in no time.

6.1 Use of Mask, Snorkel and Fins

Let's learn how to get our basic equipment ready for use, how to put it on and how to use it.

Preparing Your Gear   New equipment requires some preparation before it is ready to use. This is especially true of your face mask. It is important to your enjoyment and comfort that you see well underwater. Unless you thoroughly scour your new face mask before use, it will continually fog and significantly reduce and distort your vision. As recommended in Chapter One, toothpaste is a good cleaning agent.

Once the oily film has been removed, the lens can usually be kept free of condensation by treating it with a commercial defogging solution or simply using your saliva before entering the water. Saliva is more readily available, but the defogger is more effective. The strap needs to be adjusted so it is snug, but not tight. The snorkel should be attached to your mask strap on the left side, using a snorkel keeper as shown on the following page.

All you need to do to prepare your fins for use is to adjust the straps for a snug, comfortable fit. Be sure to wear boots when making the adjustment if boots are being used. If the fin straps are "oily," you may want to wash them in soapy water to remove the film so the straps will not slip in the buckles and become loose in the water.

Mark your personal gear for identification. This can be done with colored tape, colored markers or special paint available at dive stores. Many times gear is similar in a group of divers. If yours gets mixed up with others, you may end up with the wrong items. Mark your gear to save time and trouble.

Scour your new mask to rid it of the oily film which causes it to fog easily.

If you must walk while wearing fins, walk backwards and shuffle your feet.

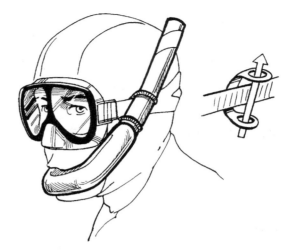

Correct configuration for snorkel attachment.

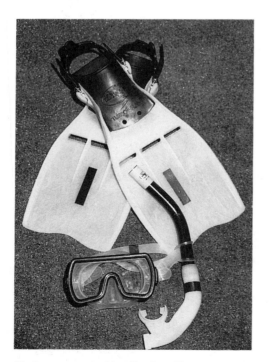

Mark your gear for identification. Tape can be used as shown. There are also special markers available at your dive store.

Looking Back

Check off each of the following items when you have completed it:

☐ 1. Removal of film from mask lens
☐ 2. Adjustment of mask strap
☐ 3. Attachment of snorkel to left side of mask
☐ 4. Adjustment of fin straps, if any
☐ 5. Marking of equipment for identification

Donning Your Snorkeling Gear   Your equipment should be donned at the water's edge. Avoid walking about while wearing fins; you can easily lose your balance and fall. If you must move short distances out of the water while wearing fins, shuffle backwards rather than trying to walk forward.

Boots, if used, should be put on first. Both your feet and the boots should be either totally dry or soaking wet. If only one or the other is moist, the boot will be difficult to pull into place. Sit down while you are putting on your boots.

The mask and snorkel are positioned next. Place the mask on your forehead, position the strap high on the crown of your head, reposition the mask into its proper place on your face, then re-adjust the strap to a lower position. This method is recommended because it works well both with and without a hood. Place the snorkel in your mouth and adjust the position of the snorkel in its keeper so the snorkel mouthpiece remains in your mouth when your mouth is opened widely. If this can't be done, get it as close as possible. The idea is to eliminate or minimize tension by the snorkel on your mouth.

Your fins are donned last. If you can sit at the edge of the water and put them on, that's best. If you must stand, steady yourself by holding onto something or someone during the process. For either sitting or standing, a "Figure 4" position of the legs is recommended (as shown in the photograph on the following page). It is best that both your feet and the foot pockets of the fins are wet when donning fins. Be sure to work your foot as far into the foot pocket as possible before pulling the strap or heel of the fin into place. Trying to don fins by pulling them on with the strap or the heel can damage the fins or cause the straps to slip or pull out.

Mask Clearing   Perhaps you were introduced to mask clearing in the Entry Scuba Experience and can already clear your mask underwater while breathing from scuba. You should also be familiar with the basics of clearing water from

Right, To don a mask while wearing a hood, position the mask on your forehead (A), position the strap on the crown of your head (B), settle the mask into place on your face (C), then make a final adjustment on the strap (D).
Below, When properly adjusted, the snorkel will remain close to the position in which it is used even when the mouth is opened widely.

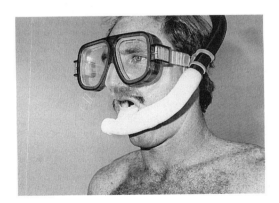

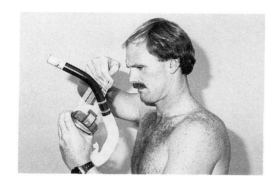

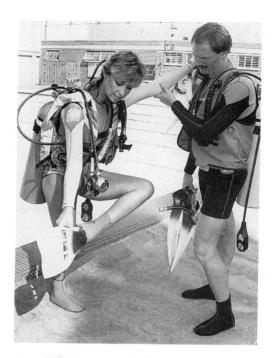

If a hood is not used, you may be able to don a mask in just a couple of motions as shown.

different types of masks. We will review the key points and then concentrate on some useful details for clearing a mask as a skin diver and as a scuba diver.

When skin diving, if some water seeps in, you can simply wait and pour it out when you surface, or you can clear the mask of water while underwater. But remember, the only air available is that in your lungs. Underwater mask

The "Figure Four" position is recommended for the donning of fins for both sitting and standing situations.

clearing by a skin diver at depths exceeding pool depths is a rather advanced skin diving skill. If you can do it, great, but the ability to do so is not essential at this point.

You will recall that the water inside your mask is displaced by air. The air rises to the top of the mask and water flows out the bottom. In a purge valve mask, the water flows out the one way valve in the nose of the mask, so the head is tilted forward during the clearing process. With a non-purge valve mask, the head is tilted back while air is exhaled into the mask so the water can flow out of the mask over the edge of the skirt at the bottom of the mask.

Remember that you must begin exhaling before tilting your head back so water will not run up your nose. A steady exhalation is more effective than short, strong bursts of air which tend to escape instead of remaining inside the mask.

It does not take much air to clear a mask completely. When you become proficient, you should be able to clear your mask several times with just a single breath of air. With this in mind, you will want to reach the point where you can comfortably clear your mask at least twice when starting with a full breath.

Getting the water out of your mask is one of the most important of all diving skills. You need to practice until you are completely comfortable with it and can execute it automatically. Practice in shallow water — three to four feet (1-1.5 m.) — where it is safe to overweight yourself slightly so you will not have to fight buoyancy problems while perfecting the art. When you can clear your mask several times on a single breath, you will be amazed at how little air and effort are required.

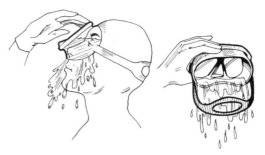

When clearing a mask of water, the water is literally "poured out" as air displaces it. This is why tipping the head back is important during mask clearing.

Remember to begin exhaling before tilting your head back when clearing a mask of water.

Snorkel Clearing   The snorkel allows you to conserve your energy and the air in your scuba tank while at the surface. It is a valuable part of your diving equipment. When you have mastered the skills of snorkel use, you will also have developed some skills which will be useful to you for scuba diving as well. The breathing and clearing techniques will help you to learn to use your regulator more effectively.

Water can enter the open end of a snorkel as you snorkel at the surface. This can occur from wave action or from inadvertently dipping the end of the snorkel below the surface. If this

happens, you need to be able to clear the tube of water so you can resume breathing. There are three ways to clear a snorkel at the surface. Removing the mouthpiece and pouring out the water is one of them. It can require considerable energy and, if done repeatedly, identifies a novice diver.

Another method of purging a snorkel of water is called the "blast" method. It involves a short, forceful breath of air which blasts the water from the snorkel tube. The technique is very similar to that used to launch a pea from a pea-shooter.

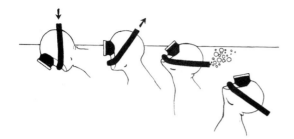

After blasting the water from the snorkel, inhale cautiously through it. If any water remains in the tube, you can inhale past it if you do so slowly. The blast can then be repeated forcefully to rid the snorkel of any remaining water. This is another skill which becomes automatic with practice.

When you make breath-hold dives beneath the surface and then ascend, you can use yet another snorkel clearing technique which requires less energy and which can rid the snorkel of water completely in a single breath. The technique is called the "displacement" method and is performed as follows:

The head is tilted well back during your ascent. This should be done anyway so you can watch above you as you ascend. With the head back, the snorkel will be inverted. A small amount of air is exhaled into the snorkel as you near the surface. This air will expand as you ascend and "displace" the water inside the tube. When you surface, the snorkel will be empty. All you have to do is keep it that way while getting the snorkel into an upright position. To do this, exhale while you tilt your head forward and into a face-down position at the surface. This must be done just as you reach the surface. If done earlier, it will be ineffective because water will pour into the open tube. Once you catch onto this technique, you will be amazed at how easy it is to clear a snorkel when ascending as a skin diver.

Swimming With Fins   Fins provide us with thrust and stability in the water. When fully equipped for diving, we need to use the powerful muscles of our legs for propulsion, not only to overcome resistance to our movement, but also to free our hands for other purposes. Imagine trying to take pictures or pursue some other activity if you had to swim with your hands. The sooner you can overcome the beginner's tendency to swim underwater with your hands and arms, the sooner you will begin looking and feeling like an experienced diver.

Fins can be moved in a variety of ways to provide propulsion. The principles, however, are always the same. Your legs should be extended and the blades of the fins pointed behind you. Thrust against the water slowly and powerfully for as long as possible during each stroke. Quick, short kicks are inefficient for scuba diving.

Top, More efficient than blast clearing, displacement clearing takes advantage of air expansion and gravity to reduce the effort needed to clear a snorkel.
***Center**, "Blast" clearing a snorkel literally blasts the water from the tube.*
***Bottom**, For displacement clearing, keep your head tilted well back until your faceplate reaches the surface, then exhale while rolling your head forward.*

The flutter kick is shown in the series of pictures below, and is the most commonly used kick. Note how little the knee is bent. If the knees are bent too much and pulled toward the stomach, the fin will merely slip back and forth in the water and little or no thrust will be produced. The fins should sweep the water away behind you, and the power portion of your kicking stroke should be during the downward motion. Speed is not the objective. Moving steadily without overexertion is your goal.

When moving at the surface, you will need to modify the flutter kick slightly. The fins can only provide propulsion when pushing against water, so you will need to shorten the upward portion of your kick stroke to keep the fins underwater. You can also swim on your back or side while using the flutter kick. This allows a wider stroke, keeps the fins underwater and is a good change of pace from face-down swimming.

There are other strokes which can be done with fins. Your instructor will teach you the most

popular of these — the Dolphin kick. This is an undulating motion performed with your entire body and with your feet together. Just imagine a wave passing through your entire length. It is a good idea to learn more than one way to kick with fins so you can change methods if your muscles tire from one type of kick. You should also learn how to swim with just one fin so you will be able to function if a fin breaks or is lost.

Surface Dives   When you want to get below the surface, various types of dives are used to initiate your descent. The following surface dives apply best to skin diving. As you will see when

Note the position of the legs and fins. Variations of the flutter kick for surface swimming. When you swim on your side or back, wider strokes can be used than when swimming face-down.

The most commonly used kick - the flutter kick.

we cover scuba descents, the best way to go down is to simply sink feet first, but this doesn't work when skin diving.

The principle involved in performing a surface dive is simple — invert yourself, get as much of your legs as possible above water and let the weight of your legs push you beneath the surface. Kicking wastes energy and will not help you to descend until your fins are underwater. (Be sure to remember to deflate your buoyancy compensator before attempting to make a dive, or you will pop right back to the surface.) With the main ideas in mind, let's look at two versions of headfirst dives.

Headfirst surface dives can be executed from either a swimming or a stationary position. If you want to descend while swimming along at the surface, simply bend forward at the waist until the trunk of your body is vertical, then lift your legs above you to form a straight, vertical line in the water. The weight of your legs, combined with your forward motion from swim-

ming, will carry you well below the surface where you can begin kicking to continue your descent.

If starting from a stationary position, you first pull your knees to your chest in a tuck position, then roll forward using your hands to get into a head-down position. You then extend your arms and trunk downward and your legs upwards. You should be in the same position at this point as you would be with the swimming dive. Both dives should be carried out as one smooth, continuous motion. It is helpful to imagine you are trying to stand on your hands when you are beginning a surface dive. It will soon come quite naturally.

The Dolphin kick is an undulating motion performed with the feet together.

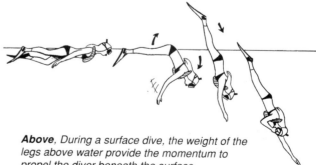

Above, During a surface dive, the weight of the legs above water provide the momentum to propel the diver beneath the surface.
Below, A surface dive executed from a swimming position. Note the height of the legs above the surface.

To make a surface dive from an upright position, pull your knees to your chest and invert yourself while holding the tucked position.

Looking Back

See if you can recall the following key concepts concerning the use of your mask, snorkel and fins.

1. Briefly describe how to walk if you must do so when wearing fins. _____

_____

2. List two ways to prevent losing your balance when you are donning your fins:

A. _____

B. _____

3. In what direction is the head tilted when clearing a purge valve mask? Why? _____

_____

4. Name three methods of clearing a snorkel, including one which is not recommended.

A. _____

B. _____

C. _____

5. Which if the snorkel clearing methods requires the least amount of energy? _____

_____

6. List three things you should *not* do when swimming with fins:

A. _____

B. _____

C. _____

6.2   Use of Scuba Equipment

In this section you will learn how to prepare scuba equipment for use. You will also learn correct techniques for donning gear, various breathing patterns and disassembly procedures. Learning these skills will increase your confidence in the use of self-contained breathing equipment.

Assembling Your Scuba Equipment   Scuba gear consists of a tank, a backpack with intergrated BC, and a regulator. By learning a few simple rules and practicing them, you will be able to assemble these items correctly and efficiently. This is one of the areas to observe to determine if a person is a competent diver.

If the pack is not on the tank, you will need to attach it. Look for the opening in the tank valve. When the pack is oriented correctly on the tank, the opening where the air comes out of the tank will be facing toward the backpack. Your first step then is to orient the pack properly when positioning it on the tank.

The next step is to secure the backpack band which holds the tank. There are many types of bands with many different locking mechanisms. Your instructor will show you how your's works. The important thing to remember is that the band must grip the tank tightly so the tank cannot slip out of the pack while you are wearing it. After securing the pack to the tank, grasp the top of the backpack and try to move it up and down on the tank. You should not be able to move the pack. If movement does occur, you need to tighten the band.

The pack must also be mounted at the correct height on the tank. If the tank is too high, your head will be bumping the valve as you swim and, if too low, the tank will hang too low on your back. Your instructor will point out the height adjustment

Give a tug on the backpack to make sure the pack is secure on the tank.

for the type of pack you will be using. Remember the position of the band for subsequent water skill sessions.

The next step is to attach the regulator to the tank. The procedure is illustrated in the series of photographs. Note particularly the following points:

1. The regulator must be oriented so the second stage hose comes over your right shoulder. It helps if you will place the tank in front of you with the pack facing away from you. If you then imagine that you are standing behind the person who will be wearing the tank, you will be able to orient the regulator correctly.

2. Open the tank valve briefly before attaching the regulator. This discharges any water which might be in the valve opening and keeps it from being blown into your regulator first stage.

3. After the regulator seat has been carefully positioned over the "o-ring" (a black or white rubber ring used for high pressure seals) on the tank valve outlet, the first stage of the regulator should be tightened onto the valve, but only

finger tight. When the air is turned on, the high pressure air will tightly seal the regulator.

4. The tank valve operates like a faucet. It is opened by turning it counter-clockwise and closed by rotating it in the opposite direction. When opening the valve, slowly open it all the way, while aiming the pressure gauge away from your face, then turn it back from its fully opened position a quarter of a turn. When closing the valve, do so gently. Excessive closing force will damage the seat inside the valve. Close the valve just tightly enough to shut off the flow of air.

5. Be sure to check the pressure gauge after turning on the air to make sure the tank is filled. Do not hold the pressure gauge toward your face or other persons when you first open the tank valve. The regulator should also be tested to make sure it is functioning properly. Typical problems can include "free-flowing" (a constant flow of air from the mouthpiece) or a stuck exhaust valve. Your instructor will show you how to handle minor problems such as these. Sometimes the o-ring will not seal properly when the air is turned on. Don't be alarmed by loud, hissing air rushing from the tank. Simply turn the valve off and get assistance from your instructor to correct the problem.

When your scuba equipment is assembled, tested and ready for use, lay it down with the backpack facing up while you prepare the rest of your gear. If you leave the scuba unit standing, it may fall over or get knocked over and the valve or regulator could be damaged, not to mention someone's toes...

Donning Scuba Equipment   Develop the habit of having your buddy assist you with your scuba unit. Your buddy should help you don your tank and you should help your buddy with his or her tank. The shoulder straps should be loosened so they will slip on easily. Your buddy should hand you the ends of the waistband once the tank is in place on your back. The regulator hoses should be placed on your shoulders so they will not be trapped under the strap when the waistband is secured. You should bend forward and balance the tank on your back while you pull the slack out of the straps before securing the waistband. The tank should feel balanced and secure. You can test the height adjustment of the tank by tilting your head back

A

C

B

D

Procedures for setting up your scuba tank. Open the valve to rid the opening of water (A), orient the regulator so the hose will come over the right shoulder (C), attach the low pressure inflator before turning on the air (B), check the air pressure and regulator operation (C), and lay the unit down until ready to use it (D).

while standing. If your head hits the tank valve, the tank is mounted too high in the backpack.

Exceptional Breathing Techniques   For the most part, breathing from scuba is just a matter of breathing slightly deeper than normal. This becomes automatic with experience. Of course, you must remember to always keep breathing so you won't trap expanding air in your lungs during an ascent. There are a few situations, though,

where your breathing must be modified. Such situations include removal of the regulator from your mouth, breathing from a free-flowing regulator and sharing air with a single mouth-piece. Let's address these situations and find out how to handle them properly.

If the regulator must be removed from your mouth for any reason, you must remember that you still have compressed air in your lungs. You must overcome your natural tendency to hold your breath or the air in your lungs can expand during an ascent and damage your lungs. To be sure that no air expansion problems can occur, develop the habit of exhaling a tiny stream of

bubbles whenever you are breathing compressed air and the regulator is not in your mouth. Whenever possible, the regulator should remain in your mouth, but you will discover a few situations where removal is required.

Whenever a regulator is removed from your mouth while underwater, the mouthpiece will flood and will need to be cleared of water when re-inserted into your mouth. The quickest and easiest is to simply exhale into the regulator, as you do in snorkel clearing. The air will rise to the top inside the regulator chamber and will force the water out the bottom where a non-return exhaust valve is located. Note that the regulator needs to be in an upright position in order for all of the water to be cleared from the chamber.

If you do not have enough air in your lungs to clear the mouthpiece, you can clear the chamber by depressing a button on the front of the

Remember to exhale whenever the regulator is removed from your mouth.

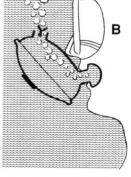

When donning your scuba tank on land, get your buddy to give you a hand. When the tank is in place, bend over and place the hoses on your shoulders while securing the waistband.

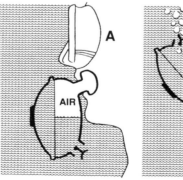

With the regulator in the normal position, water will be cleared from it by an exhalation (A). If the regulator is inserted upside down, however, as in (B), the air will escape through the exhaust valve without displacing the water. Be sure the regulator is in an upright position when you are clearing it.

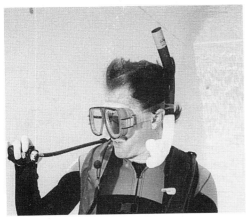

With the mouthpiece pointing up, a regulator will free flow in water. By pointing the mouthpiece down when the regulator is removed from your mouth, the loss of air can be prevented.

regulator housing. This is called the "purge button" because it purges the water from inside the regulator. You need to block the mouthpiece opening with your tongue while depressing the button so the water will be forced out through the exhaust valve and not into your mouth and throat. That's all there is to regulator clearing.

The preferred way to share air with another diver is to give the person in need of air a second mouthpiece from which to breathe. This extra item of equipment is highly recommended.

To commence buddy breathing, reach for one another on the side opposite the regulator to ensure proper linkup, allow receiver two or more initial breaths, then exchange the regulator every two breaths thereafter. The receiver guides the mouthpiece into place by placing a hand over the donor's hand.

Top, *To breathe from a free-flowing regulator, place it lightly against your mouth, breathe as needed, and allow the excess air to escape.*
Bottom, *One method of recovering a regulator.*

If, for some reason, an extra second stage is not available, it is possible to share air by exchanging a single regulator. This procedure is shown in the series of photos and will be further explained and demonstrated by your instructor. Basically, it involves passing the regulator back and forth with each diver taking two breaths. For the first exchange only, the diver in need of air may need to take additional breaths to re-

establish controlled breathing. Thereafter, each diver is to take two breaths only. The buddies should hold onto one another during the exercise. The diver who is not breathing from the regulator should always be doing something. Do you know what it is? If you said exhaling tiny bubbles, you were correct.

When a regulator starts delivering air continuously, it is said to be free-flowing. Fortunately, this is about the only problem you might ever have with a regulator, and it is not a serious one. You should not dive with a free-flowing regulator, but if one starts flowing continuously during a dive, there is a way you can breathe from it while you ascend. If the regulator is sealed in your mouth, the free-flow of air from the tank can build up enough pressure to damage your lungs. To prevent this, simply remove the mouthpiece from inside your mouth and place it against your lips, breathe the air you need and allow the excess to escape in the form of bubbles. When you reach the surface, have your buddy close your tank valve so you don't drain all of the air from your tank.

There is another situation where your regulator is occasionally removed from your mouth. A means of inflating your buoyancy compensator with low pressure air through a hose from your regulator is very desirable. In the absence of a low pressure inflation system, the alternative is oral inflation. In this situation, you will need to remove the scuba mouthpiece, exhale into the buoyancy device, then re-insert the scuba mouthpiece, clear it and repeat the process as needed to achieve the desired buoyancy. Remember to keep sufficient air in your lungs to be able to clear the regulator.

In your course, you have probably learned how to recover the regulator hose from behind your shoulder. You can reach back over your right shoulder with your right hand, grasp the hose where it comes from the tank and slide your hand along the hose to the end where the mouthpiece is located.

There is an instance on every dive when the regulator should be removed from your mouth...when you surface. When you get ready to descend for a dive, your snorkel is replaced in your mouth with your regulator mouthpiece. Upon surfacing, but not while ascending, the regulator should be replaced with the snorkel. You will practice snorkel/regulator exchanges at

Top, *Another method of regulator recovery.*
Bottom, *Snorkel/regulator exchanges should take place without lifting the face from the water.*

Oral inflation of the BC under water.

the surface until they are simple and easy to perform.

The exceptional breathing situations don't appear very difficult, do they? They're not. You need to learn them, however, and when you can handle the exceptional situations, the normal ones will be just that much easier.

Disassembly of Your Scuba Gear After diving, you will need to disassemble your scuba equipment and rinse it with clean, fresh water.

The rinsing procedures are covered in the equipment section. Let's find out how to disassemble the gear.

The first step is to turn off the air. Which way do you turn the valve knob? Clockwise is correct. Before you can remove the regulator from the tank, you will have to relieve the air pressure inside the regulator. It is virtually impossible to unscrew the regulator first stage from the tank valve until you do. How can you relieve the air pressure? Just push the purge button on the regulator second stage and allow the air to escape. You can then unscrew the regulator from the tank. After removing the regulator, be sure to dry and replace the protective cap which goes over the inlet on the first stage. Keep water from entering that inlet

because it can affect the efficiency of your regulator if allowed inside

With the regulator removed from the tank, all that remains to be done is to secure the straps on the backpack so the straps will not drag and get in the way. The straps should be wrapped neatly around the pack and buckled into place.

Using scuba gear is really very easy. The hard part is getting it on, and even that becomes easy with experience. Aside from developing proper breathing habits for various circumstances, there isn't much else you need to learn to use scuba gear itself. It is the combining of the scuba equipment with everything else that requires instruction and practice. When it all comes together for you, it is sure worth the time you invest in your training. With help from your NAUI Instructor, all of the separate skills of diving will come together for you.

Proper disassembly of scuba gear includes purging the system of pressure and drying the protective cap before positioning it over the first stage opening.

Looking Back

1. There are three points to keep in mind when attaching a backpack to a scuba tank. List two of them.

A. _____

B. _____

2. How should a regulator be oriented when mounting it on a scuba tank?_____

3. A scuba tank valve is turned on when rotated in a _____ direction.

4. List two recommended steps to be taken as part of the donning of your scuba unit.

A. _____

B. _____

5. What action should you take whenever a scuba regulator is removed from your mouth underwater? _____

6. List two methods of clearing a regulator of water.

A. _____

B. _____

7. How many breaths should be taken by each diver when air is being shared with a single regulator? _____

_____

8. What is the main thing to avoid when breathing from a free-flowing regulator? _____

_____

6.3 The Downs and Ups of Diving

There are two categories of descents in diving and four categories of ascents. You will become familiar with them in this section. You will be introduced to them in training, and you will be able to perform them in open water by the end of the course. Descending and ascending are

Descend together and feet first when scuba diving.

among the most important skills you will acquire during your training, so concentrate on the points presented in this section and put forth extra effort to develop them during confined water work.

Descending   There are many beautiful and exciting places to visit underwater, but you have to be able to make a descent to reach any of

them. The following are some procedures for descending properly.

You and your buddy should descend together. In fact, you should remain eye-to-eye throughout the descent. If one has a problem in equalizing pressure in an ear, the other should wait while it is being corrected. Continuous buddy contact is important.

When you and your partner have agreed to leave the surface and descend, preparations must be made. You will need to exchange your snorkel for your regulator, note the exact time so you can keep track of the amount of time you are under water (reason explained later), and deflate your buoyancy compensator. You already know how to exchange your regulator for your snorkel and how to recover and clear the regulator of water.

It helps to look at the BC exhaust valve to see if air is escaping. Leaving the valve open when no air is coming out allows water to enter.

With the regulator in place and cleared, you are ready to note the time prior to initiating your descent. During training you may not have a timing device but you may simulate checking the time by tapping on your wrist with one finger. This helps you remember to note the time when you do have a timer and helps remind your buddy to do the same.

The next step is to deflate the buoyancy compensator (BC). When you are weighted correctly you will sink only when all of the air has been vented from your BC and you have exhaled. You first have to get all of the air out of your BC. To do this, the exhaust must be the highest point in the BC. It will help if you will look at the deflator — if possible —so you can see if air is escaping. Get all of the air out, but close the valve once the air is exhausted. After the BC is vented, exhale to start your feet-first descent. It will take a few moments for anything to happen. So hold your exhalation until you start sinking, then take a quick breath and exhale again. Keep your lung volume low during the first few feet of your descent. If you cannot get down by exhaling, you may need to add weight if it is available. Descending feet first provides better orientation, buddy contact and makes it easier to equalize pressures than if descending head first.

Before you start down, and continually throughout your descent, you will need to clear your ears and equalize pressures. The exact techniques and what to do if your ears won't cooperate are covered elsewhere in this book, but at no time should you continue a descent if any discomfort is felt. When done correctly, no discomfort should be experienced during a descent.

The rate of your descent should not be rapid. The recommended maximum rate is 75 feet per minute — a little over one foot per second. Remember that you and your buddy should descend together.

When you are wearing exposure suits and make descents in open water, there are other considerations. You will lose buoyancy as pressure compresses your suit, so you will need to add some air to your BC from time to time to maintain neutral buoyancy. You should never sink out of control but should be able to stop at any time by taking in a full breath of air.

The compression of your suit can affect your weight belt. As your circumference decreases, your belt can become loose and shift position. The belt should be checked as you descend and when you reach the bottom. Your fins should be moved very little, if at all. Control should be maintained by buoyancy, not by kicking. Fin movement will stir up clouds of silt as you approach the bottom and will ruin your visibility. If you inhale maximally and continue to descend, you are too heavy and should add air in the BC.

Since there are so many things happening at once during a descent, your first descents in open water will be controlled. This means you will descend on a line or along the contour of the bottom to help you control your progress while you learn to equalize pressure, maintain buddy contact, establish neutral buoyancy and perform the other parts of a proper descent. When you

Equalize pressure early and often and control your rate of descent.

Your first descents will be controlled.

can do these things, you will be introduced to free descents — vertical descents in water with no reference or anything to hold onto. When you can execute free descents in a controlled manner, you will be well on your way to becoming a qualified diver. Start going through all the steps of descent in your mind. This pre-visualization will help speed your learning. Picture yourself remembering every point and doing everything smoothly and correctly. This mental exercise will help you learn proper descending techniques quickly.

Ascents   For every descent you make you will also have an ascent. You need to know standard ascent procedures, procedures for assisted ascents and procedures for ascending in emergency situations. You should rarely, if ever, need to make any of these ascents except the standard one, but you should be familiar with the procedures for exceptional circumstances. Practice them so you will feel confident and be prepared to handle any problems which occur.

Look up, reach up, come up, and control buoyancy during an ascent.

Normal Ascents   A normal ascent consists of swimming slowly to the surface with your buddy while looking up and around, maintaining neutral buoyancy and breathing regularly. There are several steps to be taken to accomplish this. You and your buddy should agree to ascend by responding to the "up" hand signal. If you have introduced air into your BC to compensate for suit compression, a couple of kicks should lift you enough to allow you to gain additional buoyancy. The deflator for your BC should be held in your hand throughout the ascent, and air expelled from time to time to maintain a slight degree of buoyancy.

The rate of ascent should not exceed 60 feet per minute. This is only one foot per second and is much slower than the rate at which you are naturally inclined to proceed. You should not pass the smallest bubbles from your exhaust as you rise through the water. It will help to time your ascents at first and to compare them to the depth so you can gauge your rate. You will have to develop a feel for the correct rate. Your instructor will help you do this. The ascent rate is important because it allows gas which is dissolved in your tissues under pressure to come out and be expelled without causing problems. If you ascend quickly, the gas can cause a condition known as the bends.

Keep looking up and around as you ascend. It is a good idea to extend one hand upward as well. Remember to maintain contact with your buddy throughout the ascent. Upon surfacing, the elapsed time of the dive should be noted. You should also establish buoyancy by partially inflating your BC. Remember, too, to exchange your regulator for your snorkel.

Maintain buddy contact throughout your ascent.

Top, *An octopus assisted ascent. Note position and contact.*
Bottom, *A buddy breathing ascent, which should be maintained all the way to the surface once initiated.*

Assisted Ascents   If you forget to check your pressure gauge and run out of air at depth, you have several ascent techniques from which to choose, depending on the situation. Two of the techniques are carried out with assistance from your buddy. These will now be introduced, then two independent methods will be presented.

The preferred dependent method of ascending when your own air supply is depleted unexpectedly is by breathing from a secondary regulator provided by your buddy. This means your buddy has an extra regulator and that you

are close to your buddy underwater and knowledgeable in the use of the secondary regulator. Your buddy may elect to give or have you take the extra regulator or he or she may want to use the primary one. The exact procedure will vary with equipment configurations and personal preference, but the important point is that the procedure be worked out in advance and agreed upon by both divers. You need to know which regulator to use, where to find it and, if you are to use the secondary regulator, how it is attached.

Breathing from an extra regulator is just as easy as breathing from your own, but ascending is more difficult because you need to coordinate your ascent with the person supplying you air — changes in buoyancy can be large. Contact is important, both physical contact and eye contact. Extra regulator configurations vary considerably, so position yourself comfortably in front and to one side of your buddy after acquiring the mouthpiece. Then carry out the ascent, incorporating the various parts of a standard ascent. Once you have the extra regulator and are positioned properly, this assisted ascent is quite easy to do.

The other type of dependent ascent also involves sharing your buddy's air. If your buddy does not have a secondary regulator, you may have to share air by exchanging a single regulator. This procedure is somewhat complex, but it is useful in certain circumstances. You are already acquainted with the skill of sharing air by exchanging a regulator. This same technique, called "buddy breathing," can be used while ascending but you need to carry out the skills of air sharing and ascent simultaneously. This can be done fairly easy with training and practice, but frequent practice is required in order to make buddy breathing a viable option as a shared air ascent. If your buddy is not equipped with a secondary regulator, you should rehearse buddy breathing techniques before entering the water and again just beneath the surface at the beginning of every dive to renew the skill and to coordinate procedures.

Several points must be kept in mind during a buddy breathing ascent. First, the person without the regulator must be exhaling to prevent air from expanding in the lungs and causing an injury. Next, buoyancy must be controlled by both divers. Continuous physical contact is

An emergency swimming ascent is similar in many ways to a regular ascent.

essential. Finally, whenever a buddy breathing ascent is initiated, it should be continued all the way to the surface. Trying to change techniques during an ascent results in confusion. You will be able to perform a buddy breathing ascent easily by the completion of this course. Just remember to practice occasionally so you will be able to recall all of the associated details.

Independent Emergency Ascents   If you find yourself without air and unable to obtain air from your buddy, you will need to make an unassisted ascent. In shallow water, this is not difficult and, in fact, is preferred to a dependent ascent. A controlled emergency swimming ascent is simply a matter of swimming to the surface while preventing the air in your lungs from overexpanding.

Lung volume is maintained at mid-volume. To control lung volume, you need to keep the airway to your lungs open by exhaling continuously. You must control the rate of exhalation, however, or you will have too little or too much air in your lungs. Unlike emergency practice in confined waters, when you left the bottom after breathing in, you will begin your ascent following an exhalation and an ineffective attempt to inhale. Keep the regulator in your mouth, exhale through it to control the rate of exhalation to maintain your lung volume so it is neither low nor high. Attempt to inhale briefly from time to time during an emergency swimming ascent. As the water pressure decreases during your ascent, some air may be available from your tank. This type of ascent resembles a normal ascent quite closely. The big difference is that your breathing is regular during a normal ascent. It is hard to imagine exhaling air as you ascend through water and surfacing with plenty of air in your lungs, but that's exactly what it is like with this type of ascent.

An emergency swimming ascent from shallow water is not difficult, but if you find yourself in a situation where you do not feel you will be able to exhale all the way to the surface, greater than normal buoyancy should be established to aid your ascent. The extra buoyancy can be achieved by discarding your weight belt or by inflating your BC if it has an air bubble or CO_2 cartridge for that purpose. Generally, buoyant emergency ascents are only used from deeper depths when no extra source of air is available.

Since there are numerous independent and dependent options, if you find yourself without air, you must be wondering which one should be used and when. This is dependent upon the situation but the following guidelines should help in deciding which ascent is most appropriate. Let's first establish some general rules:

• The emergency procedures for a dive need to be discussed and agreed upon prior to the dive. You need to know what signals will be used, what equipment is available and how to do what you agree on.

• The best independent procedure is the use of back up scuba. Carry a pony bottle and second regulator. This is the easiest and safest method of reaching the surface if you find your primary scuba without air. Simply place the back up mouthpiece in your mouth and continue breathing while ascending.

• An independent emergency swimming ascent is a good choice if the depth is less than 40 feet and if your buddy isn't close to you with an alternate air supply.

• A buoyant ascent is appropriate if an alternate source of air is not available and the depth is greater than 40 feet.

• The most highly recommended dependent ascent is octopus breathing from your buddy's air supply.

• The least desirable dependent option is buddy breathing. This could be used if you were deeper than 50 feet (15 m), your buddy is nearby, you and your buddy were proficient in buddy breathing and no alternate source of air is available.

You need to discuss emergency procedures before the dive and agree upon them.

Develop proper descent and ascent techniques from the outset of training.

It should be obvious that preventing depletion of your air supply in the first place is the best course of action. Monitor your submersible pressure gauge frequently — more frequently the deeper you dive — to avoid running out of air. Then all of your ascents can be normal ascents and you won't have to concern yourself with decisions regarding emergency ascents.

Looking Back

It is time to review descents and ascents to see if you can recall some of the key points concerning them.

1. List three steps you should take to prepare for a descent:

A. _____

B. _____

C. _____

2. List three actions to be performed during every descent:

A. _____

B. _____

C. _____

3. List three actions to be performed as part of a normal ascent:

A. _____

B. _____

C. _____

4. How do you know which of your buddy's two regulators to use during an assisted ascent?

_____

5. What is the primary prerequisite to ensure that a buddy breathing ascent will be executed properly by trained divers? _____

6. When is it appropriate to choose a buoyant emergency ascent? _____

6.4 Controlling Buoyancy

If you had to select a single skill for determining a person's diving ability, buoyancy control would certainly have to be considered. It consists of numerous sub-skills which can be learned quickly by understanding and applying basic principles. Once developed, buoyancy control makes diving much easier and adds to the safety and enjoyment of diving.

Equipment Preparation   Buoyancy control equipment consists of your Buoyancy Compensator (BC) and your weight belt. You need to be familiar with your BC and able to set up your weight belt before using them in the water.

The use of a low pressure inflation system on the BC is highly recommended. You should know how to connect and disconnect the low pressure hose and how to operate the inflator mechanism. You should also learn the various ways in which the BC can be inflated and deflated, and practice them out of the water. Become thoroughly familiar with your BC before using it; do the same whenever you use a new type of BC.

The way you set up your weight belt is important. It can affect your comfort and safety. You want to have the correct amount of weight and you want the weights to be balanced on the belt. The length of the belt is important. Some means to keep the weights from slipping on the belt is helpful.

With experience, you will be able to estimate the approximate amount of weight required for different situations. Initially, your instructor will suggest an amount for you to try. Adjust or select a belt which, when two inches (5 cm) are allowed for each weight and six inches (15 cm) of excess strap is included, will be the correct length. String the weights onto the belt as shown so they will be balanced over each hip, and so the area in the middle of your back will

When setting up your weight belt, balance the weights and secure them to the belt.

be clear. The weights may be kept from slipping by threading clips onto the belt as shown in the photo or you can put a twist into the belt as it is passed through the last weight. This will keep the weights from sliding off the belt when it is handled in the water. The final step is to try the belt to check the length and the position of the weights.

Donning Buoyancy Equipment   The main thing to keep in mind is that your weight belt must be clear for removal in case you need to establish positive buoyancy quickly. With some buoyancy jackets, it is easier to put the weight belt on before donning the jacket. Just be sure that nothing is placed over the weight belt, such as a BC crotch strap, which will prevent the belt from falling clear if released.

The recommended method of donning your weight belt out of the water is to hold both ends of it and to step through it. You can then lift the weight belt into position on your back and hips and let gravity hold it there as you bend forward and fasten the buckle. The same principle applies in the water. You should lie face down when positioning the belt so the ends of the belt

will have no tension on them and so they can be fastened easily.

A right-hand release is standard for weight belts. This can be achieved by placing the buckle on the left side when you don the belt. You should develop the habit of always handling a belt by the end without the buckle. This will prevent loss of weights. If you always hold the end of the belt without the buckle in your right hand, you will find that you will end up with a right-hand release whenever you don the belt.

When your buoyancy compensator has been donned, check its adjustment to make sure it will not ride up on you when inflated in the water. To check this, lift up on the device then make adjustments as needed.

When all your equipment is in place, take a moment to familiarize yourself with the location of the controls and releases. You should be able to find them all without looking at them.

When wearing a BC jacket, it is easier to don the weight belt before the tank. Stepping through the belt is suggested.

Adjust the belt length so there is only about six inches (15 cm) of excess strap.

Note that their position will change in the water. Your instructor will show you some ways to quickly locate them.

Testing Your Buoyancy   Buoyancy testing at the surface begins with your BC completely deflated and your lungs full of air. You assume an upright, motionless position in the water and relax. If weighted correctly, you will float at eye level in the water. Adjustments in weight may be required to reach this point. As a final test, you should exhale after you are floating at eye level. If you sink, you are weighted just as you should be. Look up as you do this part of the exercise. As soon as you sink, swim back to the surface and establish buoyancy by adding air to your BC. Learn to dive weighted correctly. It is tempting to wear extra weight because at first - especially while training in a swimming pool - it seems easier to function underwater when overweighted. It will, however, prove to be a disadvantage and perhaps even a hazard in the long run.

Your buoyancy changes underwater due to the compression of your suit, your BC, items collected and air used from your tank. You will frequently be changing and testing your buoyancy beneath the surface. To check your buoyancy underwater, assume a face-down

To find your BC hose underwater, get in the habit of reaching for the point of attachment and following the hose to the controls.

A

B

When weighted properly, you will float at eye level with lungs full (A) and sink when you exhale completely (B).

Top, To determine neutral buoyancy on the bottom, adjust buoyancy so you rise during inhalations and sink during exhalations.
Bottom, Be sure to vent expanding air from your BC during ascents. The exhaust must be the highest point.

position in the water and breathe slowly and deeply. When your buoyancy is correct, you will start to rise in the water slowly following your inhalations and will start to sink following each exhalation. Your breaths must be very long and slow before this response can be noted. Air will need to be added or vented from your BC to achieve this state. Keep in mind that with air in a BC and when wearing protection suits, buoyancy will vary with depth so you will need to check your buoyancy whenever you change your depth.

Controlling Your Buoyancy   There are quite a few factors which affect your buoyancy in the water. You should be aware of all of them and know various means available to you to remain in control of your buoyancy at all times.

The principal means of controlling buoyancy are with the amount of weight worn, the amount of air in your BC and the amount of air in your lungs. You can control your buoyancy just by varying the average amount of air in your lungs. You should keep breathing, but you can take shallow breaths to be less buoyant or deeper breaths to be more buoyant. Frequently, your breathing pattern can be used to control buoyancy until adjustments can be made with your buoyancy compensator. For example, if you feel yourself beginning to drift up in the water, you can exhale completely to stop the upward progress, then vent some air from your BC to rid yourself of excess buoyancy.

As you pick up objects underwater and carry them with you, it will probably be necessary to increase your buoyancy to offset the weight of the items. Heavy objects should not be carried in this way. Excessive buoyancy will result if a heavy object is dropped and a runaway ascent can occur. With even fairly light items, keep in mind that you will become buoyant if you set the items down on the bottom.

When you have compensated for buoyancy at depth, note that the air in your BC will expand as you ascend. Thus, your buoyancy increases as the depth decreases. Whenever you move upward in water, especially in shallow water, it will be necessary to dump air from your buoyancy compensator to keep from being carried to the surface out of control. If you find yourself rising through the water, exhale, turn into an upright position and vent air from your BC. The upright position is required because the exhaust valves in BCs are located at the top and you cannot get the air out of the device if it is inverted.

If you have air in your BC at depth, you will need to release air as you ascend. How much and how often will depend upon the situation and the depth, but you can gauge your buoyancy by your progress through the water, coupled with your swimming efforts. Slow your fin kicks from time to time to test your buoyancy. If you float up without kicking, you are too buoyant. If you start sinking, you have released too much air. You will learn to gauge this with practice and should strive to be able to control your buoyancy so well that you can stop at any depth at any time and remain suspended while

motionless. This is an evaluation of your buoyancy control and will be part of your open water training. When you can do this, you are demonstrating the ability that you need as a diver as far as buoyancy control is concerned.

Looking Back

Remember that buoyancy control is one of the most important skills. See if you can recall the key concepts related to the topic.

1. List four considerations involved in setting up a weight belt for use.

A. _____

B. _____

C. _____

D. _____

2. What is the most important thing to keep in mind when donning the weight belt? _____

_____

The second most important? _____

_____

3. List four steps involved in testing your buoyancy at the surface:

A. _____

B. _____

C. _____

D. _____

4. What are four major factors which affect your buoyancy?

A. _____

B. _____

C. _____

D. _____

5. How do you stop an unplanned buoyant ascent? _____

Hovering motionless in the water is a demonstration of good buoyancy control.

6.5   Entries and Exits

Every time you go diving, you will need to get into the water and to get out. The situations in which you will do this are numerous, so varied techniques are required. There are some general entry rules which apply, several entries which apply to the majority of situations and some general procedures for exiting the water. You will now become familiar with these to gain an overview of what is involved in getting into and out of the water. You will learn specific local techniques from your instructor and will practice these, as well as the commonly used procedures, during your water skill sessions and open water training.

Preparing to Enter   Start your entry procedures by timing your preparation with your diving partner so both of you will be ready to enter at the same time. When you are both suited up, you will be eager to get into the water, but you must pause long enough to inspect each other's equipment. You need to familiarize yourself with how your buddy's gear is fastened, how it operates, and will need to ensure that it is operating correctly. To conduct an equipment inspection, it helps to start with the tank valve and work your way down, checking three major areas as you go. The areas are:

Check your own gear and your buddy's before every dive, no matter how experienced you become.

1. Check to make sure the tank valve is turned all the way on then backed off slightly. Make sure the regulator hose is oriented over the right shoulder and that the regulator functions correctly when the purge valve is depressed. Check the submersible pressure gauge to make sure the tank has sufficient air for the dive. Also, check the tank to make sure it is secure in the backpack.

2. Check the buoyancy compensator. Make sure the low pressure inflator hose is connected and that the mechanism functions properly. Note how to operate the controls on the BC, and make sure it is properly inflated or deflated for the type of entry you are going to make.

3. The third major item to check is the weight belt. Be sure it is clear for ditching, that it is secured with a right-hand release and that no hoses are trapped beneath it.

These are the major items to inspect, but do take a few moments to check your partner from head to toe to make sure that all equipment is donned properly. It is usually easier to correct a problem before a dive than it is to correct one after you have entered the water. No matter

Any entry which gets you safely into the water without affecting your equipment is a good entry.

The controlled seated entry. You simply turn and lower yourself into the water.

how experienced and skilled you become as a diver, you should always have your buddy inspect your gear before a dive and you should always do the same for your buddy.

Entries When both you and your buddy are prepared and ready to enter the water, there are some rules which will *almost always apply*. In most cases, your BC should be partially inflated to provide buoyancy. Your mask should be held firmly to avoid flooding or dislodging. You should breathe from your regulator during the entry. And, you should ensure that the entry area is clear and sufficiently deep for the type of entry you have selected.

There is only one objective for an entry — to get yourself into the water with the minimum amount of effort and with the minimal effect on you and your equipment. Any entry which accomplishes this is a good entry. Several commonly used entries will be presented. Your goal is to be able to determine when it is appropriate for each of them to be used.

The seated entry is easy and very controlled. Whenever you can sit at the edge of the water, make final preparations and then lower yourself

into the water, it is a good choice to opt for this entry. Example situations include the side of a swimming pool, a ledge at water level in a quarry, or a water level boat dock. When seated, you are not as likely to lose your balance as you can when standing. You are also close to the water, so the impact of your entry is minimal. To perform the entry, apply the general rules, place both hands on the same side on the entry edge and turn and lower yourself into the water. This should be one continuous movement. The entry is simple, easy and effective.

Top, *The giant stride entry. Do not jump or hop —
just step out while holding your mask and looking
straight ahead.*
Center, *The back roll entry. Disorientation can occur.
Also, be sure to keep the legs pulled in to avoid hitting
your heels.*
Bottom, *Wading entries are used in many locations.*

Giant Stride Entry   When entering from a
boat or dock where the distance to the water is
not more than six or seven feet (2 m), the giant
stride entry is recommended. (For heights
greater than six or seven feet (2 m), your legs
should be brought together before you reach the
water.) This involves stepping off into the water,
landing in the stepping position, and pulling your
legs together to stop your downward momentum
to remain at the surface. This entry is appropriate when the depth of the water is known to be
deeper than seven feet (2.1 m), with no objects
underwater that a diver might strike while
entering. When carrying out the entry, look at
the water first to check the entry area, but look
at the horizon during the actual entry. Do not
step or leap from the platform, just step out with
one bold step. Leave the trailing foot behind
you. Both feet will enter the water at the same
time. It is especially important to apply the
general rules during this entry. Once you are in
the water, swim clear of the entry area, exchange your regulator for your snorkel and
watch as your buddy enters.

Back Roll Entry   This method is used from a
small boat where standing to enter could result
in an injury from loss of balance. The entry is
performed by sitting with your back to the water
and pulling your knees to your chest as you roll
backwards into the water. A couple of problems
can occur if you are not careful. Keep your legs
tucked to your chest until in the water. If you
extend your legs as you roll backwards, your
heels can clip the edge of the entry area. Also,
you may experience some dizziness as you roll
into the water. This results from spinning the
fluids in the equilibrium centers in your ears as
you turn. Don't be overly concerned, you will re-
orient in just a few seconds. Emphasis on the
general rules is important. Always remember to
make certain there is nothing behind and below
you before you roll into the water.

Wading Entries   Wading into the water is an
easy method in many areas. There is less
impact and disorientation than with the giant
stride and back roll entries, which are used
when you are going directly into water over your
head. When you can walk into shallow water to

begin a dive, it is an easy entry technique, but some precautions are necessary. Depending on the location, it may be acceptable to wade to waist-deep into the water and then don your fins. In other areas, the fins should be put on before entering the water.

Find out what is recommended for a particular site, then adopt the accepted technique. Whether wearing fins or not, shuffle your feet along the bottom rather than stepping. This detects holes and rocks or obstructions, helps prevent loss of balance and will chase bottom-dwelling animals from your path. It is a good practice in wading entries to lie down and start swimming as soon as possible. Typically, this is when the water is about knee deep. Also, if you lose your balance during the entry, remain prone and start swimming rather than exerting yourself to stand again.

For entries through surf, you will require training. In general though, you will need to time your entry to coincide with a lull or low point in the wave action. Keep your knees bent, pause as the force of the wave is encountered, watch the approaching waves continuously, and avoid stopping in the surf zone. Duck under breaking waves while breathing from your regulator. If a float is used, it must be trailed behind you on a line. This is only a brief introduction to surf entries to advise you that special instruction is definitely a prerequisite. If you are trained and certified as a NAUI Openwater I diver in an area without surf conditions, you will need additional training in surf entries and exits before attempting to dive in surf areas such as are found in California.

Below, Surf entries require training and practice and vary in technique from place to place.
Right, To exit from deep water, remove tank and weights first, have buddy hold tank, then exit and pull in heavy gear. Buddy then exits. Note that fins are worn until after exiting.

Exits Just as an airplane which goes up must come down, a diver who enters the water must exit from it. Procedures vary greatly depending on the situation. We will provide some general rules and offer some methods which are useful for typical occasions.

Conditions can change during a dive so you should take a minute or two to assess the exit area before proceeding. During this time you should make sure all of your equipment is in place and secure. It helps to think out the steps of the exit in advance as well. If you will be exiting onto a boat or from water too deep for you to stand, it is a good idea to first remove your weight belt and then your scuba unit before trying to climb out of the water. Any items you may be carrying should be handed up first, followed by the gear being removed. If wearing a horsecollar BC and using a low pressure inflator, remember to disconnect the low-pressure hose before removing the tank. Your fins should remain in place as long as possible. If you must lift yourself out of the water, use your fins to help. If you are exiting on a ladder, keep your fins on until you are ready to climb the ladder, then hold onto the ladder while removing them.

When the exit area is a flat area or a platform, and wave action is present, your approach to the area should be coordinated with the wave action so the water movement will help lift you onto the exit area. Factors such as this point out the need for local orientations to diving procedures.

When wading out of the water, simply reverse the entry procedures. Swim in as far as possible before standing. Breathe from your regulator. When you stand and start moving, shuffle your feet along the bottom. Keep your knees bent to maintain balance. Usually it is a good idea to wear your fins and to keep all other gear in place until you are clear of the water. In surf, it is often practical to exit by crawling from the water. Avoid allowing your enthusiasm to discuss the events of the dive to interfere with concentrating on the exit procedures. It is not uncommon for equipment to be lost during exits due to inattention. Be patient and save your discussions until you and your buddy are out of the water. Also, if you exit onto a charter boat, do not tarry in the exit area. Collect your gear and move away so others can exit.

It would take an entire book to present all of the considerations for entries and exits and to describe and depict all of the accepted techniques. We have merely attempted to introduce

Above, During wading exits, walk backwards and shuffle your feet. It is recommended you keep all gear in place until well clear of the water.
Right, To exit from surf on a steep beach, a crawling exit is probably the best method.

the topics in this section and to impress you with the need to learn the entry and exit techniques which are unique to each area. You will learn local methods from your instructor, but you should not assume you know how to enter and exit the water everywhere. Always get an orientation of the diving procedures for every new site and region.

Looking Back

1. When preparing to enter the water, what are the three major areas to be checked during the equipment inspection?

A. _____

B. _____

C. _____

2. List three general rules which apply to entries:

A. _____

B. _____

C. _____

3. What is the objective of an entry? _____

_____

4. Give an example of when it is appropriate to use each of the following entries:

A. Giant Stride _____

B. Back Roll _____

C. Seated _____

5. List three general rules which apply to wading entries:

A. _____

B. _____

C. _____

6. List two actions to be avoided during exits:

A. _____

B. _____

6.6   Gear Handling

Typically, you will don your scuba equipment out of the water, go diving and remove your equipment after exiting the water. However, there are instances where you may need or want to don or remove and replace your equipment in the water. For example, you may discover that it is easier and cooler to don your tank in the water. Or the boat you are using may be too small to permit much equipment handling. An item of gear may require adjustment in the water, and that necessitates removal before the adjustment can be made. If your scuba unit gets caught in something, you may be able to free it by removing the unit so you can see the problem and correct it. It is fairly common to remove some of your equipment in the water prior to exiting. As you can see, there are many reasons why you need to become proficient at working with your equipment while in the water.

Handling Scuba Gear   Removal of the scuba unit in the water is as simple as removing a jacket. The waistband is released, the shoulder strap is released and the tank is slipped from the left shoulder and then from the right shoulder. Good control and balance can be maintained if the tank is brought forward under the right arm as shown in the photo. If the BC is attached to the tank, it should be only slightly inflated. If the BC is not attached to the tank, be sure to disconnect the low pressure inflation hose from the BC before removing the tank.

To don the scuba tank at the surface, follow the procedures outlined in the photographs. Pay particular attention to the following points:

1. Be slightly buoyant when donning scuba at the surface. If the BC is attached to the tank, vent most of the air so you can work easily with the unit. It is difficult to don a very buoyant scuba unit. Retain some buoyancy, however, so you won't sink while putting on the tank.

2. Don't forget to re-fasten the shoulder strap before donning the tank.

3. Work with the tank in front of you as shown.

4. Breathe from your regulator while donning the tank, even when doing so at the surface. There are two ways you don your tank: you can put it on like a coat, or you can raise it up and duck beneath it. In either case, the regulator should be in your mouth during the donning process. If the tank is being put on over your head, the entire hose — from the first stage on the tank to the second stage in your mouth —

A

D

B

E

C

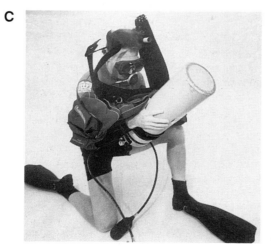

Remove tank under the arm. Be sure the regulator hose is between your arms when replacing the unit. Keep lung volume low to gain stability. Learn to complete the exercise without changing location.

must be between your arms. If a loop of the hose is on the outside of your arm, the hose will end up trapped beneath your shoulder strap when you lower the tank into place.

5. When the tank is in place on your back, locate the waist straps and pull on them to position the unit. Before securing the straps, check that the shoulder straps are not twisted and that all of your hoses are clear. Learn to buckle the waist strap by feel because it is not easy to see your waist while wearing a mask.

Removing and replacing the scuba unit underwater is similar to the technique used at the surface. Buoyancy is the difference. You do not want the scuba unit to be buoyant when working with it on the bottom. Your overall buoyancy should be slightly negative. Just as you prepare to don the unit, it helps to exhale fully and to breathe shallowly as you position the unit. It is best to work at a slow, steady pace.

It is desirable for you to be able to handle your equipment independently, but there is nothing wrong with obtaining assistance from your buddy when a problem arises. An extra set of hands and eyes can be quite useful and can save time.

To don your tank at the surface, be slightly buoyant, duck under the tank as you raise it, make sure the snorkel is clear, and lay back on the unit when securing the waistband.

Weight Belt Handling   Handling a weight belt in the water can seem very awkward, but if you will keep a couple of key points in mind, you will find with practice that working with this item isn't as difficult as it seems at first. The weights are going to want to go in a direct line to the bottom. When you remove the belt and hold it, the belt will swing to a vertical position and tend to pull you over in the water as it tries to sink. This problem can be offset by holding the belt close to your mid-section. Gravity also pulls on the belt when you are trying to buckle it after putting it in place. Use this to your advantage by assuming a face-down position so gravity keeps the belt in place across your back. In this way, there will be no tension on the buckle while you tighten and secure it. Just these two ideas will make working with your belt in the water an easier task.

Removal of a weight belt in the water is sometimes more difficult than it seems. Belts tend to get caught on the most unexpected things. For this reason, if a belt is being discarded in order to gain buoyancy in an emergency, it is important that you not only release it, but that you pull clear of yourself and your equipment before releasing it.

If you are not discarding the belt, but only removing it to hand it out of the water or to make an adjustment on it, hold it by the end without the buckle. This will prevent any weights from sliding from the belt.

When donning the belt, keep the end without the buckle against your mid-section while holding it in your right hand. Then tip yourself to the right and roll to the left while turning to a horizontal position (refer to photos), you will be able to maneuver the belt into position across your back. Make sure, of course, that the weight belt is between the tank and your back and not over the tank. It is then simply a matter of making sure the belt is free of twists, that the weights are in the correct position and of securing the buckle. Some divers prefer to hold both ends of the belt in one hand. To place the belt behind the back, grasp the ends of the belt in either hand and pull the belt into place. If this is done, immediately turn to a face-down position as the belt is pulled against your back.

The same procedures for donning a weight belt apply at the surface and underwater. Be careful not to drop or lay the belt down underwater, however, because you will instantly become buoyant and may float to the surface.

Mask Removal and Replacement   You may be wondering why you would want to remove your mask underwater. Generally you would not, but someone else may inadvertently do it for you. Your mask can be bumped and dislodged or it may get caught on something and be pulled free. You should be able to calmly relocate and replace the mask with ease.

Your vision without a mask is not good, but you can see. Make use of your eyes. Learn to open them while working without a mask. They will be more useful than you might think.

To replace the mask underwater, orient it into the correct position, then grasp it by the strap on either side. Place the seat of the mask on your

A

B

C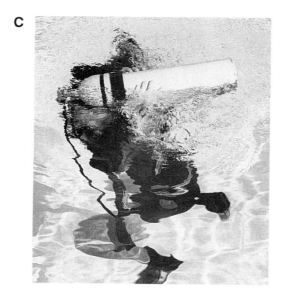

D

E

To don your tank at the surface, be slightly buoyant, duck under the tank as you raise it, make sure the snorkel is clear, and lay back on the unit when securing the waistband.

forehead and hooking the strap over the back of your head. Move the mask down into position on your face then clear the area under the skirt all the way around the mask. Items to be cleared include hair and the hood, if a hood is worn. Then clear the water from the mask before positioning the strap (or you can re-position the strap first). This method of working the mask into position in stages is recommended because it works well both with and without a hood.

Handling Fins in the Water   If a strap on your fin works loose or pulls free, you should be able to remove the fin, correct the problem, replace the fin and continue. With a little thought and practice, you will be able to do this easily.

It may be easier to correct a fin problem on the bottom than it is to fix it at the surface, so you may choose to work with your fin while underwater. You may also find it easier if you will remove at least one glove, unless the water is extremely cold, so you will have more dexterity to work with the strap and the buckles. When working with a fin at the surface, establish buoyancy so the need to kick will be reduced or eliminated. Your instructor will probably have you do exercises with one fin removed just to get you accustomed to functioning with a single fin.

Soon you will feel confident with your ability to handle your equipment in the water. The more you practice and the more experience you get, the easier it will become. Your goal is to make working with your equipment as easy as your instructor makes it look. If you need to fight with your gear, there is something you do not understand. Learn to work slowly and deliberately. Think of the steps involved in handling an item of gear, then execute them one at a time. You will do well. It is just a matter of time, practice and developing a feel for it.

Top, Assume a face-down position when positioning the weight belt to keep tension off the ends while securing the belt.
Center, When ditching the weight belt, pull it clear of yourself before discarding it.
Bottom, Handle your weight belt by the end without the buckle to avoid loss of any weights.

To don a weight belt in the water, hold the end at your mid-section, roll it into place (help it under the tank) and maneuver into a face-down position to adjust and secure it.

3. What two points should be recalled to make weight belt handling easier in the water?

A. _____

B. _____

4. List the five recommended steps for replacing a mask underwater:

A. _____

B. _____

C. _____

D. _____

E. _____

Looking Back

1. What is the primary difference between donning your tank at the surface and donning it underwater? _____

_____

2. How can you keep the regulator hose from becoming trapped when you don your tank over your head? _____

_____

_____

6.7   Open Water Skills

You have learned many skills in this NAUI course. They have been learned under controlled conditions to prepare you to dive in open water in your area. You may be diving in the ocean, in a lake or river, or in some other body of water, but the conditions are likely to be quite different than those in which you learned the needed skills. There will be greater changes in pressure and buoyancy because of greater depth. The visibility may be less. There will be currents and wave action. We will now preview some open water skills.

Buddy System Techniques It is easy to keep track of a diving partner in controlled conditions where visibility is good and the area is limited. Unless a few proven techniques are employed, however, maintaining buddy contact will not be as simple in open water. You want to have fun and it isn't fun if you are looking for your buddy most of the time. By applying the following procedures, you and your buddy can remain together without detracting from your enjoyment.

Begin by discussing the dive beforehand and agreeing on the purpose, the activity and the general course to be followed. This coordination will prove beneficial.

As much as possible, you and your buddy should maintain the same position with respect to one another once you reach the bottom. Diving abreast is preferred to a leader/follower configuration.

When a direction has been established, both members of the dive team should maintain that heading until a change of direction is suggested by a signal and acknowledged. When you know the direction of travel, you will have a general idea of where to locate a buddy if you become separated.

If separation occurs, you should search briefly for your buddy at the bottom, then ascend a few feet and look for bubbles. The total search time should not exceed one minute. If unsuccessful in reuniting during that time, surface and wait for your buddy to do the same. You can then get back together, descend again, and continue the dive. This is the fastest and best method for locating a lost teammate in most situations.

As you and your buddy gain experience together and get to know one another, it becomes easier to remain together. You will become familiar with each other's diving styles and will be able to function as a true team with minimal effort required. Developing this harmony should be your goal because diving with a good buddy is diving at its best.

Navigation Above the water, you constantly employ simple navigational procedures. You use maps, street signs and landmarks to help locate a destination and to aid you in returning to your point of origin. There are no street signs

Learn to keep your eyes open when your mask is removed.

You should be able to make minor adjustments to all of your equipment while in the water.

If you lose a fin or if a strap breaks, you can use a Dolphin kick with the legs crossed at the ankles.

Always discuss your dive beforehand and review all signals to be used.

A buddy is very helpful for equipment problems such as when a tank slips from its pack.

It is easier to maintain buddy contact if you will maintain the same relative position to one another throughout a dive.

Know the established procedures and follow them if you become separated from your buddy underwater.

underwater, but there are navigational aids which can be used to help you keep track of where you are while diving. We will introduce you to some of the fundamentals of underwater navigation. You can learn more about this very useful skill in a NAUI Underwater Navigation Specialty Program.

You will want to learn to use natural aids to navigation. These can soon become as useful as street signs to you. If you know that ripple marks on the bottom form parallel to shore and are closer together the closer you are to shore, you will have one reference. If you will note the relative position of the sun and the shadows at the start of the dive, you will have another. The back-and-forth movement of water caused by wave action near shore is called surge. Its movement is toward and away from shore. Depth of the water is another useful indicator. Underwater "land marks," such as an unusual formation, a large unique plant, an unusual crevice or a wreck become points of reference on a dive. By paying attention to such natural aids while diving, you and your buddy can keep track of your position underwater and will be able to return to the starting area without having to surface. You can avoid a long surface swim by ending your dive at a predetermined location. To know where you are and to be able to get where you want to go is the objective of under-

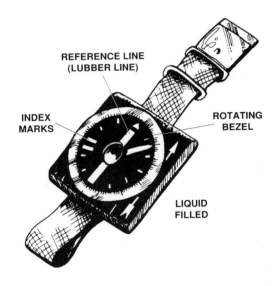

REFERENCE LINE
(LUBBER LINE)

INDEX
MARKS

ROTATING
BEZEL

LIQUID
FILLED

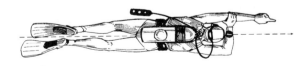

Top, A typical compass.
Bottom, It is important that the compass be aligned with the center line of your body.

water navigation. By recognizing and using natural aids to navigation, you should be able to do this. This is called piloting.

When natural aids are not available or cannot be used, such as when diving at night or in limited visibility, a compass and depth gauge are used as references. Not only do they help you find your way by dead reckoning, they allow you to navigate very accurately. The depth gauge is equivalent to the altimeter in an airplane. It tells your vertical position in the water. The compass serves as your relative direction indicator.

Learn to recognize natural navigation aids such as unique formations and the direction of the sunlight.

An underwater compass is liquid filled, has a reference line called a "lubber line," and should have some means of setting a reference course with a movable index point. Because a compass is magnetic, you should realize that it will be affected by metal objects in close proximity.

For use, the compass must always be oriented in the same direction relative to its use. The lubber line must be in line with the center line of your body. Compasses may be worn on the wrist, held in your hand, or mounted into an instrument console along with other gauges. Where the compass is carried is not critical, but making sure that it is aligned properly for reference is. When referencing a compass, always check first to make sure you are lined up with the reference line, and that the compass is level.

A compass provides relative directional information and can serve as a reference for maintaining a selected direction. Both are accomplished by referring to the direction of the needle which, without deviation, points to magnetic north. If you point the reference line of your compass toward shore and the compass needle points to the left, you will know that whenever the needle is pointing left you are swimming toward shore. Conversely, if the needle is pointing to the right, you are heading in the opposite direction — away from shore.

You can see why it is helpful to set a reference on your compass at the beginning of a dive. If you decide to start a dive in a certain direction, you can set the moveable reference marker on the compass so it is aligned with the needle when the reference line of the compass is pointed in the desired direction. By keeping yourself aligned with the lubber line and the compass needle aligned with the reference marker, you will be able to maintain your desired

To set a reference course on a compass, point the reference line in the desired direction, then align the index marks with the needle.

The compass can be held in both hands and extended in front of the diver.

When you measure your air consumption, you will see how much air you use in a given period of time at a constant depth.

course very accurately. You should look across the top of the compass as it is being used rather than down on it. Usually you will only need to reference the compass occasionally to make sure you are on course. If you want to navigate precisely, such as when returning to the boat at the end of a dive, you will need to reference the compass frequently.

As the dive progresses and you follow your chosen course, a point will be reached when you need to start back so you will have enough air to reach your final destination. Your return heading, called a "Reciprocal Course," is easily obtained if your outbound course was a straight line. All you need to do is turn yourself until the compass needle is directly opposite the original reference marker. Then you will be heading in the proper direction. What you are simply doing is making a 180° turn, and the compass enables you to do it very precisely.

What if you don't travel in a straight line during the dive? If you will follow a course, such as a square or a rectangle, and keep track of the turns made, you will still be able to navigate quite well with practice. This is another reason why the constant reference of the compass is so useful. What if no particular pattern is followed? The compass will still be helpful because you and your buddy can surface near the end of the dive, point the compass in the direction you wish to go to reach the exit point, set the heading with

the movable reference marker, submerge and follow the heading to your destination.

Simple navigational techniques such as those just presented make your diving safer and more enjoyable. By knowing where you are underwater, you will not only be able to avoid long surface swims at the end of a dive, you will also be able to relocate interesting areas. You will save time and air so you can devote it to enjoying the objective of your dive. Be sure to learn well the basics of navigation taught in this course and to learn more about underwater navigation in your NAUI continuing education courses.

Measuring Air Consumption   As discussed in part seven of Chapter Two, it is useful for you to measure the rate of consumption of your air for your dives until your rate stabilizes and you are familiar with how long your air will last at various depths and for various activities. To do this, you will need to measure the amount of time used at a constant depth for a given period of time. During your training dives, your instructor will conduct one or more air consumption measurement exercises. The instructor will indicate the starting and stopping times and provide the depth information. All you need to do is write down the starting and ending pressures. Following the dive, calculate your air consumption for the depth,

Equipment inspections before every dive are required and are important.

convert it to the surface use rate, and record it in your log book. You will learn the procedure by actually doing it, and will be able to conduct your own air consumption measurements as soon as you obtain the necessary instrumentation.

Open water training involves the application of all the skills learned under more controlled conditions plus the introduction of new skills needed for diving — skills which can only be learned in the actual environment. When you can comfortably perform the basic skills of diving in open water as well as skills presented in this section, you will be qualified for certification as a scuba diver and be able to learn even more about diving in other courses. You will find that your open water dives will be fun as well as provide an evaluation of your skills. You will realize even more why divers are so enthusiastic about their endeavors.

Looking Back

1. List three recommended techniques which will help to maintain buddy contact while diving:

A. _____

B. _____

C. _____

2. Briefly list the steps to be taken to reunite if you become separated from your buddy while diving:

A. _____

B. _____

C. _____

D. _____

3. List three natural aids to navigation:

A. _____

B. _____

C. _____

4. List two principles to be applied when using a compass for underwater navigation:

A. _____

B. _____

5. Define a Reciprocal Course: _____

_____

6. What three instruments are required in order to measure air consumption?

A. _____

B. _____

C. _____

$\mathit{7}$ *Diving Safety*

It is a good idea to be prepared for anything you want to do. The idea is even better when it comes to diving. Not only is safety a concern, but you want to have the best possible dive with minimum problems. In order to do this, you need to plan your dives. We first need to define planning. It is all the arrangements and plans you make for a dive from the time you decide to go diving until the planned dive or dives is/are complete.

We will break the task into three parts: *Planning to Dive, Preparing to Dive and Making a Planned Dive*. You will want to know what to do and how to do it so you can enjoy all the benefits of a well-planned dive, including having all needed equipment in good working order, knowing what to expect at the dive site, avoiding last minute rushing, and in some instances, just being able to go because you made reservations ahead of time for a popular activity. Yes, when you, your equipment, and your buddy are well prepared for a dive, you have the best possible chance of having a safe and pleasurable experience, which is the goal of recreational diving.

There are many things to do in diving. You should select one activity (and only one) as the purpose of your planned dive. It is unwise (and can be unsafe) to combine activities on a dive. If you try to spear fish and take pictures, you are not likely to do either very well. Your first step, then, is to decide the purpose of your dive and who your buddy will be. It helps greatly if you and your buddy have similar interests.

7.1 Planning Your Dives

Once you and your buddy have decided on the objective of the dive, you need to agree on the location. An alternate location should also be discussed in case conditions are unacceptable at the primary location. Keep in mind points such as marine life preserve areas, boat traffic, and courtesy to fishermen when deciding

Select only one activity when planning a dive.

where to pursue your underwater goals. (See *Diver Etiquette* in Appendix.)

If the dive site is unfamiliar to you, research is in order. Books are available that provide information on popular locations. You should also find a contact in the area to obtain knowledge about the proposed site. Sources include dive resorts, dive stores, dive clubs, and diving instructors. The more you can learn in advance, the better prepared you will be.

When feasible, it is a good idea to go look at the dive site in advance. This will tell you a great deal about accessibility, parking, fees, conditions, facilities, and entry and exit points. You may also find divers there who can point things out and explain the best procedures for diving at the location.

After deciding on what you want to do and the location, you and your diving partner should select the date and time for the dive. Remember to check conflicting activities, including the night before you plan to dive. It is unwise (and unsafe) to go diving the morning after attending a party you had forgotten was planned when you scheduled your dive. The time of day for your dive is also a consideration. Local winds may be light in the morning and strong in the afternoon, or vice-versa. If you can, try to schedule your dive during the high tide.

Your next step is to make some phone calls. These calls include reservations for a plane, boat, hotel, etc. You may want to get information on the dive site at the same time if you speak to someone who knows the area. Take some time to obtain emergency contact information as well. The information you should have will be presented later in this chapter.

When you have acquired knowledge about the planned dive, you can determine the equipment needed. For example, if the water temperature is different than that in which you usually dive, you may need to obtain a different type of protective suit and change the amount of weight you will wear to assure good buoyancy control throughout the dive. An estimate of the water temperature is a particularly useful bit of information you should make sure you obtain.

It is a good idea to prepare a list of things to do to prepare for your dive. Keep it handy so you can add to it as thoughts come to mind. Develop a checklist which will be useful to help in planning future dives as well. Do not rely on your memory. (See Appendix for sample checklist.)

You need to inspect your equipment to make sure it is in good condition and ready for use. Make any minor repairs which you are qualified to make, such as replacing dried and cracked straps on your fins. Have any sophisticated equipment with problems serviced at your dive store well in advance of your dive trip.

Avoid waiting until the last minute to buy items you will be needing for the dive trip. Typical items include tickets, air fills for your scuba tanks, film, sun screen lotion, seasick pills, and a fishing license. Determine what you need, write it down, and get it in advance. This includes some spare parts for your diving equipment. Having an extra mask strap or an O-ring for your tank can save a lot of time and frustration if they are needed at the dive site.

As the day of the dive draws near, it is helpful to check the weather trends, water conditions, and the long-range weather forecast. Your

When feasible, visit the intended dive site a day or so before your dive to check the conditions, access, etc.

You should begin every dive with the good, confident feeling that comes with being properly prepared.

NAUI Instructor will advise you about available sources for such information. If you know in advance that the weather may be bad on the day your dive is planned, you may be able to avoid wasting a trip.

Finally, remember to get yourself, as well as your equipment, ready to go diving. Be fit for diving. Exercise to develop stamina. Practice skills to keep them sharp.

It may seem like a lot of trouble to plan a dive, but it becomes easy and fun to do after a few times. You will enjoy talking diving with your buddy and with others from whom you seek information. There is a good feeling that comes from being well prepared to do something. To get the most from diving, you should arrive at your selected dive site with this feeling.

Preparing to Dive   With all of your plans and long-range preparations completed, it will be fairly easy to complete the last minute details of preparing to go diving. Let's identify those details.

The day or evening before your scheduled dive, gather all of your equipment and personal articles together in one place. Use of a checklist is recommended. Your gear should be packed into two bags: one for your diving equipment and one for your personal items, such as towel, jacket, snacks, camera, and clothes — things you want to keep dry. Your weight belt should not be packed with your dive gear. The easiest way to carry it is to wear it. Your backpack should be mounted on your tank. The tank can also be carried by wearing it. It is helpful to pack your diving equipment in the reverse order of which it will be needed. Put the fins, which are donned last, on the bottom; and your exposure suit, which is donned first, on top.

A last minute check of weather and water conditions is recommended, as is providing someone who is not going on the dive information on your destination and estimated return time. If you are unusually late in returning, assistance can be summoned to look for you. Don't forget to notify the person if you are going to be late intentionally.

Be sure to get a good night's rest prior to your diving activities. You want to be well rested, be in good health, and have a good feeling about the dive.

Making a Planned Dive   When you and your buddy arrive at the selected site, there are plans which need to be made prior to entering the water. First, evaluate the conditions to determine if they are acceptable for your planned activity. If conditions are unfavorable, either travel to an alternate location or abort the dive. Don't be afraid to say that you don't feel good about diving in poor conditions. The purpose of a dive is enjoyment, and it isn't fun if conditions are bad.

When you decide to dive, you must then plan the dive itself. This includes discussion and agreement on the following points:

1. One member of the dive team should be the leader in charge of decision-making for the dive. Generally, this person will decide when

Keep yourself fit for diving through regular, related exercise.

Learn to pack your gear in the opposite order it will be used.

to change course, when to begin the return leg of the dive, and when to surface. Partners can always make suggestions, but it should be agreed that most decisions be up to the dive leader. The person in charge does not necessarily need to be the most experienced or the most qualified member of the dive team. The person most familiar with an area should lead on the first dive, then the buddies or team members can take turns leading on subsequent dives.

2. You need to agree on the activity and the objective of the dive. Discuss what you want to do, how you want to do it, and any special signals you may need to use. Standard signals, which will be presented in the next part of this chapter, should also be reviewed. Communicate as much as possible before the dive because it is much more difficult to do so after you descend beneath the surface.

3. Your next step is to outline the course to be followed on the dive. Where will you enter? What pattern will you follow, and for what distances? What will be your limits for depth, time, and air supply? Where do you intend to surface? Where is your exit point? You should both understand the course to be followed and agree upon it.

4. Finally, discuss contingency plans, emergency procedures, and accident management.

Outline the general course or pattern to be followed on the dive.

Agree on what to do in a situation where air is needed underwater. Agree on what to do if a buddy pair gets separated underwater. (A good rule is to stop, listen, and retrace your previous course for up to one minute. If contact is not made, both members should surface and get together.) Every effort should be made so divers do not separate. However, if it should happen, and quick contact is not made at the surface, another course of action is necessary. Agree on how help can be summoned, if it is needed. Discuss the steps to be taken if an accident or injury should occur. Have local emergency contact information and make sure you know the location of the nearest phone. It is a good idea to make sure the phone is working. Take some time to be prepared for emergencies because there isn't much time available if one does occur. Diving is safe, but accidents can happen. Be ready for them.

Dive Your Plan   It is very important that you carry out the plans you have made. The dive plan should not be abandoned part way through a dive. If something occurs to alter your plan, terminate the dive long enough to make new plans, rather than trying to change them underwater. You and your dive buddy must coordinate while diving. This is difficult even when you are in agreement on what you intend to do. If one member of the team varies from the dive plan, confusion will result.

Plan ahead while diving. Remind one another of the limits you have agreed upon. Keep carrying out your plans throughout the dive. You will feel rewarded when you can do what you set out to do and end a dive exactly where you planned. Accept dive planning and the ability to execute your plan as a challenge. This adds enjoyment to the dive while making it much more effective and safer.

There are many benefits when you are prepared for a dive. It is worth the time it takes to properly plan and prepare. As you work with others to coordinate your activities, it will become easy; you will find enjoyment in the preparations as well as the dive. We hope you always make plans for your dives. All good divers do.

Plan your dive, then dive your plan.

Looking Back

1. List three reasons why dives should be planned.

A. _____

B. _____

C. _____

2. List ten steps of long-range preparations for diving.

A. _____

B. _____

C. _____

D. _____

E. _____

F. _____

G. _____

H. _____

I. _____

J. _____

3. List four steps of last-minute preparations for diving.

A. _____

B. _____

C. _____

D. _____

4. What is the first step to be taken upon arrival at the selected dive site? _____

5. List five items you and your buddy should agree upon before diving together.

A. _____

B. _____

C. _____

D. _____

E. _____

7.2 Communications

You probably already know it is not easy to communicate underwater. The need to communicate as much as possible prior to making a dive was emphasized in part one of this chapter. There are some standard signals used for communication which you need to know. The following will introduce you to some other means of communicating which work well for diving.

Standard Hand Signals   The NAUI Diving Hand Signals are standard in the diving community in the United States and are also recognized in many other countries as well. As a certified diver, you should be able to correctly identify and use each of them. Once you start using them, they will be easy to remember.

When hand signals are given, they should be displayed distinctly and acknowledged by repeating the sign or responding with the "OK" sign. In addition to standard hand signals, local and personal hand signals are popular. For improved communications, some divers learn sign language to expand their vocabulary for underwater communications. Hand signals should be reviewed before dives and in any new area.

Recreational Diving Hand Signals

OK!?   STOP   UP

DOWN   I'M OUT OF AIR   LET'S BUDDY BREATHE

DANGER   LOW ON AIR   HELP (SURFACE)

OK (SURFACE)   OK (SURFACE)   PICK ME UP (SURFACE)

Other Means of Communicating   There are a number of ways to communicate while diving, both at the surface and underwater. Let's examine the available means for each of these locations.

At the surface, various forms of visual and audible communication can be used. Some of the standard hand signals are surface signals. A diver should not wave to anyone while in the water because this is a distress signal.

Divers are occasionally recalled from a dive with a special flag, depicted below. When flown, it means that all divers who surface are to return to the exit point.

Audible communications are possible, although yelling is not effective for long distances over water. A whistle produces a sound which can be heard at considerable distance, and not much energy is required to produce the sound.

A repeated series of four short blasts on a whistle is the standard distress signal.

In addition to hand signals, underwater communications include written messages on underwater slates — a handy way to prevent a trip to the surface — communication by touching to gain someone's attention, or to let a diver know you are nearby, and audible signals. Sound signals include rapping on a tank to gain attention or the use of some noise-producing device to serve as a pre-arranged recall signal. If the recall signal is heard while underwater, you should surface and look to the exit point for instructions. It does not necessarily mean you should exit.

The key point to keep in mind is that in order to be effective, the signals to be used must be discussed and agreed upon before diving.

Top, Acknowledge signals given to you underwater. *Center*, Don't wave while at the surface . Waving is a diving distress signal. *Bottom*, The diver's recall flag, which is blue with a white center.

A slate is a helpful means of communicating.

Looking Back

1. List four means of communicating underwater.

A. _____

B. _____

C. _____

D. _____

2. List three means of communicating at the surface while diving.

A. _____

B. _____

C. _____

3. What action should you take when given a hand signal underwater? _____

_____

_____

A cramp can be relieved by quickly stretching the affected muscle. Massaging also helps.

4. What is the most important point regarding diving communications? _____

_____

_____

7.3   Diving Nuisances

A nuisance is defined as an annoyance, and that is just what the following diving nuisances are. If you will keep in mind that most problems can be overcome if you will stop to analyze them and cope with them calmly, you will also come to view perplexing situations as mere annoyances.

Cramps   Cold, exertion, restricted circulation, or a combination of these, can lead to cramps, which usually occur in the legs. Prevention is best. Avoid becoming chilled or exhausted, or wearing protective clothing which is too tight. If a cramp is experienced, the recommended action is to stretch the cramped muscle and massage it. For cramps in the calf or in the foot, it is usually effective to pull on the tip of the fin while straightening the leg, as shown in the photo. This stretches the muscles which usually cramp. Once a cramp has been removed, rest and recover, then proceed at a slower pace. It may also help to employ a different kick to help keep the cramp from returning.

Entanglements   Entanglements typically occur in plants, fishing line, or fishing nets. It is imperative to have a knife available so you can cut yourself free, but that should not be your first reaction to an entanglement. The first step is to determine where you are caught and, if possible, what the source is. You may be able to free yourself by pulling the plant, line, etc., clear or by getting your buddy to free you. Frequently, you can reverse direction and achieve freedom. Remember that you have buoyancy control, which allows you to move up and down, thus providing another dimension of movement. It is most important that you remain calm while working to free yourself.

One of the most likely points of entanglement is at the tank valve area on your scuba unit. Unfortunately, you cannot see this area. Your buddy can, though, so try to use his or her eyes

Remain calm if entangled. There is no rush, and hurrying only compounds the problem.

and hands to help you. If your buddy — for some reason — isn't near, you can free yourself. Avoid turning in the water while entangled. This will only make matters worse. The proper action is to remove your scuba unit, free it, and then don it again and proceed.

If none of the above actions clear you of an entanglement, then consider using a knife to cut yourself free, but use caution and work slowly and deliberately. Panic is your worst enemy, not temporary entanglement.

Equipment Problems These problems include equipment which is or becomes improperly adjusted, which comes undone, or which is lost while diving. A good diver can handle all of these nuisances, so you will want to learn how to handle them. Your instructor will help you develop this ability by giving you equipment problems to solve as your training progresses.

Nearly any piece of equipment can be adjusted while in the water. If you need to make an adjustment, think first about what needs to be done, then work slowly to make the adjustment. If you get excited and find yourself working hard, stop the activity, recover and think, and start

It is often easier to make equipment adjustments on the bottom than at the surface.

again slowly. Working with your gear in the water is good practice to keep many of your diving skills sharp.

Lost equipment could include mask, snorkel, fins, or weight belt. While each is valuable and needed for diving, you should be able to either recover a lost item and continue, or reach the surface and safely exit the water without the missing item. Practice swimming with missing items of equipment, and you will develop the techniques needed to allow you to handle this diving nuisance.

Air Starvation   This has been presented before, but because of its importance, we are going to re-emphasize it. Any time you find yourself feeling starved for air, or as if the regulator is not delivering enough air, stop what you are doing, relax, and concentrate on breathing slowly and deeply until you regain control of your breathing. The feeling of air starvation will pass.

Coughing and Choking Underwater   Breathing while in water can result in some water being inhaled, so you need to know how to handle a situation where you start coughing or choking. You should first know some steps you can take to minimize the possibility of choking. The first breath you take after clearing a snorkel or a regulator should be shallow and taken cautiously. You can also raise your tongue to the roof of your mouth to form a barrier to keep drops of water from going through your mouth and into your throat.

If you do cough, you can do so into a snorkel or a regulator. Keeping the mouthpiece in place while you recover can help you avoid drawing in more water and increasing the problem. If you will swallow several times in rapid succession,

your recovery will be quicker. The main idea is to develop trust in your regulator. You can cough or sneeze into it and through it. Instead of spitting it out, hold it in place. You will quickly learn how to avoid inhaling drops of water and how to recover if you do.

Temporary choking can occur if water tries to enter the windpipe leading to the lungs. For a few moments it may be difficult or impossible to breathe without considerable effort. Training without a face mask underwater usually conditions divers so this phenomenon is unlikely to occur. If it should, however, you must deliberately relax your body and wait for your airways to relax before resuming proper breathing.

Seasickness   This is definitely a nuisance. If you can avoid it by use of safe medication, do so. When the situation is serious, do not try to cure the problem by diving, which is frequently recommended by well-meaning divers. Vomiting underwater is hazardous and should be avoided if possible. Several recommendations to reduce problems caused by motion illness are included in the section on Boat Diving. These actions may help control the problem. A comforting note is that with time and experience most people adapt and overcome motion sickness.

Disorientation   Disorientation — not knowing where you are — can occur in several ways while diving. Sensory deprivation, especially in poor visibility or night diving, can produce feelings of dizziness or vertigo. Ear problems

If you choke on water, you can cough into the regulator until you recover.

Disorientation problems are rarely serious. The typical problem is not knowing your relative position when submerged.

and the inability to equalize easily while ascending are common contributors.

Novice divers should postpone night and poor visibility diving until they have acquired confidence through good visibility diving experiences. All divers need to exercise reasonable caution if they are aware of ear problems which might preclude the ability to equalize middle ear pressure. The most common vertigo occurs during ascent, when one ear equalizes more rapidly than the other. Understanding this phenomenon is important. Sensations of vertigo will pass in a few moments, but it is important that the diver not allow himself/herself to become excited or nervous due to lack of awareness that vertigo can and does occasionally occur.

The two most important actions to take if disorientation occurs are to overcome dizziness and discern which way is up. To overcome vertigo, hold onto some solid object or hug yourself until the dizziness passes. To discern which way is up, watch your bubbles or the position of a small amount of water in your mask.

Disorientation problems are rarely severe. The most likely problem you will face is not knowing your position underwater relative to the exit point. This can lead to the need for a long surface swim at the end of the dive. This type of disorientation can be avoided by use of natural and compass navigation, which are presented in the Skills chapter and further developed in your Advanced training. Develop the ability to know where you are and you are not likely to experience the nuisance of disorientation.

Being able to handle these annoyances without stress signifies you are a good, safe, skilled diver. By the time you complete your training, you should feel capable of handling the problems just described. This feeling of confidence will make you feel much more relaxed so you can more fully enjoy diving.

Looking Back

For each of the following nuisances, list at least one correct action you can take to overcome the problem.

1. Cramp in the leg _____

2. Entanglement _____

3. Air starvation _____

4. Choking _____

5. Lost item or gear _____

6. Extreme dizziness _____

7. What is the primary advantage of being able to cope with the nuisances described?_____
_____
_____

7.4 Helping Other Divers

In part three of this chapter, you learned how to take care of yourself by overcoming various nuisances which can occur while diving. As a diver, you have two responsibilities to your buddy: the first is to keep problems from occurring, and the second is to help your partner overcome any problems that occur. Problems may be classified as either minor or emergency. The following paragraphs describe how to assist a buddy in overcoming minor problems. In the next part of this chapter, you will learn how to

When you feel competent you enjoy diving the most.

perform rescues in emergency situations. While the situations described are rare and should be prevented before they occur, you need to know what to do, just in case.

The Three Primary Steps   Even though it seems strange, most diving problems occur at the surface rather than underwater. If your buddy is in distress at the surface, there are three actions you should take to assist. First, help your companion establish buoyancy. There are several ways to do this. If you can instruct your buddy to get buoyant and obtain a correct response, that is best. If your partner does not respond to instructions, extending a surface float to him or her is an excellent alternative method of quickly providing buoyancy. When neither of these options is workable, you will need to use

the person's weight belt and/or BC to fulfill your task. Approach your buddy from the left side or from the back and try to inflate the BC with the low pressure inflator. If unsuccessful, reach around the person, release the weight belt, pull it clear and discard it. Work from a position where your companion cannot easily grasp you. Once your companion has become buoyant, move out of touching distance and proceed to step two.

The second step is to get your buddy to rest and breathe deeply. Have your buddy discard any hand-carried items or give them to you so you can discard them if necessary. Give assurance and encouragement. Help your buddy recover and overcome the difficulty without your direct help if possible. Be buoyant yourself and remember to control your own level

A

B

C

Top, To assist another diver, first get the person buoyant or provide buoyancy.
Center, If you want to inflate another diver's BC, do it from behind.
Bottom, When the troubled diver is buoyant, try to get him/her to take it easy and regain control.

Two versions of the tired swimmer's carry — with the hands on the shoulders and with the fins on the shoulders. The biceps push (C) is also an effective assist.

of exertion. Your main task is to remain close to your buddy and give optimistic encouragement and advice.

The third step is to provide assistance as needed. You are first to try to get your buddy to solve his or her own problems. If this isn't possible, or if your directions are not followed, you will need to provide assistance. Your help may consist of working out a cramp, solving an equipment problem, or assisting the person to the exit point.

If you need to help your buddy through the water, various swimming assists and tows can be used. Two variations of the "Tired Swimmer's Carry" are shown in the photos. If your partner does not feel comfortable with this arrangement, he or she can be moved by grasping the upper arm as shown and pushing the person along. This assist provides control and allows good eye and voice communication between you and your buddy. A diver should not be allowed to swim to the shore or boat alone. You and your buddy should practice swimming assists from time to time. You need to learn how to function as both the diver needing assistance and as the one providing it.

Looking Back

Briefly summarize the three rules for assisting a distressed diver.

1. _____
2. _____
3. _____

7.5 Diving Rescues

Most of the time divers can keep themselves out of trouble. If not, they can overcome their problems independently or with help from their buddies. Most emergencies in the water are preventable, and many occur because divers violate the rules of safe diving. You must be aware of the fundamentals of rescuing an incapacitated diver even though it is unlikely you will have to apply what you learn. If it should be necessary for you to rescue someone, at least you will have some idea about how to proceed.

Administering mouth-to-mouth artificial respiration in the water. Note how the "victim" is signaling "OK" during the exercise to let everyone know that no actual emergency exists.

Further training in diver rescue techniques is included in NAUI continuing education courses and is recommended.

You should have some training in first aid and in artificial respiration. Everyone — diver or not — should be prepared to administer first aid, especially Cardiopulmonary Resuscitation (CPR). If you have not taken courses to acquire these skills, or have not refreshed your knowledge for years, you should complete the programs which are readily available to the public through the American National Red Cross and the Heart Association.

One kind of diving emergency is where a diver is unconscious and perhaps not breathing. Possible causes include drowning, a lung expansion injury, a head injury, or drugs in the system. Such injuries are rare, but you need to be able to help if your buddy or another diver is unable to care for himself or herself.

Unconscious Diver at the Surface   If the person is unconscious at the surface, you should make contact with him or her and establish buoyancy for yourself, then pull the person to a face-up position and establish buoyancy for him or her. This can be accomplished by ditching the weight belt and inflating the BC if more buoyancy is required. The victim's mask should be removed, and you should ensure that he/she is breathing. If the victim is not breathing, call for assistance and administer artificial respiration as shown in the photos and as taught by your NAUI Instructor. The ventilations must be continued as you transport the victim to the exit point. If the distance to assistance is very long, consider ditching the victim's tank. Since this can be time consuming, tank ditching should be done only if necessary. It is best to wait for assistance before removing someone from the water unless the person requires CPR (see Appendix), which cannot be administered effectively in the water. Training and practice are needed to be proficient at in-water artificial respiration. You will learn the basics of it in this course.

If unconsciousness occurs underwater, your primary concern must be transporting the victim to the surface. If the diver is breathing, simply

Above, Surfacing an unconscious diver. The most important thing is to get the person to the surface.
Below, You will learn the basics of in-water artificial respiration as part of your NAUI training.

hold the regulator in place while you swim the person to the surface. If the regulator has fallen out of the victim's mouth, leave it out. You will probably have to make the person buoyant in order to swim him or her up without overexerting. This can be accomplished by inflating the BC or ditching the weight belt.

During the ascent, hold onto the victim. Don't worry about expanding air inside the victim's lungs; it will escape naturally from an unconscious person. Your major concern is to bring the victim to the surface where you can administer first aid. Do not waste time worrying about trapped air in the lungs. Upon reaching the surface, turn the victim to a face-up position, open the airway by tilting the head back, and check for breathing. If the diver is not breathing, begin artificial respiration immediately.

In-Water Artificial Respiration With the victim at the surface and buoyant, hold the victim with one hand while using your other hand to push the person's head back and open the airway. The mouth should be quickly checked to be sure it is clear of obstructions. The person's head can be turned slightly toward you to make it easier to seal your mouth over his or hers for mouth-to-mouth respiration. After the customary two full breaths, ventilations are continued at a rate of 12 breaths per minute — one every five seconds. Again, training in first aid, CPR, lifesaving, and diver rescue will be helpful and is recommended. Care must be taken to prevent water from entering the victim's mouth and being blown into the lungs. Unless the distance to shore or a boat is short, emphasis should be placed on keeping water out of the diver's lungs and on maintaining mouth-to-mouth resuscitation rather than on rapidly transporting the victim without attempts to ventilate. You will have to learn to pace yourself so you will not become too exhausted to be of assistance. By the end of your entry level course, you will be able to perform the fundamentals of in-water artificial respiration, but additional training and practice will be required for you to become proficient. Even your NAUI Instructor has to practice regularly to maintain skill proficiency.

Looking Back

The following points emphasize the important aspects of handling diving emergencies:

1. According to the section just completed, what is a diving emergency, by definition?_____

_____

2. List four types of emergency training recommended in this chapter.

A. _____

B. _____

C. _____

D. _____

3. What is the first action you should take when providing assistance to an unconscious diver at the surface?_____

_____

4. How do you prevent a lung expansion injury in an unconscious person when bringing him or her to the surface?_____

_____

5. What are the two most important points regarding in-water artificial respiration?

A. _____

B. _____

7.6   Emergencies and First Aid

To be a qualified buddy, you must be able to assist your partner, rescue him or her, render proper first aid, and manage an emergency situation. While few diving accidents are life-threatening, just as in most physical activities, injuries do occur. You need to be prepared to cope with injuries ranging from cuts and bruises to wounds from aquatic animals to respiratory and cardiac arrest. You may be the only person available to offer immediate assistance.

Being Prepared   To be prepared to handle emergency situations, you need training, emergency equipment, emergency contact informa-

Training and frequent practice are required to perform effective rescues.

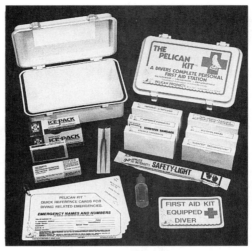

A commercially produced Diver's First Aid Kit is available in dive stores.

tion and plans, and the determination to take action.

An overview of emergency training was presented earlier in this chapter. You should strive to update your training in first aid, CPR, and diving rescue techniques periodically. Practicing with your dive buddy several times a year is a good way to keep emergency skills sharp. It is surprising how quickly an ability is lost if it is not applied occasionally.

Equipment for emergencies can be extensive, but as a minimum, you should have a first aid kit available. Recommendations for the contents of a kit are listed in the Appendix. Several first aid kits designed especially for diving are available on the market. Other useful equipment includes a continuous-flow oxygen unit (oxygen is extremely valuable for the treatment of serious diving injuries), cloth or space blanket, and a supply of clean fresh water. Your emergency equipment should be ready at the dive site and be replaced promptly after use.

Oxygen is extremely valuable as part of first aid treatment for serious diving injuries, such as air embolism, bends, and near drowning. Some states prohibit the use of oxygen resuscitators by non-medically trained personnel. However, continuous flow units are readily available, and

may be used without restriction. Dive boats are usually equipped with emergency oxygen systems. Check with your instructor about the laws in your area. NAUI believes oxygen is vital in effecting first aid on site as recommended by diving medical advisors.

You need to know how to call for help. In some areas, a special number is available for reporting a diving emergency. In most regions, however, you will need to know who to call for medical attention, for recompression treatment in a chamber, or for other emergency needs. There is a nationwide emergency network of hyperbaric chambers and diving physicians that can help provide consultation, transportation, and treatment through a single emergency telephone number. The network is known as DAN — Divers Alert Network — and the 24-hour emergency number is (919) 684-8111. You should acquire local emergency contact information for diving. Write these numbers and the DAN number on a card, tape coins for calls to the card, and include it in your first aid kit.

The last requirement for preparation is the determination to act in an emergency. People tend to stand and watch as an accident occurs. You must decide in advance that you are going to take action if present at the scene of a diving accident.

Basic First Aid Procedures

First aid should include the following:

1. A quick examination of the victim to determine the nature and extent of the injuries.

2. Treatment for life-threatening emergencies such as cessation of breathing.

3. Treatment for less serious injuries and shock.

4. Arrangement for medical care and transport.

There are five major injury categories for which you should be prepared to administer first aid. You must be able to stop severe bleeding, maintain respiration if a person has stopped breathing, maintain circulation if a person's heart has stopped, treat for shock (a factor in all serious injuries) and render first aid for serious diving accidents (such as lung expansion injuries and decompression sickness). Emergency training will teach you how to properly respond in the first four areas.

First aid for air embolism and decompression illness includes laying the victim down, maintaining respiration and circulation, treating for shock, administering oxygen (if available), constantly monitoring the patient, and transporting to the nearest recompression chamber.

NAUI recommends that you participate in a NAUI Rescue Techniques course where you can learn and practice how to handle accident management.

Aquatic Life Injuries   General first aid training does not cover this area. Here are some general guidelines. These are intended only to make you aware that you need to find out from local diving instructors how to treat injuries which you could receive from aquatic animals in places you may dive.

Aquatic life injuries are classified in three major categories: Punctures, stings and bites. Puncture wounds can be caused by sea urchins, spiny fish, or sting rays. If possible, any material in the wound should be removed. Toxin may be injected and should be treated by soaking the wounded area in water as hot as can be tolerated for a period of 20 minutes. Just as some individuals are allergic to bee stings, some divers may be hypersensitive to marine wounds. Medical attention is recommended.

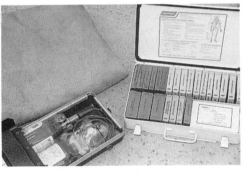

Emergency equipment — first aid kit, oxygen, and a blanket.

First aid for stings, such as those from jellyfish or coral, includes removal of the stinging materials, application of vinegar or diluted ammonia, and application of a baking soda paste. Medical attention is required if the injury is serious or if the victim shows signs or symptoms of allergic reaction.

If a diver is bitten by an aquatic animal, first aid can range from the control of bleeding to simple antiseptic cleaning of the wound. Medical attention is required if the injury is serious or if the patient shows signs or symptoms of allergic reaction.

Aquatic life injuries are as varied as the diving environment. You need to know what wounds

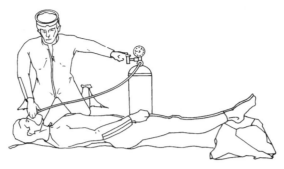

Top, *First aid procedures for a seriously injured diver.*
Center, *Learn the first aid procedures for the marine life in the area where you will be diving.*
Bottom, *Rescue Diver is one of the specialty ratings required for the NAUI Master Scuba Diver rating.*

are likely to occur in a given area and the first aid for them. Even more important, learn how to avoid being wounded.

Looking Back

1. What are the four requirements to be met in being prepared for a diving emergency?

A. _____

B. _____

C. _____

D. _____

2. List two recommended actions, in addition to completing emergency training courses, to ensure your skills will be adequate for a diving emergency.

A. _____

B. _____

3. List four recommended items of first aid equipment for diving emergencies.

A. _____

B. _____

C. _____

D. _____

4. What are the name and telephone number of the national network for diving emergencies?

_____

_____

5. Briefly describe first aid procedures for an unconscious diver. _____

_____

7.7   Safety in Summary

What is the overall impression you have of diving safety thus far? Do you feel it is primarily a matter of knowing the rules and following them and of being prepared? If so, your conception is correct. Having an awareness of safe diving practices — both generally and locally — and having the desire to follow them, will do more than anything else to ensure your safety. If something unexpected should occur, being prepared to deal with it can make it inconvenient rather than insurmountable.

Diving safety is, first of all, an attitude.

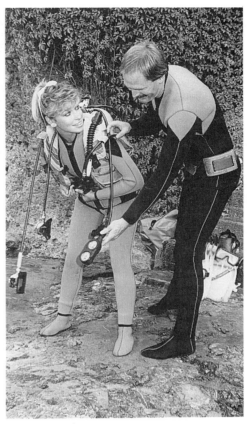

If you will follow safe diving practices, there is little to fear in diving.

Diving safety is primarily an attitude. When a diver respects the environment, wants to be properly prepared for diving and for emergencies, wants to follow the buddy system and other safe diving practices, safety is simply a by-product of the attitude. You must develop a desire to abide by NAUI Safe Diving Practices, which will be presented in the following paragraphs (and which are summarized in the Appendix). By applying these principles, you will see for yourself that the saying, "Diving safety is no accident," is not merely a play on words.

Safe Scuba Diving Practices   You need to be trained for what you do in diving. You must resist the temptation to teach others unless you become certified as a NAUI Instructor. Your training should continue with advanced and specialty courses as well as refresher courses to keep your knowledge and skills current.

Only dive when feeling well, both mentally and physically. A regular physical exam by a diving doctor is recommended. Do not dive under the influence of drugs, including alcohol. Keep yourself in good physical condition, know your limits, dive within them, and maintain a reserve of energy and air as a margin of safety. If you become cold, tired, ill, or low on air while diving, exit the water to be safe.

Your equipment must be maintained properly and checked before each dive. Have it serviced professionally as recommended. Use all recommended equipment when diving. Be properly weighted when diving and avoid diving overweighted. Do not loan your equipment to friends who are not certified to dive.

Know the location where you will be diving. Respect the environment and avoid dangerous dive sites and poor conditions. Fly the dive flag to warn boaters of your presence, then dive near the flag. Exercise moderation with regard to depth and time limits.

Stick to your plans. Do not exceed agreed-upon limits for time and depth.

Take the time to properly plan your dive, then follow your plan. Know the rules of the buddy system and abide by them for enjoyment as well as safety. Dive regularly or renew your skills before diving after a period of inactivity. Your dives should be logged to help you remember details and experiences.

When you look at all the things you have to do to dive safely, they may seem overwhelming. It is similar to driving a car. You have to learn and practice a great many things in order to drive safely, but as you apply the correct principles, it soon becomes second nature and does not require a great deal of effort. It is the same with diving safety. If you will take the time to follow the safe diving practices presented by your NAUI Instructor from the outset of your training, they will soon become part of your routine procedure and will be accomplished with little effort. Make this your goal now and you will set yourself on a safe course through the hazards of diving. Safety is an attitude. This is reflected in the NAUI motto, "Safety Through Education."

SECTION 3

Get involved with a dive club or other divers in your area as soon as you complete your course.

Looking Ahead

By now you have acquired or nearly acquired the knowledge, skills and experience to allow you to safely scuba dive. Your dream of being able to parallel the adventures of an astronaut is becoming a reality. You are about to acquire NAUI credentials which will be your passport to the underwater world. It has taken study and physical effort to develop the needed ability. You can be proud of all you have accomplished. It is now time to look ahead. What should you do after you have obtained certification? What can you do to increase your skills and to keep informed? To what activities will you apply your diving ability? Let's find out what is available.

Involvement We recommend you become involved with other divers right away. Local dive clubs are an excellent means to find diving companions, learn about the local area and be introduced to many diving activities. Be sure to inquire about joining a dive club in your area.

For a larger perspective on diving and to get involved as part of a national organization of divers, we recommend you join the NAUI Diving Association (NDA). This provides you with an excellent news magazine, offers educational programs and an international conference, saves you money and identifies you as part of a large, collective voice of recreational divers. You will receive an application to join NDA. Join

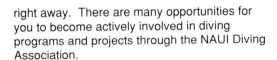

The NAUI Diving Association is a good source of information and educational products. You should join as soon as possible to keep in touch with the latest developments in diving.

right away. There are many opportunities for you to become actively involved in diving programs and projects through the NAUI Diving Association.

Developing a Special Interest   It is exciting to don scuba equipment and explore the world beneath the surface of the water, but you will soon find that diving is really a means to allow you to do something in the underwater world rather than being an end in itself. Soon you will want to inspect old wrecks, take pictures, take game, collect things, find treasure or dive in unusual places. Such challenges make diving exciting and rewarding. Specialty areas can be learned much more quickly and easily through training than by trial and error.

One of the reasons you should get involved with local divers and with NDA is to learn what the special diving interests are in your area and how to be introduced to them. When you have an underwater objective, your enthusiasm for

Specialty diving is exciting and rewarding.

diving will multiply many times over and you will have some of the best times of your life developing and refining your interest area.

There is little to compare with the feeling of accomplishing a goal you have set in the underwater world. Getting the perfect picture of

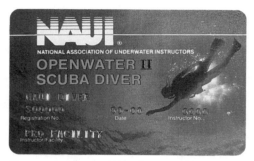

Your next goal - the NAUI Openwater II rating to increase your skills and experience.

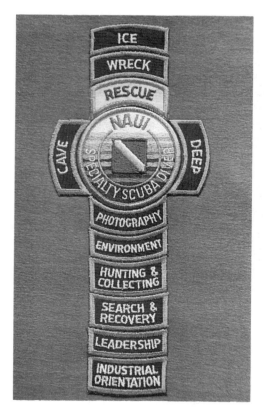

Develop interests through professional NAUI Specialty training.

an elusive subject, finding a rare object, locating an ancient wreck, or capturing a prize fish for your home aquarium. Imagine the excitement and satisfaction you can experience, then realize that relatively few people learn how to dive and will never feel the exhilaration you experience because of your success in "inner space." Diving can provide some of the most cherished moments of your life, and these moments are usually related to a special interest area. Learn about the "special" activities of diving, and get involved.

Additional Training   The best way to remain involved in diving after this course is to continue your diving education. We hope you realize that while you will be prepared as an Openwater I diver to dive unsupervised under conditions similar to those encountered during your entry level course, there are many other aspects of diving you need to learn or to further develop. You should consider your initial certification as a "License to Learn" how to dive. Experience and additional training are needed.

To gain diving experience, an orientation to a variety of dive sites in an area, and an opportunity to meet new diving friends, you might want to take the NAUI Openwater II course. This is a dive oriented, 12-hour course offering six open water scuba dives and an environmental orientation to some of the special dive sites in your area.

When you have completed the Openwater II program, we suggest the NAUI Advanced Scuba Diver course. This provides you with an additional eight supervised dives, acquisition of other useful skills, amplification of knowledge and further introductions to specialties. Underwater navigation, limited visibility or night diving, search and recovery, light salvage techniques and deep diving procedures are included. Every diver should graduate from an Advanced Diver course. At this level, you have the knowledge, skills and ability to safely enjoy diving in a variety of conditions and locations. All that remains is for you to get specialty training in at least one specialty course.

You can learn diving specialties by taking a NAUI sanctioned course or by attending the school of experience. While experience is said to be a good teacher, it frequently gives you the test before the lesson. This results in frustration and wasted time. It can also be unsafe. To get the most from a diving specialty and to get it as quickly as possible in today's fast-paced world, complete a NAUI specialty course. This way you will quickly achieve success in your endeavor and will be able to take advantage of your NAUI Instructor's years of experience in your area of interest.

With the acquisition of Advanced and Specialty ratings, you will probably want to seek the highest non-instructional rating in recreational diving — the NAUI Master Scuba Diver rating. You'll need a year of experience plus a minimum of 25 logged dives, but you can set it as your goal right now.

Perhaps you will want to get involved in a leadership role in diving. This is a special interest area not yet mentioned, but it is one of the best. It is personally rewarding to help others realize the dream of becoming a diver or of having an underwater adventure. NAUI has the finest leadership programs and training

available. If you find that diving becomes more than a hobby to you, keep in mind that through NAUI there are many opportunities to work as a professional. By becoming qualified as a NAUI Divemaster or Instructor, you can profit from your diving ability, training and experience. Your instructor is an example of this and he or she will be glad to provide you with information on leadership training programs.

Diving is constantly changing. Equipment is constantly being improved and new types are being developed. Physiological discoveries keep changing our understanding of the effects of pressure upon us. Continuing education is important. You should belong to NDA, subscribe to diving magazines, attend diving seminars and conferences, take refresher courses every year or two and obtain the highest level of certification possible. Get all the training for diving you can so you will be able to get all the diving you can from your training.

Leadership ratings aren't for everyone, but you may aspire to become an instructor. NAUI offers several leadership ratings.

With good equipment, a good buddy, and proper preparation, you are ready for a great time.

Words can't describe the feelings. Welcome to NAUI's world - "Inner space."

Responsibilities   When you are certified as a NAUI diver, you will continue to learn about diving through your diving experiences. Bear in mind that you have certain responsibilities to yourself, to your buddy and to others. The following is a partial list of what is expected of you as a NAUI diver:

1. Keep yourself mentally and physically fit for diving.

2. Continue your diving education.

3. Use complete, correct, well maintained equipment.

5. Know your dive site and avoid or abort diving in hazardous conditions.

6. Be prepared to handle emergencies.

7. Always dive with a buddy and remain together while diving.

8. Avoid running low on air, control buoyancy at all times and ascend properly.

9. Keep conservation in mind with regards to the environment.

10. Demonstrate proper etiquette to boaters, fishermen and the general public.

Now it is time to look ahead to fun, adventure, and all of the excitement you envisioned when you started this course. That strange, wonderful world of "inner space" is now accessible to you and waiting for you to enter. Enjoy yourself and fulfill your responsibilities as a NAUI diver. We look forward to working with you again soon in your next NAUI course.

Answers to Review Questions

1.1 The Primary Items

1. Fit, comfort
2. Purge valve
3. Small inside diameter, sharp bends, excessive length

1.2 Scuba Equipment

1.

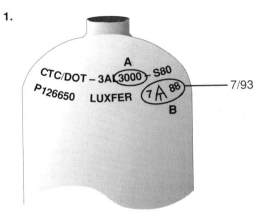

2. Tank, tank valve, regulator, extra second stage
3. J valve is a reserve valve; K valve is a non-reserve valve
4. Regulator hose, submersible pressure gauge hose, extra second stage hose, BC low pressure inflator hose
5. Ease of breathing
6. Depressing purge button while rinsing regulator
7. Extra second stage, redundant or back up scuba unit. Extra second stage is used more frequently. Redundant scuba unit.

1.3 Buoyancy Systems

1. Horse collar - C, Back flotation - B, Buoyancy jacket - A
2. C, low pressure inflator
3. Salt water, dirty water, or chlorinated water inside the BC will cause damage

1.4 Weighting Systems

1. The quick release
2. To keep the weight belt fitting snugly on a diver when the diver's suit is compressed by pressure

3. An integrated weight system requires maintenance to keep the release mechanism functioning properly

1.5 Protective Clothing

1. Heat loss, cuts, scrapes, stings, and other injuries
2. Dry suits are warmer because water is excluded and the diver is insulated by a layer of air as well as insulation
3. Dry suits require more weight than wet suits
4. A hood is of greatest value

1.6 Diving Instruments

1. Capillary gauge
2. Initially and occasionally
3. A pressure activated switch automatically starts and stops the timer as you descend and ascend
4. Timing device, depth gauge, compass, and submersible pressure gauge

1.7 Diving Accessories

1. To cut rope or line under water
2. To display the flag only while diving and to dive near by the flag
3. May be required for proof of recent experience; for documentation of diving experience for leadership positions or ratings
4. Underwater slate, game bag, underwater light, marker buoy, spare parts

2.1 Water Compared to Air

1. 20% oxygen, nitrogen
2. False
3. False
4. 6.4 pounds (.08 x 80)
5. By streamlining to reduce cross-sectional area
6. Since air increases in density as depth increases, there is more resistance to the movement of air for breathing
7. A. Water conducts heat rapidly
   B. Water has a greater capacity to absorb heat

2.2 Pressure

1. 34, 33
2. Five
3. Three atmospheres

2.3 The Primary Effects of Pressure

Pressure	Volume	Density
Doubles	Halves	Doubles
Triples	One-third	Triples
Halves	Doubles	Halves
Quadruples	One-fourth	Quadruples

2.4 Buoyancy

1. Volume of the object, density of the object, density of the water
2. Change amount of weight worn; change amount of air in BC; changing amount of air in the lungs; changing equipment worn
3. Decrease
4. Remove weight

2.5 Thermal Effects

1. Conduction and respiration
2. Lowering the temperature of the air
3. The saliva reduces the surface tension of water so it does not allow beads of moisture to form on the mask lens
4. To prevent dehydration which can be caused by breathing dry scuba air
5. As the temperature increases, the pressure inside a scuba tank will increase

2.6 Other Effects of Water

1. Larger, closer
2. The diver would not be able to determine the direction from which the sound was coming
3. Cold numbs your sense of touch, and you will be wearing gloves

2.7 Air Consumption

1. Depth, activity, body temperature, lung volume, anxiety, breathing habits
2. 29 psi per minute (1300/20 = 65 X 33 /40+33 = 29)
3. To determine when your breathing rate stabilizes, to be able to estimate the duration of your air supply, or to learn how factors affect your breathing rate

3.1 Your Body in Depth

1. Ears, sinuses, and lungs
2. It would be difficult or impossible to equalize pressure in your sinuses

3. Exhale into your mask to equalize pressure in it and eliminate the mask squeeze

3.2 Equalization of Pressure

1. Squeeze
2. A. Sudden, extreme vertigo
   B. Ear infection
   C. Permanent hearing loss
3. Swollen or congested sinuses as when you have a cold
4. Mask squeeze
5. The most common ear clearing technique, known as the Valsalva method, is attempted exhalation against closed nose and mouth
6. Failing to equalize pressure in ears during descent, and by means of a very forceful Valsalva maneuver

3.3 Air Expansion Problems

1. Reverse block
2. Prevention
3. Holding your breath or not breathing properly
4. Neutral

3.4 Respiration and Circulation

1. Carbon dioxide
2. c. Slow and deep
3. Stop all activity, rest, and breathe deeply
4. Keep the regulator in place

3.5 Thermal Considerations

1. Conduction and respiration
2. Insulation, eating well two hours before diving, moderate exercise while diving
3. Shivering
4. Recommended: Warm, dry clothing, warm drinks, warm bath. Not recommended: alcoholic drinks, warm bath after deep dive

3.6 Secondary Effects of Pressure

1. Have tanks filled with compressed air only
2. Have tanks filled at a reputable air station
3. Dive within time and depth limits for various depths
4. Limit diving to depths shallower than 100 feet
5. Ascend to shallower water
6. Cold, shorter duration, narcosis, decompression sickness

3.7 Health and Fitness Considerations

1. You must be able to perform at full capacity while diving
2. A woman should not dive when pregnant or when effects of menstruation are bothersome
3. False
4. Dive regularly
5. Medications only mask the symptoms of your illness, but the illness still exists, affects your physiology, and can be hazardous.

4.1 The Varying Environment

1. Temperature, visibility, currents, plants, water movement, animals, seasons, weather, bottom formations, shoreline configuration, and bottom composition
2. Can reduce visibility, can change temperature of the water, can set water in motion, can affect dive procedures, can affect the activity of the dive, can affect equipment used or needed
3. Dive new areas under supervision, learn in advance as much as possible about a new diving area, be trained for specialized diving

4.2 The Water

1. An abrupt transition from a warmer layer of water to a colder layer of water
2. Locality, season, weather, water movement, bottom composition
3. Disorientation

4.3 Water Movement

1. Tides, gravity, winds, earth's rotation
2. False
3. True
4. Swim parallel to shore until clear of the current

4.4 The Bottom

1. An extension of the shoreline formation, charts, other divers
2. Entry and exit techniques, activity of the dive, anti-silting techniques, amount of swimming required during dive, amount of life encountered
3. Mud and silt are easily stirred and reduce visibility
Sandy bottoms are relatively barren.
Rocks provide a good base for animals and plants.

Coral can cut and sting a diver.
Each type affects entry and exit techniques.

4.5 Aquatic Life

1. False
2. A. Learn to identify hazardous life forms in the area where you will be diving
   B. Move slowly and look carefully while diving
   C. Stay clear of that which can hurt you
   D. If you don't know what something is, don't touch it
3. Helps you know what to look for; helps you know where to look for it
4. What you take has an impact on what will be available in the future

4.6 Boat Diving

1. Go with an experienced diver or group to learn correct techniques; study boat diving procedures and get training if possible.
2. A. Take suitable medication
   B. Get fresh air
   C. Watch the horizon
   D. Stay near the center of the boat
   E. Lie down with your eyes closed
3. Training in boat operations and seamanship

4.7 Other Considerations

1. A. Use sun screening lotion
   B. Keep out of sun as much as possible
   C. Wear protective clothing
2. A. Learn of possible entanglements
   B. Be on the lookout for possible entanglements
   C. Advanced planning
3. A. Display the dive flag
   B. Dive in the vicinity of the dive flag
   C. Pause during ascent to listen for approaching boats

5.1 Nitrogen Absorption and Elimination

1. Ingassing is the process of accumulating increased nitrogen in the body under greater than normal pressures
2. Bubble formation occurs during outgassing when the pressure is reduced faster than the excess gas can be eliminated from the body
3. 20 feet (6 m)
4. 55 minutes

5. Nitrogen in excess of normal levels remaining in your body after diving

5.2 Dive Table Terms and Rules

Terms:
1. 60'/30 (18m/30)
2. 1:25, 2:20
3. 55 minutes
4. With a letter group designation
5. 15' (5m), 3
Rules:
1. 60 (18 m) 10
2. 60'/30, 50'/20, 30'/40 (18m/30, 15m/20, 9m/40)
3. 40'/40 (12m/40)

5.3 Finding Time Limits

1. 31 mins.   2. 2:29   3. 60 feet (18 m)

5.4 Using the NAUI Dive Time Calculator

(Answers provided with the questions)

5.5 The Worksheet

(Exercise is to be reviewed in class with instructor)

5.6 Special Rules and Sample Problems

1. A precautionary decompression stop is recommended for every dive.
2. 10 minutes
3. 80'/30 (24m/30)
4. 24 hours
5. 1,000 feet

5.7 Using Dive Computers

1. Shallowest depth, ascend
2. 20 feet (6 m)
3. 100 feet (30 m)
4. False

6.1 Use of Mask, Snorkel and Fins

1. Shuffle fins while walking backwards
2. Sit down, steady yourself by holding onto someone or something with one hand
3. The head is tilted forward when clearing a purge valve mask so the purge will be the lowest point in the mask and so the water will flow out at that point
4. Blast method, displacement method, and removing the mouthpiece to pour out the water (not recommended)
5. Displacement method
6. You should not swim with rapid, short kick strokes, bend the knees sharply, swim rapidly, swim with your arms, kick your feet above the surface of the water

6.2 Use of Scuba

1. The opening in the valve should be oriented toward the pack; the band must hold the tank securely so the tank cannot slip; and the pack must be mounted at the correct height on the tank
2. The regulator should be mounted so the regulator hose will come over the user's right shoulder
3. Counter-clockwise
4. Have your buddy assist you; place the hoses on your shoulders so they will not be trapped under the strap when the waistband is secured; bend forward and balance the tank on your back when working with the straps; test the height adjustment
5. Blow a continuous stream of small bubbles so you will not be holding your breath with compressed air in your lungs
6. Exhalation; use of purge valve
7. Two, except receiver may take up to four during initial exchange
8. Do not seal your mouth around the regulator when breathing from a free flowing regulator

6.3 The Downs and Ups of Diving

1. Exchange snorkel for regulator; note the time; deflate BC
2. Maintain eye-to-eye contact with buddy; equalize pressure in air spaces often; control buoyancy; control rate of descent
3. Signal buddy; agree to ascend; note time; look up; reach up; swim up; control buoyancy; ascend at 60 feet per minute
4. You and your buddy should agree before the dive which regulator is to be used
5. Recent practice with the person with whom you may need to buddy breathe
6. When no source of air is available and the depth is greater than 40 feet

6.4 Controlling Buoyancy

1. Amount of weight; distribution of weights on belt for balance; amount of excess strap; means to prevent slipping of weights

2. The weight belt must be clear for removal in an emergency; the belt should be donned so the release operates right-handed

3. A. Deflate BC completely
   B. Have lungs full of air
   C. Hang upright and motionless in the water
   D. Adjust weights to float at eye level with lungs full and to sink only when lungs are empty.

4. A. Amount of weight worn
   B. Amount of air in BC
   C. Amount of air in your lungs
   D. Object picked up and carried
   E. Suit compression at depth

5. Exhale completely, swim down to overcome buoyancy, invert and dump air from BC

6.5 Entries and Exits

1. A. Air supply: valve, regulator hose orientation, regulator function, submersible pressure gauge, tank security in pack
   B. Buoyancy compensator: low pressure connected, function, operation of controls, partially inflated
   C. Weight belt: clear for ditching, right-hand release, no hoses trapped underneath

2. A. BC should be partially inflated
   B. Mask should be held firmly
   C. Breathe from regulator during entry
   D. Be sure entry area is clear and sufficiently deep

3. The objective of an entry is to get yourself into the water with a minimum amount of effort and a minimal effect on you and your equipment.

4. A. Use Giant Stride when the distance to the water is several feet
   B. Use a Back Roll entry from a low, unstable platform or small boat
   C. Use Seated Entry whenever you can sit at the edge of the water and lower yourself into the water

5. A. Determine when it is best to don fins for the location
   B. Shuffle feet along bottom rather than stepping
   C. Lie down and swim as soon as possible

D. Time the entry to coincide with a lull in wave action
   E. Trail float behind with a line

6. A. Don't take tank off without disconnecting low pressure hose to a horse collar type BC
   B. Don't remove fins until absolutely necessary
   C. Don't exit with items in your hands
   D. Don't talk about dive until out of the water
   E. Don't tarry at the exit point after exiting water

6.6 Gear Handling in the Water

1. You want to be positively buoyant at the surface and negatively buoyant at the bottom

2. Have hose entirely inside your arms

3. A. Hold the belt close to your midsection
   B. Assume a facedown position so gravity will keep the belt in position across your back

4. A. Orient into correct position, then grasp strap on both sides
   B. Place seat of mask on forehead and hook strap over back of head
   C. Position mask on face, then clear area under skirt
   D. Clear water from the mask
   E. Reposition strap

6.7 Open Water Skills

1. A. Discuss dive beforehand and coordinate
   B. Maintain a general heading until both agree on new direction
   C. Maintain same relative position with respect to one another

2. A. Search briefly
   B. Ascend a few feet and look for bubbles
   C. Total search time not to exceed one minute
   D. Surface and wait for buddy

3. A. Sunlight
   B. Ripples
   C. Natural formations

4. A. The lubber line of the compass must be aligned with the center line of your body
   B. Have a reference setting on the compass
   C. Look over a compass rather than down on it

5. A reciprocal course is a heading 180 degrees from an original heading, e.g., in the opposite direction from which you started.

6. Submersible pressure gauge; depth gauge; timing device

7.1 Planning Your Dives

1. A. To have the best possible time
   B. To have a safe experience
   C. Having all equipment in good working order
   D. Avoid last minute rushing
2. A. Determine purpose of the dive
   B. Select dive buddy
   C. Determine location plus alternate
   D. Research dive site if it is unfamiliar
   E. Select date and time for the dive; schedule on calendar
   F. Make any necessary reservations
   G. Obtain emergency contact information
   H. Determine needed equipment
   I. Inspect equipment to ensure readiness
   J. Purchase advance items (tickets, air, film, license)
   K. Inventory spare parts kit
   L. Check long-range weather forecast
3. A. Check weather and water conditions
   B. Ensure you are physically and mentally ready to go diving
   C. Collect all equipment and use checklist to prevent omissions
   D. Pack equipment in reverse order in which it will be used
   E. Pack personal items in separate bag from dive gear
   F. Leave information on destination and ETR with someone
4. Evaluation of diving conditions to determine suitability for diving
5. A. Decide who will be in charge of the dive
   B. Review hand signals
   C. Agree on the general course to be followed on the dive
   D. Agree on entry and exit locations and techniques
   E. Agree on emergency procedures

7.2 Communications

1. Hand signals, sign language, underwater slate and pencil, tank rapping, noise-producing device, touch
2. Hand signals, flags, whistle, voice
3. Acknowledge the signal by repeating it or responding with "OK"

4. Signals must be reviewed and agreed upon before diving

7.3 Diving Nuisances

1. Stretch and massage cramped muscle; proceed slowly with different swimming stroke after recovery
2. Determine where you are caught, try to get clear by reversing direction or sinking, try removing scuba unit, cut yourself free with knife as last resort
3. Stop all activity, rest and breathe deeply
4. Keep mouthpiece in place, swallow several times in rapid succession
5. Recover lost item if possible or surface and exit water
6. Hold onto a solid object or hug yourself until the dizziness passes
7. A feeling of confidence helps you relax so you can enjoy diving

7.4 Helping Other Divers

1. Establish buoyancy
2. Help diver overcome difficulty if possible
3. Provide assistance as needed

7.5 Diving Rescues

1. When a diver is unconscious and perhaps not breathing
2. First aid, CPR, diving rescue, life saving
3. Establish buoyancy for yourself
4. Don't worry about it because the air will escape naturally
5. Keep water out, maintain the breathing cycle

7.6 Emergencies and First Aid

1. Training, equipment, contact information, determination to take action
2. Update training periodically, practice frequently with buddy
3. First aid kit, oxygen, blanket, supply of clean fresh water
4. (919) 684-8111
5. Lay diver on the back with legs only elevated, maintain respiration and circulation, treat for shock, administer oxygen if available, monitor patient constantly, transport patient to nearest recompression facility

Diver Etiquette

As a responsible diver you should:
• Manage your equipment and vehicles as compactly as possible so you do not block sidewalks, driveways or public accesses. Maintain a tidy equipment area to avoid a "cluttered" look at the dive site.
• Take care with spear guns. Loaded spear guns are forbidden while on land and any spear should be restricted from crowded beach areas.
• Ask before using or crossing private property, whether to gain access to a dive site or for recreation after a dive.
• Not change clothes in public. Be discreet and use vehicles, changing robes or tents. Think of others passing the site or using the beaches.
• Try and create a "good guy" impression about divers. Talk pleasantly to interested non-divers who are curious about your sport. Be careful of your language and behavior, particularly the use of alcohol or drugs before a dive.
• Not violate the rights of others to enjoy the environment, run businesses or have a pleasant town to live in.
• Obey the laws, whether they are fish and game regulations or designated parking and access areas. Cooperate with local peace officers.
• Not litter beaches or otherwise destroy property. Beach environments are often fragile ecological systems that require your careful use if they are to survive.
• Patronize local merchants. Divers can have great positive economic impact on an area from restaurants to dive stores to motels. Good economic rapport with a community means continuing good communications and accesses for divers.
• Begin your dives early in the day for optimum diving conditions, less crowded beaches, more parking and more freedom of choice of dive sites. Do not exceed your diving capabilities in selecting your dive site. Ask local residents or divers about possible dive sites. Rely on their knowledge of water and bottom conditions.
• Only take game you can use. Collect as little as possible, clean fish only in designated areas and dispose of wastes properly.
• Be helpful to other users of our aquatic environment. It makes you, as a diver, better than the faceless crowd and gains respect for your sport. It also removes many of the "hassles" of diving and makes you a happier, thus calmer, safer diver.

NAUI Safe Boat Diving Practices

1. Select a Coast Guard licensed boat that is fully equipped with the required safety equipment and has diver support and safety equipment.
2. Ask to receive Boat Diving Techniques Training as a part of your basic, sport or advanced diving courses.
3. Rely on the Skipper's knowledge of the most suitable dive sites. Plan your dive using the specific site information provided by the crew or divemaster.
4. Only sign up for trip destinations that are consistent with your ability and dive plan.
5. Arrive at the boat at least a half hour before departure. Stow your well marked gear in the assigned locations. Respect the boat facilities: no wet suits in the bunk room nor dropping tanks or weight belts on the deck.
6. Between dives, keep gear in your bag to avoid lost or broken equipment. Assist your buddy with his/her tank. Do not sit on the deck to put your tank on or you may get hit on the head by another diver's tank.
7. Use your equipment to dive easily and safely. Do not overweight yourself. Only use your BC to fine-tune your buoyancy during the dive or to compensate for a heavy game bag at the end of the dive.
8. No loaded spear guns are EVER allowed on the boat or boarding ramp. Bring a container for your game. Help keep the boat deck clean and clear.
9. Use the boat exit points recommended by the crew. Move away from the boat exit once you are in the water. Either snorkel clearly on the surface or begin your descent down the anchor line. Do not use scuba to skim the surface. If you just skim the surface, you cannot be seen by passing boats or other divers.
10. Fins should be put on last while you are waiting near the exit. Do not walk around the deck wearing fins.
11. Be sure to use a compass and submersible pressure gauge. Plan your dive so you end the dive with a reserve of air and are able to return to the boat while still underwater.
12. Be aware of changes in current conditions during the dive. Use natural clues such as seaweed. Look for current lines trailed behind the boat on the surface. Do not hesitate to pull yourself hand-over-hand back to the boat using this line.

13. Use common sense, training, and experience — ask questions if you are unsure. Allow for a "margin of reserve" and do not push your endurance limits. Watch for other divers waving one arm while on the surface. They are signaling a diver in distress. Divers who maintain personal control and are comfortable in the water have safe, enjoyable experiences underwater.

Explore the far away places.
Boat dive often.

Dive Planning

Advance Planning
☐ **1.** Determine purpose of the dive
☐ **2.** Select dive buddy
☐ **3.** Determine location for the dive plus alternate location
☐ **4.** Research dive site if it is unfamiliar
☐ **5.** Select date and time for the dive; schedule on calendar
☐ **6.** Make any necessary reservations
☐ **7.** Obtain emergency contact information
☐ **8.** Determine needed equipment
☐ **9.** Inspect equipment to ensure readiness
☐ **10.** Purchase advance items (tickets, air, film, fishing license)
☐ **11.** Inventory spare parts kit
☐ **12.** Check long-range weather forecast

Final Preparations
1. Check weather and water conditions
2. Ensure you are physically and mentally ready to go diving
3. Collect all equipment and use checklist to prevent omissions
4. Pack equipment in reverse order in which it will be used
5. Pack personal items in separate bag from dive gear
6. Leave information on destination and ETR with someone

On-Site Planning
1. Determine that conditions are acceptable for diving or move to alternate location or don't go diving
2. Decide who will be in charge of the dive
3. Review hand signals
4. Agree on the general course to be followed on the dive

5. Agree on entry and exit locations and techniques
6. Agree on emergency procedures; know location of telephone

Diving Your Plan
1. Abide by pre-dive plans
2. Think ahead while diving

Remember, plan your dive,
then dive your plan

Diving Equipment Checklist
☐ Dive Gear
☐ Gear bag
☐ Fins, mask, snorkel, and keeper
☐ Exposure suit
☐ Hood
☐ Boots
☐ Gloves
☐ Weight belt
☐ Buoyancy compensator
☐ Dive knife
☐ Scuba tank (filled)
☐ Backpack
☐ Regulator with gauge
☐ Depth gauge, timing device and compass
☐ Float, flag and anchor
☐ Dive tables

Additional Dive Gear
☐ Dive light
☐ Slate and pencil
☐ Thermometer
☐ Marker buoy
☐ Game bag

Spare Equipment
☐ Tanks
☐ Weights
☐ Mask and fin straps
☐ O-rings
☐ Snorkel keeper
☐ Tools

Emergency Items
☐ First Aid kit
☐ Phone numbers
☐ Coins for phone
☐ Oxygen

Personal Items
☐ Certification card
☐ NAUI Log Book
☐ Swimsuit
☐ Towel
☐ Jacket, extra clothes
☐ Hat or visor
☐ Sunscreen lotion
☐ Sunglasses
☐ Lunch, snacks, drinks
☐ Tickets, money
☐ Seasickness medication
☐ Toilet articles
☐ Sleeping bag

NAUI Safe Scuba Diving Practices

Being a safe, effective diver is more than merely doing a series of skills. It is also a frame of mind. Diving requires some enthusiasm and dedication before the real fun begins in open water. You will need to meet some basic health, swimming and age requirements. Then, your NAUI Instructor will train you to meet the challenge.

For safe, enjoyable skin and scuba diving you, as a diver, should:

1. Be trained in scuba diving by a certified underwater instructor and certified by a nationally recognized certifying organization.

2. Maintain good physical and mental condition for diving. Be at ease in the water. Only dive when feeling well. Do not use any intoxicating liquor or dangerous drugs before diving. Have a regular medical examination for diving.

3. Use correct, complete, well maintained diving equipment which you check before each dive. Do not loan your equipment to a non-certified diver. When scuba diving in open water, use a buoyancy compensator plus a submersible pressure gauge and/or a reserve warning mechanism.

4. Know the limitations of yourself, your buddy and your equipment. Use the best possible judgment and common sense in planning each dive. Allow a margin of safety in order to be prepared for emergencies. Set moderate limits for depth and time in the water. Save some air for use at the surface.

5. Know your diving location. Avoid dangerous places and poor conditions. Do not let ego create dangerous situations.

6. Control your buoyancy to make diving as easy as possible. Be prepared to ditch your weights, make an emergency ascent, clear your mask or mouthpiece, or take other emergency action if needed. In an emergency: stop and think, get control — then take action.

7. Never dive alone. Always buddy dive — know each other's equipment. Know hand signals and stay in contact. Be able to rescue a non-breathing buddy if an emergency arises.

8. Use a boat or float as a surface support station whenever this will increase the safety and enjoyment of the dive. Fly the diver down flag to warn boaters that divers are underwater. Slowly surface close to the float and flag, watching and listening for possible hazards.

9. Beware of breath holding. Breathe continuously throughout a scuba dive. Exhale on any ascent. Without scuba: avoid excessive "over breathing" before a skin dive; do not overexert. Know your limits and allow a margin of safety. Be sure to equalize pressure early and often during both ascent and descent.

10. If not feeling well, get out of the water. Diving is no longer fun or safe. If any abnormality persists, get medical attention.

11. Know decompression procedures, tables and emergency procedures. Make all possible dives as "no decompression" dives. Avoid stage decompression particularly on repetitive dives, at altitude or when flying after diving.

12. Continue your scuba training by taking advanced, open water or specialty courses. Log your dives and try to make at least 12 dives each year.

Sample Divers First Aid Kit

A first aid kit should be present at all dives. The contents may be simple or complex as the distance from medical assistance increases. The following items are basic and may be supplemented according to personal needs and capabilities of the user and local conditions.

General

Sterile compress pads for severe bleeding
Roll of 2" gauze bandage
Assorted Band Aids
Adhesive tape 1" wide
Assorted gauze pads (sterile)
Cotton swabs
Assorted safety pins/needles
Triangular bandage
Antiseptic soap
Germicide spray (such as Bactine)
Sea sick pills (such as Bonine or Dramamine)
Decongestant tablets (such as Sudafed)
Scissors
Tweezers and/or splinter remover
Medicated stick (such as Chapstick)
Isoprophyl alcohol (about 70% solution or commercial product, such as Swim-Ear)
Sunscreen cream (such as Max-a-Fil)
Aspirin and/or Tylenol
Loose change and emergency phone numbers

Optional

Adolph's Meat Tenderizer
Cleaning agent (e.g., Hydrogen Peroxide, Listerine)
Gauze scrub pads (such as Betadine or Phisohex)
Baking Soda
First aid book
Salt tablets
Waterproof matches
Drinking water and paper cups
Blanket
Other

Safety Through Education

GLOSSARY

When using the glossary, you find words/terms in alphabetical order with acronyms. For example: BC, listed as if spelled "BC" without regard for the spelled out words. The page number indicates the first mention in the text.

ABSOLUTE PRESSURE: the result when atmospheric pressure is added to gauge pressure (page 37).

ACTUAL DIVE TIME: the total time spent underwater from the beginning of descent until breaking the surface at the end of the dive. Does not include precautionary decompression time (page 81).

ADJUSTED MAXIMUM DIVE TIME: the Maximum Dive Time for a specific depth minus the residual nitrogen time for a specific letter group and depth (page 81).

ADT: Actual Dive Time (page 81).

AIR EMBOLISM: the blockage of the blood flow to the brain by air bubbles escaping into the blood from a lung injury (page 52).

AMBIENT PRESSURE: the surrounding pressure (page 18).

AMDT: Adjusted Maximum Dive Time (page 81).

ALVEOLI: the tiny air sacs found in the lungs (page 47).

ATMOSPHERIC PRESSURE: the pressure exerted by the atmosphere (page 37).

BACK FLOTATION SYSTEM: a buoyancy control device that is attached to the scuba tank and does not wrap around the diver in any way (page 21).

BACKPACK: a piece of equipment designed to hold the scuba tank on the diver's back (page 18).

BACKUP SCUBA: a redundant second stage or total scuba unit for use in out of air situations (page 20).

BC: Buoyancy Compensator (page 9).

BENDS: another name for decompression sickness (page 58).

BEZEL: a movable ring on a compass or watch that allows the placing of index marks (page 134).

BUOYANCY: an upward force on an object placed in water equal to the weight of the water displaced (page 40).

BUOYANCY COMPENSATOR: a piece of equipment used to provide increased volume with little increase in weight, thus providing lift (page 9, page 21, 22).

BUOYANCY JACKET: a buoyancy control device that is worn like a sleeveless jacket (page 21).

BOYLE'S LAW: the inverse relationship between pressure and volume (page 39).

BUDDY SYSTEM: a system where you never dive alone, where you always have someone to assist you, if necessary, and to share experiences with (page 139).

C-CARD: Certification Card (page 4).

CARBON MONOXIDE TOXICITY: a condition that results from breathing air contaminated with carbon monoxide (page 57).

CARDIO-PULMONARY RESUSCITATION: the first aid procedure that sustains ventilation and pulse until medical assistance becomes available (page 158).

CEILING: a minimum depth displayed by a computer to which a diver may ascend without risk of decompression sickness (page 98).

CERTIFICATION CARD: a card awarded by NAUI as evidence of completion of required training (page 4, page 5).

"CLEARING": the moving of air from the lungs to the other air spaces such as the ear and sinuses (page 7).

CO_2 DETONATOR: a mechanical device that allows the buoyancy compensator to be filled quickly with carbon dioxide to provide rapid flotation. This is an option and is not standard on all BCs (page 22, 23).

COMPASS: a piece of equipment that aids in underwater navigation by indicating the direction of true NORTH with respect to your position (page 30, page 31).

CONDENSATION: water that forms on a surface due to the cooling of air containing water vapor (page 42).

CONSOLES: devices designed to hold assorted gauges and instruments around or in line with the submersible pressure gauge (page 31).

CORAL: a polyp or polyp colony that produce a mineral skeleton. Corals are living organisms (page 6, page 11)

CPR: Cardio-pulmonary Resuscitation (page 158).

CURRENTS: water motion caused by the wind, earth's gravity, tides, and the earth's rotation (page 66, 67).

DECOMPRESSION STOP: the time a diver stops and waits at a specified depth during ascent to allow nitrogen elimination before surfacing (page 81).

DECOMPRESSION SICKNESS: the result of bubble formation in the body when one ascends without considering the nitrogen that has dissolved in the body during the dive (page 57).

DEFOG SOLUTION: a substance rubbed on the lens of the mask to keep it free of condensation. Saliva is often used as a defog solution (page 15).

DEHYDRATION: the loss of body fluids (page 42).

DENSITY: the quantity of something per unit of volume (page 34).

DEPTH GAUGE: a piece of equipment that indicates the depth (page 29, 30, 31).

DIVE COMPUTER: an electronic device that senses water pressure, measures time, continuously calculates the amount of nitrogen in several "compartments", and displays information to assist divers in avoiding decompression sickness (page 80, 97, 98).

DIVE SCHEDULE: an abbreviated statement of the depth and duration of a dive expressed as depth/time, e.g., 70 feet (21M) for 40 minutes = 70'/40 (page 81).

DIVE TIME CALCULATOR: a rotary calculator containing the NAUI Dive Tables in a format that eliminates the mathematical calculations associated with the dive tables (page 81, 88).

DRAG: the resistance encountered when moving through the water due to the water's density (page 35).

DRIFT DIVING: a dive made using a current as the primary means of propulsion (page 61).

DRYSUITS: protective suits that prevent water from coming into contact with covered portions of the body (page 26-27)

EARDRUM: the membrane that separates the middle and outer ear (page 48).

EQUALIZATION: the methods of preventing and correcting 'squeezes' (page 49).

ESE PROGRAM: Entry Scuba Experience program – a NAUI program to introduce non-divers to scuba diving. This program does not lead to certification. (page 4).

EUSTACHIAN TUBE: the tube that connects the middle ear with the throat, allowing divers to 'clear' their ears (page 48).

EXTRA REGULATOR: a spare second stage regulator to be used during out of air situations (page 10).

FINS: a piece of equipment that increases the surface area of the foot to make propulsion easier (page 8, page 14, 16).

GAUGE PRESSURE: the pressure indicated by a gauge which is the pressure relative to ambient pressure (page 37).

GOGGLES: a piece of equipment that covers only the eyes to prevent water from irritating them. GOGGLES ARE NOT AN ACCEPTABLE SUBSTITUTE FOR THE MASK (page 15).

HEAT EXHAUSTION: a condition that results from overheating that is characterized by a pale, clammy appearance and a feeling of weakness (page 55).

HEAT STROKE: a condition that results from overheating that is characterized by hot, dry, flushed skin (page 55).

HOSE PROTECTOR: a piece of heavy plastic or rubber that fits over the ends of hoses to relieve the stress caused by the weight of equipment (page 31).

HUMIDITY: the amount of water vapor in the air (page 42).

HYDROSTATIC TEST: a test required every five years to ensure the safety of scuba tanks. This test is done using water as the medium to provide pressure (page 17).

HYPERVENTILATION: breathing much deeper and more rapidly than required. This lowers the carbon dioxide levels of the blood (page 53).

INDEX MARKS: the points on the bezel of a compass that provide a place to aim the needle of the compass in order to stay on a desired course (page 142).

INTEGRATED WEIGHT SYSTEMS: systems where weight is combined with the backpack and BC (page 24).

INTERNAL VISUAL INSPECTION: a periodic inspection of the scuba tank that checks for corrosion to ensure the integrity of the tank (page 17).

LETTER GROUP DESIGNATION: a letter used to designate the amount of residual nitrogen in the system after a dive (page 81).

LONGSHORE CURRENTS: currents that run parallel to the coast line (page 66).

LOW PRESSURE INFLATION DEVICE: a device that allows the flow of air from the scuba cylinder to the buoyancy compensator (page 9, page 22).

LUBBER LINE: the 'reference line' on a compass. The stationary line that will show the direction of travel (page 142).

LUNGS: the part of the body that allows oxygen to transfer from the inhaled air to the blood. One of the body's air spaces (page 6, page 47).

MASK: a piece of equipment that holds a pocket of air around the eyes to improve underwater vision (page 3, page 14).

MAXIMUM DIVE TIME: the length of time that may be spent at a given depth without being required to stop during ascent to reduce the likelihood of decompression sickness (page 81).

MDT: Maximum Dive Time (page 81).

MEDIASTINAL EMPHYSEMA: the condition that exists when air from an over expansion injury escapes into the chest area near the heart (page 52).

MIDDLE EAR: the space in the ear connected to the throat by the eustachian tube (page 6, page 47).

MULTI-LEVEL DIVE: a dive with progressively shallower depths (page 80).

NAUI: the National Association of Underwater Instructors (page 4).

NEOPRENE: a rubber based material saturated with tiny gas bubbles that provide insulation. This material is used to manufacture environmental suits (page 25).

NEPTUNE'S KINGDOM: the sea, Neptune is the god of the sea in Roman mythology, thus his kingdom is the sea (page 10).

NEUTRAL BUOYANCY: the state that exists when an object will neither float nor sink (page 41).

NITROGEN NARCOSIS: the name given to the narcotic effect nitrogen has at deeper depths (page 58).

OCTOPUS: an extra second stage attached to the regulator for use in 'out of air' situations. An extra regulator (page 20).

"ONE ATMOSPHERE": the force of the atmosphere on the earth taken as a constant 14.7 psi (page 36).

OPENWATER I DIVER COURSE: the first course in NAUI's complete diver education program. This course leads to certification (page 4).

OVER EXPANSION INJURY: injuries caused by the expansion of air in closed body spaces (page 7).

OVERPRESSURE VALVE: an important device built into buoyancy compensators that allows the escape of expanding gas without loss of buoyancy or damage to the BC (page 22).

OXYGEN: the gas necessary to sustain life. This gas makes up approximately 20 per cent of the air (page 57).

PNEUMOTHORAX: the condition that exists when air from an over expansion injury escapes into the chest area and causes a lung to collapse (page 52).

POSITIVE BUOYANCY: the state that exists when an object is forced up by water or rises toward the surface (page 41).

PRECAUTIONARY DECOMPRESSION STOP: three minutes spent at a depth of 15 feet (5m) as a safety precaution even though the Maximum Dive Time has not been exceeded (page 81).

PRESSURE: the force of the weight of the air and water above the diver measured in pounds per square inch (page 6).

PRESSURE GAUGE: a piece of equipment that allows a diver to monitor the air remaining in the scuba cylinder (page 3).

PRESSURE RELIEF DISK: a safety device built into tank valves that prevents pressure from reaching dangerous levels. This is a one-time use device and must be replaced if the disk bursts (page 18).

PSI: pounds per square inch (page 38).

QUICK RELEASE BUCKLES: buckles that are designed to be operated with one hand, so they can be opened quickly in an emergency (page 18, page 24).

"RAPTURE OF THE DEEP": an older, more romantic name for nitrogen narcosis (page 58).

REFERENCE LINE: the 'lubber line' on a compass. The stationary line that will show the direction of travel (page 142).

REGULATOR: the piece of equipment that reduces the high pressure air in the scuba cylinder to ambient pressure (page 11, page 19).

REPETITIVE DIVE: any dive made within 24 hours of a previous dive (page 81).

REQUIRED DECOMPRESSION STOP: an amount of time specified by dive tables, a calculator or a computer to be spent at a specified depth whenever the Maximum Dive Time is exceeded (page 81).

RESIDUAL NITROGEN: that dissolved nitrogen remaining in the body as a result of an earlier dive within 24 hours (page 77).

RESIDUAL NITROGEN TIME: Residual nitrogen expressed in time already spent at depth (page 81).

REVERSE BLOCK: the opposite of 'squeeze'. The situation that exists when the internal pressure of an airspace is greater than the external pressure (page 51).

RIP CURRENT: a transitory current that results when water pushed up on the beach by waves rushes back to the sea (page 66).

RNT: Residual Nitrogen Time (page 81).

SAC-RATE: Surface Air Consumption Rate (page 45).

SALIVA: spit, sometimes used as a defog solution (page 15).

SCROLLING: a display continuously flashed by a computer between dives to provide the Maximum Dive Times for various depths in sequence (page 98).

SCUBA: Self Contained Underwater Breathing Apparatus (page 3).

SCUBA TANK: the piece of equipment that contains the high pressure air to be breathed while underwater (page 9, page 17).

SERVICE PRESSURE: the working pressure of the scuba tank. It is stamped on the shoulder of the tank; for example, with 'CTC/DOT-3ALxxxx-S80'. The 'xxxx' indicates the working pressure (page 17, page 20).

SINUSES: air cavities within the head that are lined with mucus membrane. May cause problems equalizing if blocked due to a cold (page 6, page 47).

SIT: Surface Interval Time (page 81).

SKIP BREATHING: the hazardous practice of taking a breath and holding it for a moment before exhaling while scuba diving (page 53).

SNORKEL: a tubular piece of equipment that allows a person to breath while keeping their face in the water (page 15).

SPG: Submersible Pressure Gauge (page 19).

SQUEEZE: when the pressure outside an airspace is greater than the internal pressure (page 49).

STANDING CURRENTS: currents that are regular and steady (page 66).

SUBMERSIBLE PRESSURE GAUGE: a piece of equipment that provides a read out of tank pressure during the dive (page 19, page 29).

SURFACE AIR CONSUMPTION RATE: the rate of air consumption converted to a surface rate (page 45).

SURFACE INTERVAL TIME: time spent on the surface between dives (page 81).

TANK VALVE: a fitting that screws into the scuba tank allowing the high pressure air to be turned on and off while providing a place to mount the regulator (page 17, page 18).

TEST DATE: a date stamped on the scuba tank that indicates the date of the last hydrostatic test (page 17, page 20).

THERMOCLINE: the dividing line between water of different temperatures and densities (page 64).

TIDE: the change in water level caused by the gravitational attraction between the earth, sun, and moon (page 66).

TIDAL CURRENTS: currents that accompany changes in the tide (page 66).

TIMING DEVICE: a device used to record the length of a dive; for example, a watch or bottom timer (page 30).

TOTAL NITROGEN TIME: the sum of Residual Nitrogen Time and Actual Dive Time following a repetitive dive (page 81).

TRAIL LINE: a line used while boat diving. It is let out from the stern (back of the boat) with a float attached to aid divers returning to the boat (page 73).

TRANSITORY CURRENTS: currents that are unpredictable (page 66).

VALSALVA MANEUVER: the attempted exhalation against a closed nose and mouth which ordinarily opens the eustachian tubes allowing equalization (page 50).

VERTIGO: a loss of the sense of balance, dizziness (page 48).

WETSUITS: environmental suit that allows a small amount of water to enter the covered area. This water is trapped and warmed by the body, thus providing a certain amount of protection from the cold (page 25, 27).

NAUI OPENWATER I SCUBA DIVER COURSE STANDARDS

I. **General**

This course is the NAUI entry level certification course in scuba diving.

II. **Course Objective**

The objective of the Openwater I Scuba Diver course is to provide the novice with the minimum knowledge and skills to participate in open water scuba diving activities without direct leadership supervision.

III. **Qualifications of Graduates**

At the time of successful completion of this course, graduates are considered competent to engage in open water diving activities without direct leadership supervision provided the diving activities approximate those in which the diver was trained and the area being dived approximates the areas in which trained with regards to type and conditions.

IV. **Who May Teach**

This course may be taught by any Active-Status NAUI Instructor.

V. **Prerequisites for Entering the Course**
   A. The minimum age for Openwater I Scuba Diver certification is 15. Students 12-14 years of age may be accepted in accordance with the NAUI Junior Openwater Course standards.
   B. No previous certification is required.

VI. **Required Course Minimums**
   A. Classroom hours — 11
   B. In-water hours — 17. This includes confined water and open water training. The minimum number of in-water hours may be reduced to 12 for private and semi-private instruction [one or two students].
   C. Open water dives - five. The dives may be either five scuba dives or one skin dive and four scuba dives.
   D. No more than two scuba dives to be credited toward the dive requirements for certification may be conducted on any given day. No additional scuba dives to expand student experience may be conducted until the four required scuba dives have been satisfactorily completed. Open water training may be completed in two days with a skin dive and two scuba dives on one day and two additional scuba dives on the other day.
   E. Days of training — five. The minimum number of training days is five with not more than eight hours of training conducted during any one day.
   F. All open water training must take place during daylight hours.
   G. Thirty feet (nine meters) is the maximum depth for the first open water training scuba dive. Sixty feet (18 meters) is the maximum depth for any open water training dive during the course.

VII. **Skill Performance Objectives**

The required skills which are to be performed or achieved during the course are:
   A. Confined water – Swimming skills, no equipment.
      1. Distance swim of 220 yards (201 meters); nonstop, any stroke.
      2. Survival swim of 10 minutes; drownproofing, floating, etc.
      3. Underwater swim of 50 feet (15 meters); one breath, no push-off or dive.
   B. Confined water (open water optional) – Skin diving skills; mask, fins, snorkel, BC, weight belt (protective suit mandatory for open water if needed for student comfort or safety).
      1. Distance swim of 440 yards (402 meters); nonstop, using no hands and breathing from snorkel.
      2. Bring another diver simulating unconsciousness to the surface from eight to 12 feet (2.4 to 3.7 meters) of water.
      3. Practice and perform, without stress, proper techniques for: water entries and exits, surface dives, surface swimming with fins, clearing the snorkel, ditching the weight belt, buoyancy control, underwater swimming and surfacing.
   C. Open water – Skills for optional skin dive. Students are to be equipped with open water diving skin diving equipment suitable for the area.
      1. Select, check, assemble, adjust and don equipment; perform pre-dive gear check for self and buddy; defog masks; after diving, doff, rinse and care for gear.

2. Enter and exit the water using proper techniques for local conditions.
3. Perform surface buoyancy check and make adjustments as needed to achieve neutral buoyancy at diving depth.
4. Correctly give and recognize surface hand signals for divers.
5. At the surface, remove and replace (in turn): masks, fins, weight belt.
6. At the surface, orally inflate and deflate own and buddy's BC.
7. At the surface, with face submerged, breathe through snorkel while resting and swimming.
8. At the surface, with face submerged, breathe through water in the snorkel without choking.
9. Control pressure in air spaces and buoyancy compensator for comfortable, controlled descents and ascents.
10. If representative of local diving, swim in and over weeds, kelp or other obstructions.
11. Recover an object from at least 10 feet (three meters) of water (skin diving only).
12. Use the buddy system for skin diving by remaining within approximately 10 feet (three meters) of the buddy on the surface and above the buddy's approximate location when the buddy is diving (skin diving technique only).
13. Release a simulated leg cramp from self and buddy.
14. If appropriate for the area, enter and exit the water with a float, Diver Down flag and line; use to identify the dive area while diving.
15. Demonstrate proficiency in all required skills and appropriate endurance.

D. Open Water – Scuba diving skills; open water scuba gear appropriate for the area.
1. While fully equipped for scuba diving, perform all skills from Item VII. C, except as noted for skin diving only.
2. At the surface, alternate breathing from snorkel to regulator, with face submerged, without choking.
3. At the surface, on snorkel, remove and replace (in turn): mask, fins, weight belt, scuba unit.
4. Use the buddy system for scuba diving, remaining within 10 feet (three meters) — or less, if required by conditions — of buddy at the surface and underwater.
5. Descend feet first with a minimum of hand movement using breath control and BC to control rate of descent; equalize pressure in air spaces.
6. Control buoyancy with BC, breath control and weight adjustment to hover off the bottom without support and with minimum movement.
7. Give, recognize and respond to standard underwater hand signals.
8. Repeatedly flood and clear mask of water while breathing from scuba.
9. Repeatedly remove, replace and clear regulator of water using two methods.
10. Regain a regulator which has fallen behind the shoulder.
11. Buddy breathe with another diver. Be the donor of the air and the receiver of the air. To be performed in a stationary position at a depth of approximately 15 to 25 feet (4.6 to 7.6 meters).
12. Perform a relaxed, controlled emergency swimming ascent. All equipment is to be in place and the regulator is to be in the mouth. The ascent rate should be as near normal as possible. To be performed from an approximate depth of 15 to 25 feet (4.6 to 7.6 meters) and in accordance with the NAUI OW I Scuba Diver Instructor Guide.
13. Breathe from scuba and swim underwater a total of at least 80 minutes during at least four scuba dives. The total time may be reduced to 60 minutes if the water temperature is 55° F (12.7° C) or colder.
14. Prevent exhaustion of air supply while scuba diving by monitoring an underwater pressure gauge and ascending with no less than the recommended pressure remaining.
15. Dive in limited visibility if representative of local diving.
16. Breathing normally with scuba, ascend to the surface by swimming at a steady rate of approximately 60 feet (18 meters) per minute while controlling expanding air in the BC to maintain neutral buoyancy.
17. Share air as a receiver from an octopus or alternate breathing source during an ascent from a depth of at least 25 feet (7.6 meters) while scuba diving.
18. Transport for a distance of at least 50 yards (15 meters) a buddy who is simulating exhaustion. Eye-to-eye contact between rescuer and diver simulating exhaustion must be maintained.
19. Bring a diver simulating unconsciousness to the surface from a depth of approximately 10 feet (three meters); remove victim's weight belt, mask and snorkel; simulate artificial respiration.

E. Environmental Orientation
   1. For a dive site typical of the local area, be able to identify safe and hazardous weather and water conditions, entry and exit points and underwater terrain features, such as offshore reefs.
   2. While wearing scuba diving equipment, be able to maneuver through, around or over aquatic terrain typical of the local area, such as kelp, coral, etc.
   3. Recognize and identify by common name samples of plant and animal life typically seen in local diving.
F. Air Consumption/Navigation
   1. Measure and record individual air consumption in psi/min. (or similar scale) using a submersible pressure gauge, depth gauge and timing device. Using this data, plan a safe no-required-decompression dive leaving adequate air for descent, time at depth, ascent, precautionary stop and safety margin.
   2. Using environmental navigation aids and a compass, travel underwater to a designated location or in a given direction for a set period of time.
   3. Use an underwater compass to set a bearing: follow the bearing and return on a reciprocal course to the approximate starting location.
G. Deeper Water Diving
   1. Safely plan and make a dive to a recommended depth of between 40 and 50 feet (12 and 15 meters).
   2. Properly calculate the no-decompression limit for the planned deeper water dive using repetitive dive tables. Upon completion of the dive, properly calculate a planned no-required-decompression repetitive dive.
   3. Demonstrate the use of all appropriate equipment during deeper water diving, including at least: Open water scuba gear, depth gauge, timing device, weight system, BC, alternate air source (octopus) and exposure suit, if used.
   4. Using effective buoyancy control, swim on the surface, descend and ascend at proper rates and hover at depth.

VIII. **Openwater Training Supervision**
A. An Active-Status NAUI Instructor is to personally visually observe and evaluate the performance of the skills required for each open water training dive. Following the satisfactory student performance of the skill evaluations during the second or subsequent open water scuba training dives, the instructor may delegate responsibility for supervision to Active-Status NAUI Divemasters, NAUI Assistant Instructors or NAUI Skin Diving Instructors with scuba certification, who may escort the students during underwater tours. No other supervisory responsibility may be delegated except that during any open water training dive, Active-Status assistants may escort students during surface excursions and exits and may temporarily oversee the remaining students while the instructor conducts a skill with other students.
B. An exception to the foregoing supervisory requirements is allowed during the navigational exercise required during the third or subsequent open water scuba training dive. Students may swim the navigational exercise portion of the dive in buddy pairs without direct supervision. At all other times during the required four scuba dives, students in training are to be supervised by either the instructor or by Teaching status assistants as specified in item VIII. A.
C. The maximum number of students per Teaching status assistant for the escorting of students during underwater tours is two .
D. Dives following satisfactory completion of the dives required for certification and for the purpose of expanding student experience may be conducted with indirect supervision. This is defined as the general observation, evaluation and direction of diving activities by an Active-Status NAUI Instructor. The instructor is not required to visually observe and direct the performance of skills, but must be present at the entry/exit point; approve the diving activity; oversee the planning, preparation, equipment inspections, entries, exits and debriefings; and be prepared to quickly enter the water wearing the equipment required for open water training scuba training dives (see Standards Applying to All NAUI Diving Courses).

IX. **Required Curriculum Subject Areas**
The instructor is to assure the student gains a basic knowledge of each subject area:
A. Applied Sciences — Physics, physiology and medical aspects as they relate to a diver's performance and safety in the water. Emphasis is to be placed on physical fitness, diving hazards, personal limitations and the behavior needed to function safely as a diver. Material is to be presented in terms

of practical applications, and is to include: gases, pressure, volume, temperature, density, buoyancy, vision and acoustics; the definition, cause, prevention, symptoms, first aid for decompression sickness, nitrogen narcosis, respiratory accidents, squeezes, over-exertion, over-exposure, air embolism and related injuries. Repetitive dive tables are to be covered to the extent required for students to be able to plan repetitive dives not requiring stage decompression.

B.   Diving Equipment — Purpose, features, types and uses of recreational skin and scuba diving equipment. The student is to be able to select, use and care for: mask, snorkel, fins, BC, knife, weight belt and weights, protective suit, depth gauge, watch, compass, regulator with submersible pressure gauge and alternate air source, and cylinder with valve and backpack.

C.   Diving Safety — Lifesaving and first aid as applied to diving, underwater communications, basic underwater navigation, dive planning and safety rules are also to be covered. Shock, wounds, panic and drowning are to be covered under first aid. Lifesaving is to include problem recognition, assists, transports and rescues in open water. Students are to practice self-rescue techniques.

D.   Diving Environment — Physical and biological aspects of the environment where open water training is conducted. Potential hazards should be pointed out before the students enter the water for open water training. The instructor is to nurture student awareness of the importance of conservation and the kinds of negative impact sport divers can have on the environment. Game regulations and other pertinent laws are to be addressed where appropriate.

E.   Diving Activities — The how, who, when, where, what and why of diving. Specific information on dive clubs, boats, stores, locations, books and periodicals and a limited introduction to specific diving activities should be given.

F.   Continuing Education — Students are to be told their limitations as new divers and the importance of additional training. Specific information on continuing education courses, workshops and conferences is to be provided. Use of the log book must be taught. Open water training is to be recorded by the student and all entries are to be authenticated by the instructor's signature. Students are to be told of the need to re-evaluate their physical condition and diving competence before resuming open water diving after periods of inactivity. Use of the NAUI Refresher Scuba Experience (RSE) in such cases is to be recommended.

X.   Learning Objectives

A.   Select, use and care for safe, comfortable equipment.

B.   Explain how buoyancy changes at depth with the compression of air spaces, and how to select proper weights to avoid unsafe negative buoyancy at depth.

C.   Define and explain the cause, prevention, effects, symptoms and first aid for:
1.   Squeezes
2.   Shallow water blackout
3.   The panic syndrome and associated rapid, shallow breathing
4.   Cold and heat problems
5.   Exhaustion, cramps, breathing difficulties
6.   Nitrogen narcosis
7.   Decompression sickness
8.   Contaminated scuba air
9.   Air embolism and other lung overpressure injuries

D.   Select dive sites commensurate with their diving experience and explain when to seek advice from local divers (e.g., before venturing into strange waters).

E.   Identify potentially dangerous water conditions and flora and fauna in areas where trained.

F.   Explain water movement and its potential effects on divers.

G.   Use repetitive dive tables to determine time and depth required to avoid stage decompression on single and repetitive dives.

H.   Explain the first aid treatment for shock, wounds and drowning.

I.   Explain the importance of maintaining proper physical conditioning for diving and the actions to take before resuming diving after a period of inactivity.

J.   Explain the importance and benefits of continuing diving education and identify avenues for achieving it.

K.   Record diving activities in a dive log and explain the importance of having an instructor or divemaster authenticate all entries.

L.   Perform all diving skills required in these standards with ease and proficiency.

M.   Pass a standard scuba examination with a minimum score of 75%.

Index